THE MEMOIRS

OF

SIR PATRICK JOSEPH HENRY
HANNON

(1870 -1963)

FOREWORD BY

PATRICK GODFREY HANNON

POSTSCRIPT BY

FIONA HANNON

Bibliographic information of the German National Library: The German National Library lists this publication in the German National Bibliography; detailed bibliographic data is available on the Internet at dnb.dnb.de.

The automated analysis of the work in order to obtain information, in particular about patterns, trends and correlations in accordance with §44b UrhG ('Text and Data Mining') is prohibited.

Bibliografische Information der Deutschen Nationalbibliothek: Die Deutsche Nationalbibliothek verzeichnet diese Publikation in der Deutschen Nationalbibliografie; detaillierte bibliografische Daten sind im Internet über dnb.dnb.de abrufbar.

Die automatisierte Analyse des Werkes, um daraus Informationen insbesondere über Muster, Trends und Korrelationen gemäß §44b UrhG („Text und Data Mining") zu gewinnen, ist untersagt.

Verlag: BoD · Books on Demand GmbH, In de Tarpen 42, 22848 Norderstedt

Druck: Libri Plureos GmbH, Friedensallee 273, 22763 Hamburg

© 2024 Sir Patrick Hannon

Forword by Patrick Godfrey Hannon

Postscript by Fiona Hannon

Images supplied by the Hannon and Wynne family
6 images © the National Portrait Gallery

Edited by Fiona Hannon, Peter Hannon and Michael Hannon

Alle Rechte vorbehalten / All rights reserved

ISBN: 978-3-7597-9967-8

Typesetting: Peter Hannon with VivaDesigner®
Typeset in Palatino Linotype

They still remember Sir Patrick Hannon in the House of Commons as a member who in nearly 30 years never made an enemy. … For he was a kind man.

Cyril Aynsley, Daily Express

FOREWORD

by P.G.Hannon

Ireland in 1870 was, economically, in a sad way; she might be compared to one who was in a long and slow process of convalescence after a most serious illness. Twenty-four years earlier she had been struck down by a cruel and far-reaching famine which all but broke her spirit, and claimed the lives of many of her subjects, for with this famine had come plague and pestilence. Many of those who were fortunate enough to survive were forced by circumstances to seek a new life in other parts and climes abroad. In 1846 the population was over 8 million, about half that of Great Britain; in 1852 emigration to America accounted for a reduction of 220,000, while the total effect of the combination of starvation and emigration had reduced the population to 5,788,415 in 1861 and 5.5 million in 1870.

Galway, in the West, and Queenstown as it was then called (now Cobh) in the South-west, were the principal ports from which Irish migrants set sail for the shores of America and Canada, few of whom ever again set foot on Irish soil.

This, then, was the Ireland in which on 2nd March 1870 Patrick Joseph Henry Hannon first saw the light of day. He was the first of eight children of Matthew Hannon of the townland of Tavrane in the (then) half Parish of Cloonlough in the County of Sligo. His mother was Catherine Henry, a daughter of Patrick Henry, a scholar known for his translation of Virgil direct from Greek into Irish, and a lateral descendant of the Patrick Henry associated with the American Declaration of Independence. Matthew was a small farmer in the district and his children were made to live a hard life, facing tough times when they came. As the years between childhood and manhood passed, Paddy was no exception to the rule of hard work!

It must be understood that in those times school was looked upon as a necessity of conformity with the laws of attendance and not as a means of real advantage to the student! Paddy, however, did not regard it in this light at all. To him it was the opening to an entirely different and new world where he could, and did, by sheer hard work gain knowledge above the average and thus find himself, through his own ability, able to converse with many above his station and talk with them on equal terms. He once said, "I never allowed any boy to beat me or rise above me in class if I could possibly prevent it." His willpower as a boy must have been exceptional. He was not sportingly inclined, though he later became President of Aston Villa Football Club, of which he was very proud; to him the word 'knowledge' and that alone stood in front of all his activities. It became an obsession of his to rise far above the average. He read the newspapers with avidity; he made notes in scrapbooks and diaries (nearly all of which have unfortunately been lost) of interesting items from all parts of the globe, and his mind gradually became a miniature encyclopaedia. Even in his last years it was still his delight to wrestle with "abstruse mathematical problems".

He was married in 1894 to Mary Wynne, eldest daughter of Thomas Wynne of Castlebar, County Mayo, who himself had an unusual history. Of Welsh/Irish descent, he was the son of an emigrant from Castlebar to America who had (in America) married the third daughter of Richard MacEvilly of Ballyglass, Co. Mayo. Unusually, Thomas returned to Castlebar and established himself on business there in 1861, initially as a newsagent and bookseller. He was an enterprising man and set up a photographic studio in 1867, becoming one of Ireland's best known early photographers. A circulating library soon followed, long before the days of the Public Library, with a musical library in 1879 and he became an auctioneer of cattle, sheep and horses in 1886. The business was expanded to the towns of Limerick, Tipperary, Portarlington and Loughrea. His wife Margaret and his eldest daughter Mary were also photographers, and it was Mary who took on the Loughrea establishment. It was in Loughrea that Paddy Hannon met, courted and married Mary. The photography business was made over after her marriage to her sisters, Charlotte and Martha.

Paddy was very proud of the scholastic record of his grandfather, Patrick Henry. Apart from his eldest child, Cyril (who died at six months and was named after Paddy's great friend, the Carmelite Fr. Cyril Ryan), his sons all bore the names of Greek authors – Virgil, Horace and Desmond (though Horace may have been named after his friend and patron in the Irish Agricultural Organisation Society, Sir Horace Plunkett). His two daughters were Dorothy and Mary (Violet), the younger continuing his association with the Carmelite Order as a nun for thirty-three years.

His beloved Mary died in 1928, only four days before the birth of the eldest of their three grandchildren, Patrick, Michael and Neill.

In 1931 he was married for a second time to Amy Gordon-Barrett whose father, James Barrett, he had earlier known when a student at the Royal College of Science where James Barrett was a Librarian. Amy shared his interest in agriculture, being already well-known as a poultry breeder. She also shared his involvement with the Royal Navy, being secretary of the Kensington branch of the Navy League and having founded, in 1912, the training ship 'Stork' which helped boys in blind-alley jobs to secure new careers in the Royal and Merchant Navies. Amy died in 1960, having given him the unusual experience of two Silver Wedding celebrations.

Fortunate is the man who, having attained four and a half score years, can look back upon a life of unswerving devotion to the cause of his choice. The wish of service is born in many people, but few, alas, have the necessary energy and will to fulfil their desire. At the most it is often translated into a faint dissatisfaction with their mode of life. To the boy Patrick Hannon, brought up among the fields and bogs of County Sligo, there was this ever present need to identify himself with some cause that would lead to the betterment of the people around him. To his urge for service was added an immense energy and a flair for organisation. Unlike some of his fellow countrymen, who sought a solution in the destruction of the political system before all else, he realised that practical and immediate measures could alleviate distress. So Paddy Hannon, having discovered the signpost that was to guide him towards helping humanity, set upon the road of life armed with two great attributes – desire and capability. His horizon ever widened as he strode along, until it became clear to him that service to the British Empire was the best means of serving his fellow men. From then on he devoted himself to the wide fields of economic adjustment and mutual help in Empire trade and industry, influenced, no doubt, by his sojourn in South Africa; as also to the narrow, but no less important fields wherein the British individual dwells, until his retirement from Parliament. This enabled him to relax somewhat with the happy conscience of a man who has lived by his principles and has achieved the fulfilment of a useful life.

It is hard indeed to see what could have impeded the progress of a man blessed with Sir Patrick's direct, unswerving honesty, warm friendliness and keen sense of humour. He did not fail to learn and benefit from life's good gifts and adversities and always passed on the fruits of his experience. Where he found happiness, there he invited others to share it. Where he encountered hardship, there he strove to smooth the path for others. The value he derived from the education for which he had to struggle taught him to encourage others to attain the same standard. The brilliant women whom he met and with whom he worked during his early years in Ireland illustrated women's right of independence, therefore he supported the suffragette movement.

His studies at the Royal College of Science and his natural organising ability quickly won a niche for him in the newly formed Agricultural Co-operative Society, founded by Sir Horace Plunkett. Soon, he became Assistant Secretary and chief organiser of the Irish Agricultural Organisation Society. This meant constant travel throughout the country advising, urging and planning for the advancement of the farming community. His quick grasp of a situation and his clear portrayal of it suggested that he was well qualified to study industrial methods abroad, so he was sent to the Continent and later to America to study conditions there. His next mission was to Africa where, in 1905, he was made the Director of the Agricultural Organisation in Cape Colony. Here he had to deal with wine, feathers and fruit in addition to the industries better known to him; he had also to contend with the distrust between Boer and Britisher, and the immense distances from farm to farm. Yet in essence the South African's problem was identical with the Irishman's problem and one of the chief solutions lay in safeguarding Empire trade. This drew his sympathies towards Tariff Reform and, in 1909, he became Vice-President of the Tariff Reform League. The importance of shipping followed in natural sequence to Tariff Reform and industrial safeguarding, and for seven years he was secretary of the Navy League. With the expansion of air travel, and the possibility of European War, grew the essential need for an efficient Air Force. When the Aerial Defence Association was formed, he was made the Secretary. His next centre of activity was the British Commonwealth Union. He became its Director at a time when the whole Empire, having united to face their common enemy, was now suffering from slight reaction. An element of discord had invaded the Commonwealth, fed by fears of many ex-army men now unemployed. Patrick Hannon helped to form the Comrades of the Great War Association. He then worked with Earl Haig in the formation of the British Legion, thus averting not only a great individual misery, but also much unrest.

A keen interest in politics was the natural outcome of these activities. Indeed, four years before the outbreak of the Great War he had stood as a Unionist candidate for East Bristol. He was defeated, due in no small measure to religious prejudice, but he put up a gallant fight which was duly recognised and appreciated. In 1921 he stood for the East Moseley Division of Birmingham as Conservative candidate and was elected to Parliament. For nearly thirty years he held this seat for the Conservative Party, speaking fearlessly when the occasion demanded, always furthering the interests of the Empire and the individual. In 1936 his services were recognised by Royalty and a knighthood was conferred upon him. His energies, however, were not fully satisfied by politics. The business world claimed him, and he was a Director of many companies including H.P. Sauce and the Birmingham Small Arms Company (B.S.A.). In spite of all these financial and political ties, he found the time, in some remarkable way, for a practical interest in innumerable charities, institutions and clubs. In religion also he practised devout Catholicism and was notably active as a layman in all the affairs of the Church of his fathers. As a young man in Ireland in his student days, he derived considerable pleasure and satisfaction form his many clerical friends and in the service of the Faith. Although his driving ambition during his early years in England led him to seek advancement through Freemasonry (thus incurring excommunication), he was so impressed by a sermon preached in St. Peter's Basilica during a trip with a delegation to Rome that he returned to the fold in 1933 and remained firm throughout the remainder of his life. Among his many activities in the Church, he was, from its foundation in 1942, the Treasurer of the Apostleship of the Sea, thus carrying his interest in matters nautical into his religious life.

Although the trend towards dissolution of the Empire filled the post-war era, Paddy had no cause to regret the years he devoted to Empire unity. For such service cannot but have had a considerable and prolonged interest both at home and overseas and is in itself an example for all young men to follow.

'Sir Paddy' died on 10th January 1963, at the age of 93, full of years of wisdom, and was buried, clothed in the habit of the Carmelite Order which he cherished from his youth, in the grounds of St. Joseph's Carmelite Church at Gerrards Cross in Buckinghamshire.

Sir Patrick Hannon

8 January 1948 by Walter Stoneman
(©the National Portrait Gallery)

CHAPTER 1

With all his eccentricities, I loved old Martin Marron and Kitty McDonagh, his wife. They had a numerous family, some bitterly averse to me. Old Marron had two books in which he browsed in those obscure days of evolutionary struggle – the 'New Testament' and 'The History of Rome'. The 'New Testament' was part of the residue of a dead son, killed in India. Old Marron's possession of 'The History of Rome', probably bought for two-pence in a second-hand bookshop in Boyle, was one of the events of his life. Many times the huge tome was called into requisition from its place at the head of the bed to illustrate some current event by a parallel passage from the proceedings of the Curia, and Marron's eager audience would start an enlivening discussion. Small village gatherings frequently took place in his house, and the knowledge of Roman history in the townlands became remarkable. So intrigued were the villagers by his work that boys whom I knew well were addressed as Scipio, Caesar and Anthony; a man who had the hardihood to take a boycotted farm was known for many years by the not unenviable soubriquet of Nero.

Those two books were, in substantial degree, part of my early education, but there were just two more, coming perhaps a little later, which from those remote days onwards have always given me intense enjoyment. One uncle brought me a copy of Lewis Carroll's 'Alice in Wonderland' and another uncle an edition of 'Don Quixote'. The fascinating Lewis Carroll classic was in large print, with those pictures so familiar to readers throughout the world. The 'Don Quixote' was in small type and tested my eyes severely under the wretched paraffin lamp that I used in struggling through its pages. My uncle, of whom little can be said apart from his gross vulgarity, his comparatively well-off position in life as a village shopkeeper and his complete indifference to members of his family, is best forgotten.

The ruined churches and abbeys, and the graves of long forgotten heroes which are to be found in abundance throughout the rest of Ireland, aroused my early attention and were woven into thoughts in framing my long-continued interest in Irish antiquities. The old school, to which I first went as a tiny youngster, was that which replaced an old Catholic Chapel, remnant of the penal days. The building was dark, thatched and unattractive, and without any pretence to sanitary accommodation. The arrogant schoolmaster, whose genial and kindly wife was assistant schoolmistress, exacted a frightened reverence from the more or less ragged assemblance of urchins, male and female, who met there from day to day. Both Master and Mistress may be described, without want of any charity, as uneducated in the modern sense of the word, but both had qualities which, in spite of great defects, give them a place in my memory after four-fifths of a century. There was Monitor and Monitress, pleasant specimens of peasant character. The ambition of the Monitor was to become a member of the Royal Irish Constabulary and the ambition of the Monitress was to be his wife when he became Sergeant.

A river flowed by the school, giving me the greatest delight. I loved to hear the trembling cadence of its waters which, even in those raw conditions of shadowy intellectual development, stirred some sort of poetic feeling which has lasted with me all my life. Poverty struck a severe note in my little affairs at that time and after a few years I left this little school to work on my father's farm. The sale of turf from our peat bogs, in addition to such modest help as I could render from sowing and reaping, made a grave gap in a young life which was, perhaps, a little detached from the outlook of the peasant families by whom we were surrounded. Later I entered the same school again. In the meantime, it had been reconstructed; the old, thatched building had been removed and a modern school, provided by the National Board of Education in Ireland, had taken its place. My mental development was precocious and in the process of time, aged about fifteen, I became a Monitor.

A Monitor in an Irish National School in my young days occupied a position between teaching and acquiring knowledge of primitive Science and Art. What is most pitiful to recall now is how little Science and how little Art entered into the so-called education of that time. All the same, my mind grew broadly. My tremulous entry into the fields of knowledge had its effect and, although I say it with diffidence, in the course of a single year I advanced through five classes in preparation for the annual school examination.

2

In those days teachers were rewarded by payments on results and it occurred to my narrow-minded schoolmaster that he could use my modest intellectual equipment for a few years by placing me in a class lower for examination than that to which I was entitled. The whole depressing educational regime of those disastrous years left me largely to my own resources and I read and re-read without guidance (and certainly with no help from the schoolmaster) whatever book of any quality was available. I succeeded as Monitor John McDonagh, a very memorable personality, gentle and kindly, with whom an intimacy grew that largely determined my destiny. He had textbooks in preparation for his examination, and these we studied together, side by side. As my imagination expanded, he continued to press on me the desirability of looking forward to a Civil Service career.

My appointment as Monitor was delayed for a year because of the affection that the local Inspector of Schools entertained for Irish. He forgot to forward my papers of appointment to the Education Department in Dublin. Finally, however, they came through and I entered upon my professional career with all modesty and abounding self-confidence in the enjoyment of my thirty shillings a quarter.

A happy recollection of those days is the affection that grew between the Schoolmaster's eldest daughter and myself. My poetic temperament was stimulated by her gentle kindness. John McDonagh, whose memory I revere, became Master of a small school called Deerpark, perched on the slopes of the Curlew mountains north of Boyle, looking down upon the picturesque region of Lough Key and the beautiful home of Colonel King-Harman.

In those days the Department of Science and Arts, South Kensington, influenced the elementary schools in Ireland. The Master of Deerpark had gained his certificates in Advanced Science, which enabled him to qualify his pupils for examination under that Department. I count this as my good fortune to have tramped across the ranged [rugged?] mountain sides to attend lectures at this little school, more appropriately described, perhaps, as a shepherd's cottage.

I gained Honours in Mathematics, Physiography, Geology, Elementary Chemistry (and one or two other subjects) which gave me the status, so ludicrous to me now, of a teacher in those subjects. McDonagh's own education was entirely due to his diligence, his textbooks and his limited range of acquaintance with competent educational authorities. Alas for those days! How hard one struggled to get a little learning, textbooks were as difficult to get as enlightening guidance. The process then moulded character. Modern educational facilities are different, and probably involve pupils in less strain.

The fragmentary school career of mine passed from phase to phase, remote from those stimulants which arise from constant communication with the cultured influence of superior intellects. But, in many respects, it was great fun, and there is some salutary joy in placing it on record. We had a little Post Office established in the village of Cloonloo and the Postmistress, a kindly, smiling benevolent lady of indeterminate age, became one of my great friends. I took much joy in visiting this primitive Post Office and, with Miss Rush, studied with expanding zeal the meaning and structure of Post Office administration in Ireland. This was my earliest contact with the Civil Service, which I had hoped to enter. Peace to the memory of that affectionate Miss Rush. We read an wrote and, perhaps a little diffidently, loved and talked a gathered wisdom together.

One of my duties as a Monitor was the serving of Mass for the priests who came to the local churches. The Church at Cloonloo was typical of the struggle made by the Catholics to provide schools for their increasing peasant population following the penal period. The teaching of my old Master of the Latin imperative in the serving of Mass gave me, years afterwards, many peals of crude laughter when I made a more intimate acquaintance with the language of Virgil and Cicero. However, the priests were most kind and the other servers and I slobbered [?] for years, with more or less devotion, in reciting the Latin responses in accordance with the teachings of Cloonloo. Turning to those grim times, with their melancholy, but nevertheless, genial recollections, the Irish scene was changing. The Parnell movement rose in its full commanding appeal to the sentiment of the Irish people. In the villages, small gatherings took place at which I read the newspapers of the day to the assembled half-hungry, half-expectant peasants.

Michael Davitt was one of the great heroes, and I can see as if it were yesterday his appearance on a public platform, surrounded by thousands of peasant farmers. The memory of his voice still reverberates through my brain, calling for fierce unity to exterminate landlordism, with all its attendant vices. These represented for Davitt the British regime in irish government. I once walked after a procession for the five miles to Boyle to a great 'Demonstration' as they were usually called. I can still remember T. P. O'Connor and Jasper Tully demonstrating against the horrors of Dublin Castle – the satanic instrument of Irish oppression. At the close of this 'Demonstration' I was exhausted and hungry and had to walk home, leaving the town with the same sort of feeling as David Copperfield when he undertook his first visit to London. On the broad highway I met a tall, decently dressed man with a red tie and a florid watch chain. He looked at my pitiable appearance and asked: - "Is anything the matter?" I replied that I was ashamed to admit that I was hungry. He took me by the shoulders and brought me back to a baker's shop, just at the edge of the town, where he bought me a loaf of bread for four-pence. But, while proceeding on my way, enjoying my bread, I met a fellow schoolboy for whom I entertained a strong aversion. He was equally hungry, apparently, and although I confess it with shame, under 'force majeure', I parted with half my loaf. These may be regarded by some people as extravagances in an elderly man, but I have always been interested in the effects of action, and such incidents indelibly impressed their marks amongst the shadows and pictures composing the background of my life.

In those days I became acquainted with the Station-master at Kilfree Junction named Egan, who was anxious to improve his neglected elementary education. He suggested that from time to time I might be able to come and give him instruction, and this proposition made a convincing appeal to me. He was a strange character swayed by a mixture of kindness and prejudice. He owed his position to the influence of one of the Directors of the Midland and Great Western Railway and he was anxious to make himself familiar with vulgar fractions and the rules of simple proportion to prepare for further promotion. One result of all this was that I showed every anxiety to join the Railway Service as a signalman, and so to continue instructing the Stationmaster as a member of his staff. Although I was then very young, under sixteen, I succeeded through his intervention with the Chairman of the Railway Company in becoming what was described as a Signal-learner at Kilfree Junction.

The Directors of Irish Railways made visitations from time to time upon the various branches of their railways. Before my appointment, Mr Egan suggested that I should be on the platform on the occasion of their momentous visit. I was thus introduced to the Chairman of the Board, Sir Ralph Cusack, a very delightful man who became a warm friend of mine for many years subsequently, and the Hon. Richard Nugent, uncle of the then Earl of Westmeath. It is very amusing to look back on the conferences of (as it seemed to me in those days) this great body of Railway Directors, in a waiting room of what was one of the most weird and weather-beaten stations in the United Kingdom. Mr Nugent cross-examined me on my modest educational attainments, asking me to give him the enunciation of the forty-seventh proposition of the first book of Euclid; namely that the square described on the hypotenuse of a right-angled triangle is equal to the sum of the squares on the other two sides. I gave him an immediate and clear-cut exposition of this ancient theorem, which pleased him immensely, as it did the Board. Ever since then, I can never think of that ancient Greek philosopher, Pythagoras, without feeling that in the strange vagaries of life it was early Greek culture that gave me my appointment to the bleak and uncongenial signal box at Kilfree Junction.

An immediate, joyful experience of my appointment was the visit of an official on one of his tours, who was allowed to provide watches for the Company's servants, payable by instalments to be deducted from their wages. In the course of a fortnight my beautiful new Hunting-lever watch arrived; I cannot now picture, in all the vagaries of experience I have had, any greater joy than I had in paying two shillings and sixpence for a watch, and swaggering with that beautiful watch in the presence of an assembled multitude of friends and admirers, which I did after Mass at Cloonloo Church on the Sunday following its acquisition.

Time rolled on and differences arose, and Mr Egan became dissatisfied for one reason or another with my teaching. I shall say nothing against his memory, but one meets so often in life those changes of dep friendship into the bitterness of antagonism. I cannot now mark precisely how our troubles arose, but, after a year or so, partly no doubt because of want of continuous attention to his needs, and partly because his intellectual capacity could not extract the square root of a particular function, the storm gathered … departure from Kilfree desirable!

The District Inspector of the Midland Great Western Railway was one of the great gentlemen of my youth. His name was Hildebrand. Later, in my travels in Europe (and especially in Italy) where I have met the great name of Hildebrand, I have always remembered the gentle and considerate view which that District Inspector took of my case. He arranged my transfer to Kilcock in the delightful County Kildare, the centre of a romantic region where love of horses animates every feature of local life. My new Stationmaster, Mr Perry, was a genial, kindly Protestant, with all the qualities common to his class and responsibility. He was an ideal chief and a gentle, though at the same time exacting, friend. He had a charming wife and charming children, and I had the pleasure in later years of rendering some service to his boys, one of whom became a soldier and the other a member of the Royal Navy. It was great fun being a signalman at Kilcock, an occupation chiefly of idleness. Signals received from trains going up and down were to be transmitted to the next box. One waved to the driver as he passed, received messages on the local telegraphic instrument and, in my case, studied a little Latin, advanced mathematics, some science and all Dickens' novels. What a revelation I found in the picture of life that Dickens drew for his readers out of the profundity of his experience.

At that time, I scribbled a certain amount of very inferior poetry (several volcanic specimens were printed in a paper called 'The Weekly Irish Times' and occasionally I burst into newspaper contributions under the 'nom-de-plume' of 'Kilman'. Controversy sometimes arose from points made by 'Kilman' in the press. There is a secret joy in seeing such comments, especially when the original writer is regarded by subsequent correspondents not as a raw youngster, but as an old gentleman; one who has no doubt fared hard in life and whose mature experience should have been a brake on his all-advised volubility.

Kilcock has never been conspicuous in Irish international affairs, and its residents have not taken any part in the adjustment of international relations. But we had in Ireland, in my early days, a fascinating promoter of a popular variety of entertainment named Percy French. He wrote doggerel, frequently incorporated into popular songs, and of these, not the least popular was his ditty "On Kilcock". The subject of this extravaganza was the difficulty experienced by a respected resident of Kilcock in getting into Heaven. The song expressed St. Peter's surprise when he received an application that came from a modest township, of which the great saint had never heard. St. Peter was won over on hearing that Kilcock was a Midland Great Western station. Convinced, according to Percy French, the great Saint said with a grin:- "You may come in, but you're the first that came here from Kilcock."

To me, Kilcock was of some consequence in those years when a signal box was not the only means whereby I kept body and soul together, but was also my centre of study and mental improvement. In addition, the town afforded me an opportunity to develop diplomatic relations with the local Post Office. This was in the charge of a genial lady clerk who combined her great liking for a certain 'John Jameson' with the reading of popular novels. Alas! Her assiduous attention was given more to these ploys than to her Civil Service duties, with disastrous consequences. In the intervals of my devotion to Dickens, Walter Scott and Robert Louis Stevenson I browsed, read and frequently languished over 'East Lynne', 'Lady Audley's Secret' and heaven knows how many others of that type, introduced to me by the Postmistress, and which were supposed to represent the higher grades of social life in England. My lady friend and I received an aggregate remuneration of two pounds and ten shillings a week; we dwelt with comic satisfaction upon the experience of those in the country house and on the hunting field. In general, those characters were beautiful and attractive, but frequently they proved unable to endure passion without immorality. What an influence novel reading must have had upon the half educated classed then! Hosts of youngsters were shown how far removed they were from the grandeur of life enjoyed by those whose social status was derived from either heredity or the results

8

of adventure in the fields of exploration, invention or discovery.

During my temporary residence at Kilcock, the kind superior of the Christian Brothers School gave me free access to the Science Laboratory with its admittedly limited equipment. The Christian Brothers have been a seminal force in Irish education; day to day teaching on the lines of an elementary school, steadily rising to the level of a grammar school, opened wide vistas of opportunity for many young Irishmen. In the lower grades of the Civil Service (especially Customs and Excise) many Irish boys competed with success, in striking proportion more young Irishmen than English served that branch.

I made myself familiar with every branch of Civil Service duties, and it was my constant thought that (within my age limits) I might enter upon a permanent career. These were vague aspirations of which something must be said later, when at this age of seventeen or eighteen I envisaged possibly higher levels in the public service.

My great friend at Kilcock, apart from my deeply respected lady Post office friend, was the Parish Priest. He was a magnificent example of the highly cultured and finely developed character which marked a great generation in the Irish priesthood, though in large measure they faded away in the middle and later years of the nineteenth century. There was also the local doctor, gentle, refined, always sympathetic, anxious to talk of books and pictures or, better still, the countryside. He told me scraps from the history of the locality, as well as the traditional and legendary lore that surrounded the great families of the 'Pale'. I visited churches, old ruins, ancient forts and goodness knows what else that could bring one closer to the long, tragic story of Ireland's subordination to Anglo-Saxon rule. It happened also that a local small-landed proprietor of the same name as myself took a patronising interest in me, and on more or less formal occasions admitted me to the courtesies of a very pleasant household. This might have developed in many directions to my advantage, but a patronage where one's self-respect feels at a discount never made a strong appeal to me and, although I was grateful for recognition which I never sought, and which was conferred with a touch of calculated superiority, I nevertheless felt relieved when this remote relationship came to a close.

During this time, in what might be called my evolutionary period, I studied with some care (and frequently with mixed feelings) the little jealousies, vanities and ambiguities of human character which were manifest in those around me. It was amusing to reflect on the closely drawn lines of demarcation in the urban and rural outlook of the local farmers, tradesmen, petty officials and, no less, amongst those solicitors and local officials of the County administration described by statute as gentlemen. I may, perhaps, have been rather sensitive of neglect, misunderstanding and indifference on the part of those whom I served and with whom I worked from day to day, but that early experience struck into the depths of my soul, giving me an abhorrence of snobbery which, thank God, has been with me all my life. In the small and primitive communities of those early days in Ireland, the old classification of peoples as 'tup-pence half-penny looking down upon tuppence' can never be forgotten, nor can the inferiority of the wretched 'tuppence'.

Yet I entertain kindly recollections of the Railway officers with whom I associated, both at that time and, with few exceptions, in the years that followed. My Stationmaster was, in every respect, nature's gentleman. I had a good many wiggings, partly because of my scribblings for newspapers, partly because of my offering views on subjects of which I was wholly ignorant, in addition to challenging from time to time (with ill-directed impertinence) some action or other which should have been accepted with the respect due to a senior officer.

These paragraphs on Kilcock would be incomplete without reference to a matter of delicacy that stirred me deeply, at least for a temporary period. Through a colleague of mine I made the acquaintance of a very fascinating girl who lived with her mother in a cosy, old-fashioned house close to the great Catholic College of Maynooth. Sentimental bubblings arose and assignations were made under a veil of secrecy, which was as ridiculous as they were immature. The infatuation was not long sustained, but one incident is still vividly before me.

To fulfil what was politely called an appointment, I tried to enter an evening train on the side furthest from the platform in order to escape the notice of the Stationmaster, but, unfortunately, I found the door locked. Since I could not get in, I had the thrilling experience of travelling at high speed on the outside of the coach, clutching the brass handrails for four and a half miles between the two stations. A goods train passed during that trip. No knees ever knocked together more violently than mine as I dropped from my perch onto the platform when the train stopped at Maynooth. No doubt more mature persons have taken greater risks in the service of fair ladies, but they have surely been rewarded. Mine gave me no credit at all.

The word boarding-house must surely bring recollections of misery and dejection ot many minds as well as my own. During my transition period at Kilcock I sampled the hospitality of several boarding-houses where I was acutely uncomfortable. In my first experience, the lady of the house made every phase of her lodger's welfare subordinate to the dominant demands of her husband. Subsequent experience in two other lodgings was but a repetition, except that in one of them I was also unpleasantly aware of the crowd of children: they seldom washed. My last residence was somewhat more congenial, for I lived with a thoroughly decent and respectable ex-Sergeant of the Royal Irish Constabulary and his student son, who later became a priest. The lodging-house, its occupants and the ups and downs of management have occupied volumes in fiction and there is little I could add to relieve the dismal and, I must say, vulgar atmosphere of those far-off institutions.

Two years of somewhat disjointed and haphazard reading, writing and studying at Kilcock saw my promotion to a much more important signal-box at Mullingar. Mullingar opened for me a new and stimulating chapter. It was a country town of considerable size, having a first-class school (in which classes were held under the Department of Science and Art), a Literary Institute and a local newspaper. The Stationmaster was of the highest grade in his class and, although rigid and exacting, showed interest and sympathy towards my studious activities.

Shortly after taking up duty at Mullingar, I received a cheque for two pounds for an article written for a local journal, and as the object of the article was to establish friendly relations between Railway Authorities and the working staff in all the lower grades, it brought me a measure of friendship and encouragement, at least on the side of the workers. On the other hand, the 'powers that be' at the company's headquarters looked with distinct disfavour on the oddities of a young signalman who prescribed diplomatic relations between management and junior employees. This was, I think, the first occasion on which my scribbling reached the level of a modest cash value. I had already received numerous prizes in competitions in various weekly journals and magazines in the form of books, pencil-cases and other odds and ends, but those rewards of my labour could hardly be regarded as convertible currency.

In this connection, two other incidents occurred which played some part of my life in Mullingar. The first number of the 'Review of Reviews' edited by W. T. Stead was published and I lost no time in making my presence known to its exalted editor. I also made the acquaintance of the editor of the 'Westmeath Examiner', a local newspaper edited by a great gentleman, John P. Hayden, who, in the subsequent story of the Irish National Party, was a steady supporter of Parnell. Mr. Hayden showed me great friendship, lending me books, and from week to week he welcomed my notes and comments which were of very little value. No remuneration was expected or received.

Life in my off-duty hours at Mullingar flowed pleasantly, made up of evening classes, Institute meetings, country excursions and, in one way or another, a steadily widening sphere of friendship. In the country round about there are three delightful lakes, Loughs Ennell, Owel and Derravaragh which provide splendid boating opportunities. Yet in this picturesque and attractive countryside my career was almost brought to a close. A terrifying storm struck Lough Owel one Sunday at a moment when, with three or four friends, I had rowed far out into the lake. The unexpected gale caught our boat, and it was only through the mercy of God that we reached the shore again, far removed from the place where we had embarked. I remember so clearly standing among the rock of tufty grass, panting and exhausted, but all sincerely thanking God for what seemed to us to be a miraculous delivery from the great waters. People in the neighbourhood told me afterwards of their anxiety and despair as they watched our struggle against the storm, and of how they felt that at any moment we would be overwhelmed by the angry waves.

Lough Owel enjoys a legendary position in the story of Ireland. Most Irish people will remember, and many will have sung or shouted, one of Moore's melodies, 'Let Erin Remember' in which Malachi is described as winning the collar of gold from the proud invader. The proud invader was the Danish chieftain of ferocious Viking breed, and in the conflict with Malachi was drowned in Lough Owel.

Of more dramatic concern to me was the tiny island, which in those days was endowed with fine examples of Irish Ash. On the trunk of one of those trees I carved the initials of a lady for whom I was forming a romantic attachment. Frequently in after years, I wondered if those carefully carved initials were still to be found, in what was then to me a fairy island. I suppose my primitive contribution to a speculative love affair has faded away now, but it could not have faded as rapidly as did my dreams of one divinely conceived female in the presence of another.

My life in Mullingar, as I have indicated, was full of variety, and I entered upon the sphere of manhood during my occupation of that quaint old signal-box with its levers, block instruments and Morse telegraphic equipment. But it ended in tragedy, for I was responsible for throwing a train off the rails.

The manner of my misfortune was this. A new branch railway had been constructed from Attymon Junction to Loughrea and, on the morning of the opening, a special train had been fitted to take the Chairman of the Company, the General Manager and a number of Directors to the opening ceremony at Loughrea. This special train was intended to follow the principal train of the day, the 'Limited Mail' as it was called, which made very few stops. The particular lever, number nineteen, operated what are called catch-points in railway safety parlance, connecting the main line with the siding on which the special train was waiting. It was a somewhat exciting morning already, with so many V.I.P.s about and, instead of closing the safety points to allow the 'Special' to emerge on to the main line, I left them open and pulled number eighteen instead which operated a different set of points altogether. The morning immediately became much more exciting. The 'Special', instead of quietly steaming on to the main line, steamed on to the sleepers and flopped, mercifully, on to the Stationmaster's garden. Never did any signalman receive such a shock as I did on seeing the consequence of my mistake in handling the levers.

A group of mighty people approached the signal cabin and, contemplating the full value of my misfortunes, I at once declared to all and sundry that the disaster was entirely my fault. I was promptly suspended, another signalman took my place, and I walked along the platform as if I were approaching a Supreme Court of Judges as was accused of every crime under the sun. A new 'Special' had to be fitted out and, worst of all, the special dining coach where the Directors were to have lunched could not be released from the derailed 'Special'. It rested with what appeared to be genial indifference alongside that little flower garden which I sometimes tended in my desire to show my love of flowers to the ladies who were in charge of the Telegraph office on another platform.

The result of this catastrophe was my transfer from Mullingar to a quiet, homely station rejoicing in the name of Castletown Geoghegan, where a railway crossing was operated from a signal cabin. The Stationmaster, Mr. Casserley, who had once been a signalman at Kilfree Junction, gave me a kindly welcome and we became fast friends for the rest of my railway career. His wife was also a delightful person, bubbling over with good humour, and, in the leisurely intervals between the passing of trains and the opening and closing of level-crossing gates, we chatted gaily, exchanging such gossip as spreads over a rustic community.

I took up lodgings at a farmhouse not far from the station with a simple but kindly family, at the head of which was a characteristic specimen of the decent, hard-working Irish tenant farmer. There, seriously taking up the study of shorthand, I had great fun getting dictation practice from the girls and boys of the family at varying speeds.

It fell to my lot, also, at the instance of the Stationmaster, that I should take charge of the duties of Goods Clerk which, before my arrival, had been conducted by the Stationmaster. The telegraph duties in my cabin were partly the service of the G.P.O. In a short time I became familiar with a good deal of the somewhat primitive duties belonging to a country post office. Here I was then, a sort of multiple nonentity, performing with zeal a variety of the tasks that attach themselves to a small country railway station such as Castletown Geoghegan. In these circumstances I began to contemplate higher things, and Her Majesty's Civil Service constantly loomed over the horizon in my imagination.

I also had very strongly in mind the desire to become a University graduate. How one dreams of all these things at that time of life. Fortunately, I came under the influence of an outstanding example of Irish priesthood, Fr. Nedley, whose affection and constructive sympathy meant much to me in those early days. I tackled quite seriously the study of Latin and also, in a more scattered way, French. On the Latin side I can never quite forget 'Smith's Latin Grammar', nor the series of articles which appeared from month to month in a publication which for the moment I must call the 'Popular Educator'.

No doubt some elderly people will still recall those serial publications which endeavoured to bring within reasonable compass the whole sweep of human knowledge. In those days of struggle and visionary outlook I felt myself a sort of child of fortune, where the advantages of higher education, skilled instruction, and wise guidance in reading and study were replaced only by the throb of desire to reach objectives by short cuts suited to the limits of growing intellectual vitality.

The great joy of my life in those days was the purchase of a bicycle. I can see myself now, bubbling with excitement, when this bicycle (the ancient solid tyre variety) arrived at the station and emerged from the framework of its packing to the astonishment of the station staff. In those days a bicycle was a rare possession, and consequently its acquisition was an embarrassing problem for a railway Signalman, but an attractive system of monthly payments made possession possible. My clerical friend and companion, to whom I have already referred, also possessed a bicycle and there followed for me a sort of era of travel. Both of us were interested in Irish history and archaeology, and Sunday after Sunday became days of exploration through the many-featured countryside. Routes were planned, places to be visited were discussed, old guidebooks studied and pubs located where a modest midday meal could be obtained at the least expense. Yes, life was full in those days, not the least joy of which was the expectation of Sunday.

My time at Castletown was not, even in my raw condition, entirely detached from Romance. At the next station, Streamstown, the Stationmaster had two lively and pretty daughters. Pleasant chats on our telegraphic instruments, the exchange of periodicals and books and occasional poetic quotations add a fading chapter to those far-off times for which memory is grateful. Among other activities there was my systematic correspondence with a young French student in Paris University. He wrote me long dissertations in French on his reading, his outlook on life, his friends and those parts of the history of France which he was studying. My letters were in English, occasionally requesting the more exact translation of some of the delicacies of French expression. I learned a good deal in this way, not merely of French history and the day today life of a French student, but the faculty of reading the language which, in course of time, presented little difficulty to me. This knowledge was very useful to me in subsequent years when, with the help of the Carmelite Fathers, I blundered through the lectures of Pere Lacordaire and other French savants.

My keeping of the accounts in the Railway Store was quite satisfactory and I felt, not without reason, that a Goods Office would give me more scope for the modest ambitions I harboured that a signal cabin, in spite of the incidental opportunities of companionship and educational facilities. Thus I became a Goods Clerk and was promoted to the town of Loughrea. Although proud of my new job, I left Castletown with the sadness of gracious memories. Those bicylcle rides with my beloved Padre, our endless talks on life and manners, on the hopes and fears for our country, made an island in my life from which it was difficult to project a bridge for departure. Yet this was needed. So, with my bicycle and my scanty luggage, I waved a gentle goodbye to the old signal cabin, the Goods Office, the kindly Stationmaster and his wife, the sons and daughters of the farmstead which had been my temporary abode, and the girls of the neighbouring houses with whom quarrels and reconciliations were balanced in equal proportion.

Loughrea, a town of some consequence situated on a small lake from which it takes its name, fills stormy periods of Ireland's history during the Land War and anti-British activities. In the reign of Queen Victoria it enjoyed headlines in the National press. It was the centre of violent agitation which spread through the Clanricarde estate. The Marquis of Clanricarde, who was never seen in Ireland, possessed an extensive property in South Galway, including several towns of which Loughrea was the principal. The storm that broke over rural life in the 1880s was acutely felt by the whole of the Clanricarde tenantry. The 'Nor Rent' manifesto received patent support on the estate. In sober truth, the rents had not been exorbitant, but the leaders of the Land League Movement were determined that resistance to the payment of rent should be maintained side by side with the more cruelly rack-rented people in other parts of the West of Ireland. Evictions took place on a large scale, and villages of temporary houses were erected on the fringes of the Clanricarde property to house victims of what was regarded as bitter persecution.

Those were grim days of conflict between landlord and tenant, and between the policy of Her Majesty's Government and the leaders of the Irish Land League Movement. This old sad story has been presented with peculiar force by one of the noblest and most sincere Irishmen of that time, Michael Davitt, in his 'Fall of Feudalism in Ireland', and also by an endless array of ephemeral political publications as well as more permanent contributions to modern Irish history.

But I must return to my own life in Loughrea, to the home of the Stationmaster, where I was received as what would politely be called a 'paying guest', and to my shabby little Goods Office with its concrete floor and common deal counter. The Office was adjacent to the Goods Store in which wagons were loaded and unloaded, and over which a patriarchal personality, Nat Bently, was supreme director. Nat was a magnificent person with a flowing beard; when erect he stood well over six feet. In ordinary day to day work he was gentle, helpful and sympathetic to the somewhat immature Goods Clerk. From time to time his warm affection for the great firm of Guiness developed somewhat stormy weather, and that long forgotten Goods Store would be filled with vocal extravagance. Peace be to Nat's ashes. He produced a large family, all of whom (in one way or another) found niches to fill in Railway jobs, and he ended his days in charge of a Railway crossing not far from Dublin, where the opening and closing of gates synchronised with his undeviating attachment to that famous brewery product.

My work was interesting, presenting little difficulty and allowing long periods of spare time. The Stationmaster, James Brennan, and his wife were pleasant people in their way but, as their family grew, I had to seek fresh lodgings. One of the sons of this family has become a prominent member of a distinguished Order of the Catholic Church, and if he should read my little story I would like him to know of my attachment to his father and my deep affection for his devoted mother whose spirit of self-sacrifice stood on a high level, bringing up a family on a limited income.

As the shadows of old age fall, thoughts of the past and the revival of incidents of early life flow vividly before the mind. It is very difficult to classify in order of any special appeal the various incidents, nevertheless there are standing out always those which awaken a series of thoughts on early days when, like many other youngsters, I was a dreamer of dreams. I thought I could best recall some of the story of my past by indicating the generous kindness of many friends who, in various ways, lent a helping hand along the narrow and sometimes difficult paths of my life.

It was my good fortune in my young days to become the particular friend of the Carmelite Order, and the friendship and kindly help of those venerable Fathers has been closely woven into my early life. The Order of Discalced Carmelite is one of the oldest in the Catholic Church, and the Monastery at Loughrea is the parent institution of the Order in Ireland. Spreading widespread influence over the spiritual life of the Irish people was the Novitiate of the Order, in which early training of young novices was conducted before their periods of study and religious exercises at conventual establishments elsewhere. The old Abbey at Loughrea, with all its charm under the shadows of the ancient, ruined Norman Church was, to me, a second home and a school in those far off days which are still fresh in my memory. The Abbey church in its Monastery grounds, in its forlorn, roofless condition, but with the tower still more or less intact, was the embodiment of Galway history.

My emotions were deeply stirred by the many monuments of past generations; in the graveyards surrounding the old ruins rest generations of families whose names were familiar to succeeding generations of Galway families. The warriors who fought for Irish freedom against the serried invasions of their native land sleep side by side with the sons of the Monastery who kept the Faith alive in the darkest days and who are custodians of its exemplary power and beauty in the days in which we live.

In the pages of history, it is a very long call from Mount Carmel, looking down on the waters of the Levant to the West of Ireland where, in an ivy-clad ruin of a Norman Church, maintains the sacred heritage of the same undeviating concept of Faith and sacrifice.

Among these devoted Fathers was the Very Reverend Edward Holland who was then, and at other periods, the Prior of the Monastery and who has been Provincial of the Irish branch of the Order for more than one period of office. What a wonderful time I had with dear old Father Holland. I have already mentioned the purchase of my first bicycle. This I sold for thirty shillings and replaced with a new 'Safety Bicycle', bought again on the instalment system, paying I think ten or fifteen shillings per month. This incited Father Edward to secure a machine for himself, for which in his more affluent circumstances he was able to pay the £12 which, I think, was the price of the early 'Safety Bicycle' at that time. Thus, I taught him to ride. During the summer holidays of Irish priests from their parish duties, Father Holland frequently undertook to conduct their services, and we rode gaily off together from one weekend to another; Father Edward doing all the spiritual work of the Parish at the weekend, and I discharging the humble task of small service here and there, and serving Mass on Sundays.

I owed much to my close relationship with Father Edward, and among many friendly acts he brought me in close touch with Edward Martyn of Tulira Castle, Ardrahan, who was indeed a very remarkable personality, as well as a large landowner, and with whom my friendly association was maintained until his death many years afterwards in Dublin. My affection for Father Edward became intensified during the whole of my life, and I felt utmost sorrow when, after many years, he passed away in the Monastery in Clarendon Street, Dublin. Of the Carmelite Fathers and Brothers at the Monastery it is enough o say that I was devoted to them all and they were all especially fond of me; they were always helpful in my studies in those early days when I was making a struggle to obtain a degree of the Royal University of Ireland.

The Royal University provided opportunities for external students to work through a course from Matriculation to Degree stage, and I made up my mind to pursue a programme based on the university syllabus, seeking nothing higher in the long run than a 'pass' degree. I may say here that I passed my Matriculation and First Arts Examination at Queen's College, Galway, and my Second Arts at the Headquarters of the Royal university in Dublin. Even this much would hardly have been possible without the wonderful help of the Carmelite Monastery, and the tolerance and understanding of the Railway management in giving me provisional holidays over the Examination periods. My great advantage of my early contact with the Carmelite Order in Loughrea Monastery was the use of the library which, although in many respects out of touch with renewed publications, embraced an immense collection of classic and old-world publications. I enjoyed access to it at all times, late and early, and it steadily became a gold mine to me in my continuous efforts to reach a moderate level in the study of the Classics, especially Latin.

Loughrea will always be memorable to me for one act alone. It was there that I met one of the most charming little women in the world, and it was there, on 8th August 1894, that I married her. Her people lived in Castlebar, where they had a large photographic business, and it was my very good fortune that their daughter, Mary Wynne, came to Loughrea to open a branch there. Soon after my marriage I resigned from the Midland Great Western Railway in order to devote the greater part of my time to study, and we settled down at my wife's home, Clifden House, Loughrea.

It was now my ambition to become an Inspector of Schools, and with this object in view I worked frightfully hard while my splendid little wife carried on the business. There was a small garden at the back of our house, and I have pleasant memories of the odd moments snatched from my books to learn the joys of the practical application of horticulture, experimenting with seeds and plants in all manner of ways. I learned something, too, of the scientific side of photography, in the evening hours when I helped my wife with developing, printing and enlarging.

The resident Commissioner was kind enough to nominate me for the position of School Inspector, but to my exasperation and disappointment the examination was postponed. In 1895 the course of study fro the Inspectorship of Schools was altered, and the same examination was introduced for the Civil Service. So the following year I went up to Dublin to sit for my B.A. As luck would have it, in the very middle of the examination, I brole down and had to retire with a frightful chill and temperature. After that debacle, I decided to stand for the Civil Service. I was interested at that time in a particular branch called the Boundary Survey of Ireland, and hoped I might be one of the fortunate few to attain a position in it. The examination was held at 64. Merrion Square, Dublin and there were three vacant places to be filled. It was a sad blow to me when three graduates of Dublin University beat me to fourth place by nine marks. However, I had a second attempt at a later date, and this time there was only one place and twenty of us competing for it. Again I was defeated, reaching second place eleven marks below the winner. How often since then have I thanked my Guardian Angel for, what seemed at the time, to be a severe setback to my career.

In wandering through the highways and bye-ways of one's early life, one lives again with some of the earliest patrons and sympathisers of one's earliest ambitions. In those far-off days there was no-one closer to me, and of more influence on my spiritual life and thought, than Bishop Duggan who had retired as Bishop of Clonfert some few years earlier. He had served the Church with continued assiduity and constructive purpose for over half a century, and in those days when I came in touch with him in his retirement, he was still a virile personality in full possession of his faculties. He took a great interest in me, for he was related to the Hannons, a relationship scattered all over Sligo and Roscommon, and his kindness and hospitality were very warming to a young fellow like myself.

He talked to me of the famine days, which he bitterly remembered, of the emigrant ships going to the United States with Irish men and women escaping from the destitution of a land ravished by inescapable misery. I remember so well, also, his telling me the story of how he was in Lourdes at the time that the vision appeared to Saint Bernadette. To see this humble peasant girl and hear her story was a privilege bestowed on few Irishmen, and it was with feelings of great awe and reverence that I listened to his account. The wonder of that experience made a tremendous impact on his spiritual life.

In dealing with my early friends in the Catholic Church, whose influence upon my life stimulated the wisdom of outlook and cautious appreciation of difficulties and deterrent influences, we had in Loughrea in those days, (and I believe it is still there), a Diocesan College, which aimed in some modest way at the preparation of students for the Examinations of the Intermediate Board, which at that time, and for many years after, was the directive influence in the Secondary education of Irish youth. The Head of this very small and limited College was the Reverend Martin Leahy, a very good priest but a very moderately qualified Schoolmaster. Looking back upon the past, and speaking quite dispassionately, I think it was quite true to say that the great defect of Secondary education was the limited qualification of those comprised in the teaching bodies of those Secondary Schools.

The Department of Science and Art, South Kensington, had spread its education organisation in a very limited and scattered way over various parts of Ireland, and this so-called Seminary became an Examination Centre. In addition to the Grades I had already taken at Galway and Dublin, I took advantage of the opportunities presented by this modest country school. The result was that I passed successive examinations in the Higher grades of Physical Science, Geology, Mathematics and other subjects, which in those days enabled me to exercise the qualification of Teacher, under the Department of Science and Art, in certain specified subjects. It was my good fortune to enjoy the friendship and abiding interest of Dr. Healy, Bishop of

Clonfert at the time (subsequently Archbishop of Tuam.) He showed me the greatest possible consideration from time to time, and gave me continuous encouragement in my educational struggle. I grieve to say that on one occasion I committed the grievous fault of incurring his severe admonition.

The position of Science Teacher in Limerick Scientific College became vacant and, with his commendation, I approached Dr. O'Dwyer, the Bishop at the time, and received a very favourable reception, with the promise of his patronage in receiving the appointment. I made a blunder, in my own stupid way, of writing a foolish letter thanking the Bishop for his support, which embodied some suggestions which the Bishop regarded as offensive and which he promptly repudiated. He wrote to Dr. Healy, recited my blunder and intimated that he took no further interest in my effort to secure a prominent teaching position in the Diocese of Limerick.

This was a sad blow and, at once, a warning for more careful and thoughtful writing to exalted personalities in the Catholic Church, all of whom, throughout my long life, I now acknowledge to have been my generous and unfailing friends.

In the year 1896, through the commendation of Dr. Healy, I was introduced to the Headmaster of Tuam Diocesan College and was appointed Scientific and Mathematics Master, a position that I held for the better part of two years. This brought me in contact with a new sphere of life, and with many young men who afterwards became prominent members of the Church, who have always remained my friends. I took charge of the Science classes, and in spite of the record of the School for successes in Classics in the Intermediate Examinations, introduced Science and Mathematics as subjects of interest, with some substantial measure of success.

It was a very interesting chapter in my life, to give three days a week to the work of the College and to be associated with the teaching staff, all of whom were priests, and whose friendship has continued for two generations to be an asset in my life. Numbers of my former pupils, nearly all of whom were destined for the priesthood, maintained contact with me in various ways for many years, and afterwards in the Agricultural revival in which I took a leading part for so many years, were friendly and helpful, although sometimes somewhat critical of my public activities.

The Archbishop of Tuam at that time was the venerable and eminently respected Prelate Dr. McEvilly, who was related to my wife. The Archbishop was very kind to me, saw a good deal of me at class work, paid me compliments from time to time, and invited me on various occasions to enjoy the hospitality of the various functions of the Palace. One day, when I was enjoying the hospitality of Dr, Duggan, in the company of Father O'Donovan from Loughrea and Father Lyons from Castlebar, I was introduced to that most remarkable and beloved man, Father Tom Finlay. S. J. (blessed be his memory), and within a matter of weeks the whole outlook of my life changed. It is scarcely necessary for me to mention that Father Tom Finlay was an enthusiastic advocate of agricultural co-operation, and a prominent leader of the Irish Agricultural Organisation Society under Sir Horace Plunkett. He toured the countryside, speaking at Co-operative meetings here, there and everywhere, and it was through his introduction that my life with the I.A.O.S. began.

I had been doing a tremendous lot of writing at that time, and for one whole year I reported for a local paper, the 'Tuam News', for a man called MacPhilbin, who was then Editor. On the completion of the sittings of the Recess Committee (over which Horace Plunkett presided in August 1896) I had written various articles in this and other Galway newspapers, calling attention to the value of the report and pleading for its study on the somewhat stagnant and hopeless condition which then prevailed in Ireland, and these articles drew Plunkett's attention to me.

A few words here will suffice to make readers aware of the purpose of the Committee. The recommendation made was that a Department of Agriculture for Ireland should be formed, under a Minister directly responsible to Parliament. In most cases the numerous Government Boards in Ireland were responsible only to the Chief Secretary, Horace Plunkett, in an endeavour to combine the political and industrial force of the country, collected a wonderful group of men of all shades of belief into his Committee. They had one object in view, namely the advancement of Agriculture and Industry in Ireland. There was the Grand Master of the Belfast Orangemen, Colonel Sanderson and, of course, Father Tom Finlay, a Jesuit priest. John Redmond was there, with a number of Unionists as contrast. Leading industrialists from the North and the South were also members. The report, then, was sent to the Lord Lieutenant, but it was three years before Plunkett's scheme came to fruition.

Later, when I stayed with Col. Sanderson and his wife at their home, Castle Sanderson as it was called, in Co. Cavan, they were both most hospitable and extremely kind. I remember that Mrs. Sanderson was so anxious that I should be able to attend Mass. She sent for one of the footmen at night, and said: - "Mr. Hannon wants to go to Mass to-morrow morning, and you must have the trap round here for him at whatever time he wants to go." So much for religious intolerance.

Early in 1897, Father Finlay brought me to a conference of the I.A.O.S. at which Horace Plunkett showed me great kindness, and from that time forward in greater or less degree, I took part in its activities.

The Movement was a curious mixture of idealism and practicalities, aiming gloriously for the stars with one hand, and building a stout and solid stairway to the rooftops with the other. I found that I was the servant of an organisation which 'was, essentially, a teaching body designed to educate the people, to rouse them from their lethargic state of hopeless dependence by teaching them, among other things, the almost unknown virtues of thrift and economy, and also educating them in business methods. It was a Movement in which the practical man of business, the philanthropist and the idealist alike could all find common purpose. Brotherhood, the root of co-operation, was a principle difficult to inculcate in the members of the Society throughout the country. Only too often the Irish farmer of those days imagined that the only way to better himself was first to 'beat' his neighbour.

The practical side of our work may be classified as follows: -
1. The production of butter from milk sent to the Creamery
2. The transport of cream to auxiliary creameries
3. The purchase at wholesale prices of seeds, manures, etc.

4. Provision of stud animals and costly machinery
5. The sale in bulk of pigs, grain, vegetables and so on
6. The establishment of agricultural credit Banks
7. Reform of the poultry industry
8. The acquisition of land for grazing
9. The establishment of home industries
10. Raising the social life of the people by various methods

It may be seen from this that our scheme covered a wide variety of ideas, and that we had to be thoroughly acquainted with a host of subjects. The problem uppermost at that time, one indeed which had been in that state since the disastrous famine days, was that of emigration, which was continuing on a deplorably large scale. Through force of circumstances the manhood and womanhood of Ireland were transported from their quiet homes to the alleys and dens and unknown ways of the great expanding Republic on the other side of the Atlantic. The Irishman whose intelligence was quickest to grasp the nature of the terrible evil that was being wrought, and the possibility of averting the extraordinary misfortune of finding Ireland peopled by the very old, the very young, cripples and the feeble-minded, was Horace Plunkett. His programme was to regard Ireland as a co-operative workshop, where all the zeal, energy, and enthusiasm of co-operative production might be utilised in order to market Irish agricultural products abroad.

If one Province of Ireland needed the stimulation of agricultural co-operation more than any other, the claims of Connaught were very strong; for in the remote parts of Connemara, and all along the greater part of the coast, the poverty was heartrending. I remember taking Dr. Moritz Bonn, a distinguished German professor of education and economics, on a tour of some of these desolate spots. Among other places, we visited the Aran Islands, also Clare Island, that stretch of land that lies at the entrance to Clew Bay, once a stronghold of the famous Grace O'Malley (Granuaile) but, at the time of which I am speaking, a remote and hunger-stricken region, with sea birds shrieking round its thousand foot cliffs. When Dr. Bonn had first come to Ireland to study our extreme economic condition, he was of the opinion that the Celt must soon disappear. But, having heard the intelligent discussion that invariably followed the local I.A.O.S. meetings, and having spoken with some of the frieze-coated mountain dwellers from the backward districts who advanced sensible, well-balanced opinions, though the pinch of hunger lay on their faces, he became astonished at their shrewd philosophy and did not hesitate to revise his opinion. It was my good fortune, many years later, to render him a small service. His sister had married an Italian and, after the Great War when she wanted to return to her family, was having some difficulty in obtaining permission from the authorities: I was able to get a permit for her.

The first Co-operative Society to be formed in County Galway was, if I remember rightly, in the village of Tyaquin [now Tiaquin]. The Parish Priest, with all his benevolent interest in his people, was invariably brought into play as the guiding star in every project of this nature. During Mass one Sunday he would announce that a meeting of Parishioners would take place, and would be addressed by some leading personality in the Parish and by the organiser of the I.A.O.S. The meeting took place, presided over by the Priest, and the Speaker would deliver an impassioned appeal to bring the farming community together, to improve their agricultural methods, purchase their seeds and fertilisers under more scientific direction, and enjoy a substantial price reduction through collective distribution and purchase.

Looking back, the speeches were amusing, and you could not find the exaggerative faculty of my fellow countrymen more striking than the picture described by them of the forthcoming blessings of co-operation. We usually adjourned to the local Schoolhouse, where the formation of a Working Committee for the Parish was then the leading object of consideration. Usually a 'strong' farmer was selected, and in almost every case a local Schoolmaster was invited to become Honorary Secretary. To avoid the dangers of nepotism, which was a frequent difficulty in these rural Societies, we made it a rule that no member of the local community could hold this position. It was then my business to arrange the registration of the Society under the Industrial and Provident Society Act of 1893, which had been in operation in Great Britain for covering the proceedings of Co-operative Societies under the directive control of the Co-operative Union of Manchester.

It is a mere platitude to repeat now what has been accepted for over half a century as the benevolent purpose and result of co-operation in farming. The record, in its aggregate values, has been presented in Plunkett's 'Ireland in the New Century' (1904). During my active association with that lively and sometimes fantastic movement, it was my good fortune to enjoy the delightful friendship of Sir Henry Grattan Bellew. His charming home, Mount Bellew, was open to me at all times and all seasons. Locally he received the quaint nickname of 'hull-a-bulloo' because of his breezy manner, rapidity of speech and erratic character. His charming wife, whom I can never forget, Lady 'Sophie (a sister to the Earl of Granard) was the embodiment of every quality which could be exemplified by the chatelaine of a great country house in Ireland.

We organised a Co-operative Agricultural Society at Mount Bellew that became, in some respects, a model for similar Societies in the surrounding districts. My friend Sir Henry was incessantly active, not merely in and around Mount Bellow, but throughout the whole West of Ireland, promoting the expansion of the I.A.O.S. As an example of our activity, during one Saturday afternoon Sir Henry and I addressed consecutive meetings in the villages of Ahascragh, Caltra and Ballymacward. Those were the days of laborious and uncertain transport.

In the years 1897 and 1898 there was scarcely a rural Parish in the West of Ireland in which attempts were not made, with some measure of success, to introduce co-operation in Agriculture. In almost every case Sir Henry's exertions were successful. In paying my heartfelt tribute for the courtesy and consideration extended to me in the country houses throughout Ireland, none remains so fragrant as the atmosphere which enveloped Mount Bellew. An Australian Bishop (I think he was the Bishop of Queensland) came to stay at Mount Bellow, and we became very great friends. In subsequent years I corresponded with him, and through him I received an invitation from the Government of Australia to go out there to develop Agricultural Co-operation.

The village of Ardrahan was also one of the early places to develop Agricultural Cooperation, but for some time the

Society was in a state of great disorganisation. I shall always remember Ardrahan, for the difficulty which Edward Martyn and myself had with the Secretary of the Society there. He was the Clerk of the Petty Sessions at that time and had got into financial trouble, to the misfortune of the Society, and came weeping to us in an awful state of mind, imploring our mercy. We managed to arrange matters so that there was no prosecution, and the affair was never made public; but for some months the Ardrahan Society lacked an Honorary Secretary until a suitable man could be elected.

Edward Martyn was a conspicuous figure in the Irish Revival Movement of the Drama, in co-operation with George Moore, and in those days I spent many afternoons with Martyn and Moore at Tulira Castle, Martyn's beautiful home near Ardrahan, where I was treated as one of the family.

A central body for purchase and supply of agricultural requirements had been created in Dublin, under the title of the Irish Agricultural Wholesale Society. I was a Director of that Society for some years, and recall with much satisfaction its efficient management, notwithstanding the many difficulties we had to encounter. The Secretary of each local Committee would transmit the respective needs of its members to the I.A.O.S. A single consignment was then forwarded to the nearest Railway Station, and was distributed by the Secretary, in conformity with the orders that had been placed. The formation of these Societies, which were inclined to take the place of the local shopkeeper, gave rise to vigorous opposition. The farming members, however, displayed shrewd common-sense, for they appreciated the saving effected by co-operative purchase compared with the retail prices charged by the local shopkeeper, who often had the monopoly over a wide area. But how often I had to urge the Societies to trade with the I.A.O.S., explaining that it was the department that pulled down prices, enabling them to obtain greater profit.

At one particular meeting in the town of Hollymount, Co, Mayo, I was not even allowed to speak. The members wanted to buy everything wholesale, their bread, provisions and clothing, and refused to take any notice of the letter from the Secretary of the I.A.O.S., Mr. R. A. Anderson, explaining that Agricultural Co-operation could not possibly support such a project. When I attempted to make them see reason, a man called Ryan got up and declared: - "We want no observations from strangers!"

The Priest and Chairman, Father Flatley, agreed with him in a furious speech that was directed dead against the I.A.O.S., at the conclusion of which he walked out of the meeting. But this was, of course, the exception, and indeed the turnover of the I.A.W.S. in its business relations with the Co-operative Societies increased in volume year after year.

The tremendous difficulties with which the Movement had to contend can never be appreciated by those who are unacquainted with the peculiar character of the Irish people, and with the chequered history of the country. No Movement, however harmless it may appear to be, can be started in Ireland, or exist for very long, without the entrance of Politics and Religion causing inevitable trouble.

In our case, the head of the I.A.O.S. (Sir Horace Plunkett) was a Conservative member of the House of Commons and a landlord, and those who, for reasons of their own, disapproved of the Movement, headed perhaps by shopkeepers who felt their interests endangered, lost no time in describing it as having the sinister object of detaching the Irish people from their ultimate abiding principle of Home Rule. Many of the Societies were encouraged both with financial and personal help from the local landlords, who in most cases were Conservative in sympathy. Some even promoted small industries to help their less fortunate neighbours. The result being that many people thought that the I.A.O.S. was a landlord's Movement, and shunned it accordingly. There were indeed those who thought that the landlords saw in the Movement a new means of raising their rents, and they declared that the Land Commission held the same view.

John Dillon ('Lugubrious John' as we called him), the famous Nationalist, frequently attacked the I.A.O.S., and the 'Freeman's Journal', organ of Nationalism, seldom lost an opportunity to jibe at the "Plunkettian Nonsense" as they called it. To combat this widespread feeling, and to attempt to prove that the aim of the Movement was to gather together people of widely different shades of political feeling that they might co-operate on the land for the good of their country, we endeavoured to have Home Ruler and Unionist on the same platform, urging identical plans upon their audience. I remember getting Hugh Law, the Home Ruler, down from Dublin to speak at the Gam Society, and he certainly fulfilled our expectations of him, declaring that there were fifty thousand men in the Co-operative Movement: -

"Would anyone be foolish enough to assert that these fifty thousand men were traitors to their country?"

His father had been Lord Chancellor in the Gladstone Government, and had drafted the first great measure of land reform when he was Attorney General. Hugh Law was a very charming man, with one somewhat irritating fault, that of seldom being able to make up his own mind. He had a beautiful place in Sheephaven, where George Russell (AE) often stayed and painted some of his most delightful and mystical pictures. Years later, when I had left Ireland and was in the House, Law came to see me. While we were chatting about the old days, he told me how much he had wanted to be called to the English Bar, and of the difficulty he was having in getting his papers signed. I suggested he should accompany me to the St. Stephen's Club for a meal and further chat which he willingly agreed to do. Just outside we encountered Sir John Simon. On my introducing them to each other, Sir John exclaimed: - "I remember you, you were always a Nationalist."

"He wants to become a member of the English Bar, now," I said. Whereupon Law, to my great surprise, felt in his pocket and produced the paper which he showed to Sir John who, without a moment's hesitation, took it from him, held it up against the wall in front of all the passers-by and signed it. I often think of this curious way in which Law got called to the Bar.

Religious controversy, that great element so largely and unfortunately bound up with politics in the life and history of Ireland, was kept under control by the influence of Father Finlay, who spoke from nearly every platform at Co-operative meetings throughout the country and was Vice-President of the Society. He gave himself unceasingly to the founding of branches of the I.A.O.S., and to the encouragement of industries and Societies in the North, South, East, and West. No greater testimony to his loyalty to the ideals of non-sectarianism in the Movement can be brought forward, than the formation of certain Societies in the lonely parts of Connaught, where at his instigation the only Protestants in the district were elected to the Committees. Yet, whenever possible, he worked through the agency of local Convents, founding Societies of weavers and knitters to help the poor on the Western seaboard (where they could be instructed by the nuns), or organising co-operative lacemaking under Convent teaching, such as the Carrickmacross Society whose lace has been so famous for beautiful design and texture. Many journeys I made - with him touring the poorer districts, many meetings we attended together.

My old friend, Colonel Shaen Magan, reminds me of an occasion when I accompanied Fr. Finlay to a village in Roscommon, in order to open a hall there. Let him tell the story: -

"It happened that the local priest, who should have presided, was ill, so the curate took charge. He was a thin, stupid man with scarlet hair, a pink face, and a stutter; and this is the way he introduced Finlay: - 'Tonight, my brethren, my brethren, I mean my friends, we have with us the great Father Tom Finlay. See him, my brethren, my friends - you can hear him soon. See him, this theologian, theologian, scholar, scholar, scholar, saint - in fact my friends, my brethren, he is surrounded by a halo of darkness.' Well, Father Tom made his usual excellent speech, and the village hall was duly opened. It was a pleasant evening, warm with a clear sky and a full moon, so we decided, the three of us, Father Tom, Pat Hannon and myself, to walk back to our quarters. As we went along, Father Tom says in his quiet, dry, way: - 'Pat, I don't know whether you were too much engaged with your own conceit to have realised that I have been dubbed a saint, by, I am sorry to say, a not very illustrious member of my own cloth. You must be my witnesses, for it may be of use to me in another place. It's no good asking Shaen, of course, because of course, he won't be there?'"

This witty allusion to the Colonel's Protestantism was typical of Father Finlay. It is no exaggeration to say that without the support of this remarkable priest, the Cooperative movement would never have attained its important position in Irish life for, in addition to his sheer hard work, he did much to combat the mysticism engendered by Harry Norman, which threatened to disrupt the whole organisation.

Father Lyons, of Castlebar (afterwards Bishop of Kilmore), Father O'Hara of Kiltimagh, and Father O'Donovan of Loughrea are names which spring to mind, among other priests, who worked indefatigably to bring about Agricultural co-operation among their flocks. Father Lyons was one of the first people in the West of Ireland to adopt practical measures for the enlargement of the congested holdings in his district, and he negotiated successfully with Lord Lucan for strips of grazing land. I recall an occasion at Castlebar when a meeting took place to consider the establishment of an Agricultural College in Connaught. Lyons naturally declared that the foundations should be laid in Mayo, but the Bishop of Clonfert was in favour of Galway, while the Bishop of Elphin thought that the County of Sligo should be chosen. I had the unhappy task of bringing the matter down to earth, when I told the assembly that unless we could get the co-operation of the District Councils and County Councils, we should have no chance of establishing the College at all.

Father Stephen McTernan was another pillar of co-operation in the West. Unfortunately, he had a nephew, editor of the 'Sligo Champion', who was bitterly opposed to the Co-operative Movement and, along with the editor of the famous 'Skibbereen Eagle' in the South of Ireland, lost no opportunity to revile the I.A.O.S.

Talking of priests reminds me of an amusing episode of those far-off days, when law and order still possessed a sense of humour. Those who are familiar with social life in Ireland during the latter part of the nineteenth century will have been attracted, from time to time, by incidents arising from the distillation of illicit whiskey, known as poteen. Silent warfare prevailed for many years between the Royal Irish Constabulary and the producers of this potent distillate. It was quite common to find accumulations of the paraphernalia employed in making poteen in the back yards of Police barracks. The devices employed in the enforcement of the law and in the process of capture, and the stratagems enacted to avoid discovery, reflect flashes of genius in the manoeuvres of both sides.

It was of course well known that the country gentlemen and clergy of both denominations acquired from time-to-time supplies of poteen, partly for personal consumption, but more especially as a treat for visiting friends. Even when officers of the R.I.C. were entertained, a moderate measure of well-matured poteen occupied one of the decanters in the dining-room.

A respected and well-beloved priest of Glenamaddy, in the north of County Galway, was widely known for his hospitality and known to special friends for the presence of one of the aforesaid 'decanters'. It was customary in the manufacture of poteen to provide sherry casks whenever possible which were buried in the garden, sometimes for a few years, before they reached the high standard of maturity. This esteemed Parish priest entertained the local District Inspector of Police on a particular Sunday, and greetings were passed across the table, indicating that the standard of maturity would not have a 'headache in a hogshead'.

There was much espionage in relation to this illegal product. The informer in Ireland has always been the most despicable of human creatures: whenever his identity has been revealed the opprobrious word will cling to his family for generations. In this particular instance, information was laid at Police Headquarters in a neighbouring town that a cask of poteen lay concealed in the premises of the District Inspector's host.

So it came to pass that after a jovial Irish priest's dinner, which always took place about three o'clock in the afternoon and lasted for some hours, the District Inspector returned to his Headquarters to find, horrified, that information had been lodged, and that the Head Constable (who was a sort of N.C.O. in the Royal Irish Barracks) was about to arrange a search party. The District Inspector directed the Head Constable that, in order to avoid any dangerous clash with the very popular priest, the raid should not take place before three or four o'clock in the morning. Of course, the unhappy man felt that if the raid should take place at once, his genial host would conclude that he was responsible for it. Well, he went home to his private house, discussed the embarrassing situation with his wife, got ready his pony and trap as rapidly as possible, and drove like mad back to the Presbytery where he had so much enjoyed his dinner. He roused the Parish Priest, informed him of the projected raid and begged him for God's sake to remove the concealed cask. The Priest, realising the dread situation of both host and guest, at once rose to the occasion.

He hurried to the local village Police Station, called the Sergeant and, believe it or not, invited him and his four Constables to come at once to the Presbytery and assist him in removing the dread and terrible possibility of a £100 fine and, more terrible still, assist in the destruction of the liquor contained in the cask. At three a.m. the Head Constable, who was well-known for his antagonism to the poteen making fraternity, arrived at the Priest's residence, roused the little household and gave notice of a complete search. The Parish Priest, beaming with innocence, received the raiding party and expressed his profound astonishment that such a vile charge should be brought against his public character. Nothing was found of course, because the offending cask was safely lodged at the local Police Station.

Readers may think this is a somewhat embellished Irish story, but as I enjoyed the personal friendship of that Parish Priest and the District Inspector, and had the opportunity of roaring with laughter with both of them on subsequent occasions, I can vouch for its veracity.

Another objection raised against the I.A.O.S. in certain local areas was our lack of support for the Irish language, the implication being that those who did not encourage the national language movement must be against Nationalism, and were more or less likely to be classed with the Unionists. Of course, the great impediment to Gaelic-speaking meetings was that the various European agricultural experts whom we brought in as speakers from time to time could not be expected to be versed in our ancient tongue. Their presence would have necessitated the use of an interpreter, which would have brought tedium and difficulty to the Meeting. The Irish paper 'Fainne an Lae' greatly deplored our want of knowledge of the language, and a hullabaloo was raised by the little village of Kilikinny, asking why our speakers, including myself, had not a thorough knowledge of Irish. In my tours around the country I had noticed that wherever the Irish language was spoken there was a marked superiority in the intellectual character of the people.

The man who can speak two languages, who can mingle the figurative and romantic forms of Irish with the business forms of English, is unquestionably the more thoughtful and studious. One could look in vain in the purely English-speaking districts for the intellectual rivals of those famous old Aran islanders, Bryan Gilmartin or Pat Ganly, who would recite the old Gaelic heroics by the hour. For my part, I would gladly have devoted myself to becoming an ardent student of the many treasures of literary beauty that the Irish language possesses. I was an advocate of the Irish language revival and enjoyed the personal friendship of Dr. Douglas Hyde, and took an active, but modest, part in the Language Revival. However, in this case I compromised by challenging the correspondent with whom I had become involved to guarantee a few hours of his spare time in giving Gaelic instruction to the members of the Kilikinny Society, while I in return would provide them with text-books, so that we might have a flourishing Co-operative Society and Celtic class side by side in the village. As a matter of fact we did, some three months later, appoint an Irish speaking organiser to tour the remote and primitive parts of the Province of Connaught, and I accompanied him on many occasions.

Dr. Douglas Hyde was among the prime movers in the forward surge of Gaelic study. Many years later he became the first President of Ireland. His love of the language and his research into its folklore and literature was an inspiration and guiding star to the Language Movement in those early days.

Of course, the financial question was always with us. As the Movement expanded rapidly throughout the country and our expenses rose in proportion, the Central Body of the Organisation was seldom free from the strain of financial worry. I think it was at the Annual Conference of the I.A.O.S., held in 1897 at the ancient Concert Rooms in Brunswick St. Dublin, that an announcement was made that a certain generous benefactor had contributed five thousand pounds to the funds of the Organisation. A great fuss was made of this princely gift, and it was even mentioned in the French newspapers. The net result of it was a Baronetcy. I name no names, but it was well understood at the time that outstanding persons in Irish public life who were sympathetic to Horace Plunkett's work, and were prepared to give it practical support, might be commended to His

Excellency the Lord Lieutenant for some public recognition.

Yet again the following year, at the General Meeting in the early autumn, lack of funds threatened the existence of the Society. The gloomy tone of the early proceedings engendered by this feeling was not lightened by Plunkett's quotation from a speech made by W.B. Yeats at an I.A.O.S. banquet the previous year, where he declared that:-

"We have too little confidence in one another and, despite much brave self-assertion, too little confidence in ourselves, in Ireland. We are not to be blamed very bitterly, perhaps, for we live in a disastrous country where but few things have succeeded for generations."

Plunkett however, subscribed one thousand pounds himself, and other large sums were contributed privately to enable the Movement to carry on. Yeats, like other giants of the world-famous Irish Literary revival, had much sympathy for the work of the I.A.O.S., and was an occasional and popular speaker at meetings in the West of Ireland. His most natural support was given to the establishment of village libraries, which was part of our campaign, and I recall his thin, elegant, languid figure, pale face, a black lock of hair across the forehead, standing on the platform receiving an ovation for his brilliant speech from an enthusiastic audience of farmers and farm labourers.

Another outstanding friend of those days, and a devoted protagonist of the Co-operative Movement among farmers (particularly in the improvement of the dairy industry) was Sir Jocelyn Gore-Booth. I cannot recall any of my old great friends and supporters of the Irish Agricultural revival more business-like, more carefully concerned with detail, and more anxious to provide that every under-taking should be guided by wisdom and skill, and with every attention for the detail of management. He founded three Creameries on parts of the wide estates to which his family had been attached for generations, and in every instance and at great personal sacrifice, gave time and thought and personal assistance to each of these novel features in the improvement of the Dairy industry in the West of Ireland.

Gore-Booth is a great name in the West of Ireland, and Sir Jocelyn's father, Sir Henry (whom I had the privilege of meeting from time to time), was a very distinguished example of the public spirit and leadership which was the quality in those far-off days of experiment and adventure. The Gore-Booth girls were very charming. One of whom inherited a home in Manchester and turned it into a home for old people and various other charities. She used to write to me periodically and I, on one occasion, went to visit her and spent a night there.

After I joined the I.A.O.S., and fairly early in my personal activities, I came into intimate touch with George Russell (AE), who became subsequently, as the world knows, one of the outstanding figures in the literary and cultural advancement of the Irish people. He was personally very attractive, very handsome, with a long beard, a full crop of long hair, with every aspect of a dreamy intellectual, and with total absence of interest in his personal appearance or in the garments of somewhat shaggy and indifferent quality which contributed to his personal comfort. 'AE' has been the subject of endless speculation, endless writing, endless criticism, but through it all retained the everlasting friendship of everybody that knew him. He was just as much amused at my flourishes in speech and quaint figures of illustration in presenting the doctrine of agricultural co-operation as I was intrigued by his eccentricities and wholly unfamiliar peculiarity of manner.

For many years we worked side by side, his particular branch of co-operative activity being applied to the formation of Credit Societies (which we called Agricultural Banks) founded on the Raiffeisen Plan of unlimited liability, which had been a success in the early stages of German Agricultural Reform. Nevertheless, intellect was on the highest level, and in wandering over the South Dublin mountains, I learned much, admired deeply and came more and more to develop an affectionate interest in one who was in many respects, a strange inscrutable, profoundly subtle and mystic character in the early days of the twentieth century.

I must sadly refer here to the break in our friendship and the crash of my own devoted affection, when I became a Tariff Reform candidate for Parliament. For some obscure reason, which I cannot now explain, he regarded me as having departed from the ancient Irish national outlook which he entertained so deeply, and to which he made such a stimulating and abiding contribution. I heard of his severe illness during a holiday, and the news of his death brought to an end a long, and on my side, unforgettable affection.

Among my colleagues in the I.A.O.S. during a long period of years, the most active, energetic and untiring was Mr. A. T. S. Magan. He was the son of a local landlord, who suffered a long period of oblivion with his family from the local boycott, but emerged (at the time that I knew the family) into some measure of popularity. Shaen Magan, as he was always called (and some of my friends used the name of 'Atlas', because of his initials), was well over six feet tall and was full of abounding energy and vitality. His education had been sadly neglected because of the poverty which had fallen upon the family in their period of boycott, and because his eldest brother had received a Public School education in England at an expensive outlay, which the family made a great sacrifice to undertake. With his very limited education, his total inability to spell English words correctly, and his hopeless inability to compose an intelligent letter, he was at the same time a very forceful and progressive character. He was my companion and co-helper in the greater part of the Western Counties and, although his knowledge of scientific agriculture was almost negligible he, nevertheless, succeeded on many occasions in convincing groups of farmers that their economic salvation lay in co-operative methods and the introduction of experiments with improved systems of cultivating seedlings and the use of artificial manures. He had many fine qualities, embracing unfailing loyalty to me, and an intensive affection which prevails at the moment of writing this modest tribute to our joint career.

Two of Magan's sisters were devoted and hard working young women, and the younger, Violet, became a Poultry Instructor under the Department of Agriculture and Technical Instruction, and did valuable work for the Poultry industry in West Cork and Kerry. Both of these girls, for whom I entertained the deepest personal affection, died young, but after they had in various capacities done useful social and educational work in the various districts in which they lived active lives.

The Magan family form a wonderful example of the devotion and loyalty of young Irish men and women to the service of their country, and they were not singular in their exemplary work for local charities, especially those associated with the Health service. Volumes could be written in relation to Irish families in similar circumstances who, during the period of the Land agitation in Ireland, suffered the worst usages of ill-fortune, but nonetheless contributed in their many ways to improve the condition of the frequently impoverished peasantry among whom they lived.

It was Yeats who roused the interest of George Russell in the I.A.O.S. when Russell was workjng as a clerk in Pim's drapery establishment in Dublin, and he soon became intimately associated with it. I received him when he was brought to his first meeting by Lady Gregory, and he accompanied me on a tour of the West of Ireland, in which he gradually brought the practical problems of the small farmer into alignment with his love of the fantastic and occult. His curious psychic sense was a constant source of entertainment and astonishment to his friends, and many are the quaint stories told of the 'little people' he saw on his walks round the countryside. Typical of these was the incident that happened to A. T. S. Magan when they were staying with Edward Martyn. Magan and AE were strolling over the fields when they came across a small well, which had a bush growing over it. AE stopped and exclaimed that it was very probably the home of the 'little people'. Suddenly, he went into a trance, and began describing the vivid picture that only he could see, of a very small man in a blue coat and red cap, who stood under the bush.

Mahaffey, the well-known Provost of Trinity College, Dublin, was present on another occasion when AE showed his uncanny powers, this time before a number of witnesses. The incident took place at a party, when some of the guests were chaffing AE about his trances. "I feel like going into one now," he exclaimed suddenly, and the room grew quiet as all the guests stopped talking to listen to this extraordinary man. "I am at the gates of a city," he declared, and proceeded to give a description of it.

Mahaffey said with some amazement that it was a perfect picture of Jericho, as far as archaeologists had reconstructed it. "There is a tablet at the gate. A big tablet engraved with writing." AE continued. On being urged to copy down the writing, he complied, though the form of it was unknown to him. Some years later it was shown to be an almost perfect reproduction of the newly discovered tablet outside that ancient town of Jericho.

AE also became the editor of the 'Irish Homestead', organ of the I.A.O.S., and was an ardent Socialist, which drew him into prominent association with Larkin's cause.

One of the most delightful and unforgettable personalities I met in my young life, and to whom I was indebted for much kindness, friendship, and hospitality, was Lady Gregory, of Coole Park, Galway. She is still remembered by the Irish people for her love of Ireland, and the series of glowing literary contributions which she made to Irish life and the outlook of her time. Her deep friendship for Yeats, who spent a great part of his life at Coole Park, is recalled in his writings, dramatic and poetical, during that period of his life when he made a prominent contribution to the Irish literary revival. In his wanderings through Coole Park, Yeats absorbed most of the soft and congenial, and inspiring, atmosphere of the Irish climate, and much of his best work was done either within or without the genial hospitality of Coole Park, which the hostess, whose memory he has embellished in prose and verse, provided.

Lady Gregory, was the widow of Sir William, who was one of the under-secretaries at the Foreign Office until his retirement from the public service. I have not seen Code Park for many years, but I am aware of the melancholy disappearance of that extremely happy home, which I understand has gone, to use the old phrase, 'without leaving a stone upon a stone'. Irish people in all parts of the world, still attached to all the fragrant traditions of our island story, always recall the Plays presented by Lady Gregory which so vividly illuminated the lives of the Irish peasantry, and the long traditional interest which Lady Gregory's writings made an attractive feature of Irish literary life.

She bestowed much friendship on me, and was very much attached to my first wife, for whom she conceived a touching affection, and to whom she paid various visits during her widowhood till close to the time of her death. The clouds fall heavily upon these memories of the past, but I cannot forget my Agricultural Co-operative Meetings which the presence of Lady Gregory adorned, and whose encouragement gave me, a raw young man, that stimulus which was an outstanding part of my young life.

On a summer's day, I think in 1897, in my active work, John Cronin (one of the masters in the Loughrea Diocesan College) and I started in the early morning from Ballyhaunis in Co. Mayo, on a bicycle ride through Castlebar into Westport. We put the bikes up at the local Inn, and after a short lunch proceeded to climb Croagh Patrick, 2510 ft. We spent a short time in the ancient ruins of the old Church at the foot of the mountain and then undertook the climb. It was no easy journey, and after a valiant struggle on a bright cheerful day, we reached the summit with its rude temporary chapel (a very primitive structure at that time). After enjoying the wide view over Clew Bay and the surrounding mountain scenery, we made our descent, and dear old Cronin had the misfortune of putting his foot into a trap laid for hares on the mountainside. The accident was not very serious, and we got back to the little hotel for a very welcome tea with local pancakes, and a friendly greeting and sparkling chat from the Innkeeper and his little family circle. We then mounted our bikes and proceeded to Louisburgh, where we stopped for a short time to chat to various people, talk about local historical relics and the efforts of the local Congested Districts Board to improve the social conditions of the local community.

Off again to the wild mountain pass, which brought us to the shore of the sea, which spread out in front of the Leenane Hotel. We reached the Hotel about 7 o'clock, dead tired, and were received by McKeown with customary politeness and hospitality. We were taken to the bathroom, and never have I enjoyed a bath more during my early active career. There was no room for us in the hotel, but an annexe close by provided bedrooms and, after a hearty meal, we fell into a glorious sleep which, for me, was one of the most restorative of my life.

Next day, after more talk with local people, we mounted our bikes again and proceeded to Clifden, spending some time on the way at one of the notorious settlements built by English Missionary Societies, founded with the object of Converting the inhabitants of Connemara to the abandonment of their ancient Faith. It is sad to reflect on the pitiful and painful efforts made a few generations ago to replace the Catholic Faith in the West of Ireland with a wholly unsuccessful process of attending Protestant

Conventicles. I have written a good deal about this in days long ago, and I am glad to reflect that in these days in which we now live, not a single trace of the misery, corruption and ill-directed enthusiasm now remains in those completely Catholic regions of Connemara.

What a wild, beautiful and unforgettable region surrounds Clifden, and the inlets of the sea on that part of the coast. We received a warm welcome from the Parish Priest at Clifden, one of those great reformers in the improvement of the economic life of the Western population in all the communities along the sea-board. From Clifden we went to Rosmuck, whose Parish Priest was equally ardent and hard working in support of the Congested District Board, in its various schemes of development throughout the West of Galway.

CHAPTER 2

On the farms in Ireland, as in many other countries, it has always been the woman of the household who is in sole charge of the hens, geese and turkeys that live in the farmyard. In return for her attendance on the flock she keeps the money earned by the sale of eggs and fat birds. I remember at one meeting in the West of Ireland we had been pressing the advantages of co-operation in the dairy industry, and somewhat exaggerating the benefits that might be expected when the marketing of eggs was properly and scientifically conducted.

One man in the audience shouted out: - "If you say much more, we will never get an egg to eat again, the women will keep them all for sale." There were roars of laughter when I advised the wives to give the small, un-saleable eggs to their men as a prize for good conduct.

Certainly, the industry was in great need of reform in those days and much was accomplished in this direction by some lady members of the I.A.O.S. They threw themselves wholeheartedly into the Movement. Lady Clonbrock was keenly interested in the Clonbrock and Castlegar Poultry Society; two sisters (the Misses Kenny), were most vigorous in their district, and so many others gave their time and money to help educate their less fortunate sisters. From Denmark we obtained the services of a poultry expert called Viggo Schwarz. He did a great deal to rouse the industry from the state of apathy into which it had fallen.

Apart from the more scientific methods of breeding and feeding the poultry, which he impressed upon his audiences, he had to fight against the carelessness and ignorance in the trade itself. So many of the women kept the eggs from day to day until there was a reasonable quantity to be sold, thus endangering their freshness. The eggs were often dirty and unattractive to look at, and there was little thought of proper grading or packing. Irish eggs had, for a time, such a poor name on the London market that eggs were actually imported from Russia to Ireland and re-exported as Irish eggs.

The poultry shows, which we arranged all over the country, were something of an innovation in many districts, and roused considerable excitement and rivalry among the women folk, also helping to impress upon them the necessity of proper methods in their job. In many instances, on the small farms the eggs were not sold for money, but bartered by the farmer's wife for tea or sugar, with the men who travelled the countryside from homestead to homestead gaining greatly in the exchanges. These 'higglers' as they were called, were a great menace to the trade both in poultry and butter.

Talking of 'higglers' reminds me of the notorious 'gombeen' men (moneylenders) who also played upon the farming community, making large financial gains from their ignorance. In the early Spring of 1898, I was appointed organiser of the Irish Financial Reform League, and a month or so later I was one of the witnesses at a committee of the House of Commons on money-lending at which Horace Plunkett gave evidence. At that time I had only come across three instances of 'gombeen' men, but they continued to flourish for some years after we had introduced measures to improve the economic condition of the farming industry.

The striking characteristic of the 'gombeen system' consisted in charging exorbitant rates of interest and, at the same time, putting the borrower entirely in the power of the lender. The means of obtaining small loans on easy terms for purposes of production was still unknown to our struggling tenant farmers, who were consequently driven to seek monetary advances from any source that presented itself. In his emergency, the farmer might address himself to some friends who had a certain standing at the local Joint Stock Bank and, if the interview proved satisfactory, a third person would be called in who, together with the obliging neighbour, constituted the security required by the bank. The party would then proceed to the Bank, the promissory note would be signed and the loan duly advanced. The usual amount required in those days was between £5 and £10, and very frequently even less, and the loan was for a period of three months.

The Bank charged sixpence in the pound up to £5, and the borrower had to pay for the stamp and the bill. This, however, was only the beginning of the unfortunate farmer's expenses. The party usually had to travel a considerable distance to the nearest town, on foot or by ass-cart, not returning home until the evening. In most cases the borrower was expected to give a day's work to each of his friends to make up for this, and he had to take great care to treat them to a suitable dinner in the town. Adding these small items together, it is no exaggeration to say that the amount of interest paid on a loan of £5 would equal about 42% per annum.

George Russell (AE) and myself came over, and we both gave evidence before the Money-Lending Commission of which T. W. Russell, Under-Secretary for Ireland, was Chairman. The evidence we gave was so striking that they abandoned the proceedings for further consideration of the Bill, then before the House of Commons. The shopkeeper's credit, which prevailed on a large scale, was but little less injurious to the farming community. 'Once in a shopkeeper's books, never out of them' was a trite but expressive saying among the country people in the poorer districts of Ireland. The loan was received in kind. But far too often the shopkeeper himself fixed the price of the produce brought to him by the unfortunate farmer, (the sack of potatoes, load of cabbage or whatever it might be) and instead of returning cash he merely wrote off a small portion of the inevitable debt.

This, then, was one angle of the economic condition of the Irish farming industry. Here the I.A.O.S., allied with the Raiffeisen banking system, brought about a remarkable revolution. The peasantry of Bavaria, Wurttemberg and other German states had become a prey to unscrupulous moneylenders, but marvellous results followed the introduction of the Raiffeisen co-operative credit societies. At the end of ten years they had become free and independent. What a struggle we had to educate our own farming community to the many advantages of the co-operative agricultural bank on this model.

The object was to create a society of farmers, artisans and agricultural labourers who would band themselves together to build up a credit association where money could be lent at a minimum charge. Arrangements had first to be made with the nearest Bank for a sum to be placed on current account to meet, from time to time, the demands of borrowers. Under this system the farmer not only received financial benefit, but also training in economy and thrift, the absence of which are glaring defects in the Irish character. In addition, he was taught the value of punctuality in his payments, and gradually was enabled to build up his own independence.

Many were the ways and means adopted by those who were attempting to organise a Credit Bank in their district. I remember the parish priest of Kyle, the Rev. John Gleeson, writing to tell me how he had obtained sufficient money to start the bank by opening an athletic sports contest, together with refreshments for visitors.

"But," he added plaintively, "I had to face universal criticism and cold water even from intelligent persons when I started this business, and the parishioners grumbled because I did not put the money on the roof of the chapel, or some such work. Some of them thought it a reflection on the parish, as if other parishes might think they were so poor that the priest had to get up money for them. They looked on it as a charity."

The best managed credit Banks never granted loans to pay debts or rent, and the period of the grant corresponded with the length of time that the young animal or crop would take to become marketable. Again and again it was evident to me that twice the quantity of stock could have been kept by the farmers in the congested districts, if only they had obtained the money through agricultural credit. In remote Clare Island, for example, eight small loans brought to the poverty-stricken farmers a profit of £58. Where the co-operative societies had to face organised opposition, however, they found great difficulty in getting banks to open accounts with them, and if this resistance was overcome they found that the terms offered to them were not acceptable. In these circumstances the poor farmers were a prey to such clever swindlers as those who cunningly took advantage of the interest roused in agricultural cooperation, using it for their own ends.

I remember one such fraudulent firm, calling themselves the Irish Agricultural Loan Bank, against whom we had to publish warnings, in some cases, alas, too late. They claimed to have no object other than the advancement of the Irish farmer, but in reality they had no object other than their own enrichment. An enthusiastic disciple of the Raffeisan banking system was the author, Rider Haggard, who investigated the agricultural depression in England and helped to popularise the system throughout Great Britain.

Lack of education was partly to blame for the woes of the Irish farmer, who was unable to raise himself without properly organised assistance. It was that great Irishman, Thomas Davis, who said that an educated Ireland was synonymous with a prosperous Ireland, but the task of educating the whole countryside was somewhat formidable. Some fifty years before the period of which I am speaking, the most potent influence in the lives of the peasantry was the ceilidh, or village gathering, which may be regarded as a somewhat primitive form of debating society. When the reading of newspapers became more general, the outlook of the community was widened, but there was still a complete and unhappy lack of technical education. Nowhere could the Irish farmer learn the art of farming. No children in school were taught the practical application of essential facts about livestock and soil cultivation which scientific progress had discovered. Agricultural education of a sort was indeed included in the school curriculum, but it was nothing more than a farce.

When I was enquiring into this, I visited seventy-two National schools and asked boys in senior classes if any of them put into practical effect the instruction they received. The answer was invariably: - "No".

It was not until the Agricultural Act had weathered its stormy passage through Parliament, and a Department of Agriculture and Technical Instruction had been set up (with Horace Plunkett on the Board as Vice-President), that practical and scientific measures were taken to educate the members of the agricultural industry. In 1898 the Royal College of Science in Dublin still awaited the coming of its first candidate for the Diploma because, although a certain course of studies was advised, there were no agricultural lectures. In the same year the I.A.O.S. held its first examination for creamery Managers, and it was not surprising that none of the entrants qualified, for there was no place in Ireland where they could be trained. As it was with the dairy trade, so it was with poultry keeping; very few people indeed had a thorough knowledge of all branches of this industry.

In 1899 the I.A.O.S. very kindly gave me a fortnight's leave to sit in London for the examination at the Royal

College of Surgeons, for the Diploma of the Royal Agricultural Society. The syllabus included (besides agriculture) land legislation, chemistry, bookkeeping, geology and a variety of other subjects. I was the only Irish examinee, and the only entrant who had not been trained in an agricultural college, but fortune was with me and I obtained the Diploma. The examinee who took first place was a man called Heel who, by a comical twist of fate, served under me some years later in South Africa, being transferred from Natal to the Cape for this purpose.

Some months after my return from London a sub-committee, of which I became a member, I was appointed by the I.A.O.S, to deal with the establishment of experimental plots all over Ireland. H.C. Sheringham (the gardening expert) and Lt. Col. Everard, who was particularly interested in tobacco growing, were fellow members. My work in this direction was chiefly in the West of Ireland, where many plots were laid out to experiment with such things as artificial manures for potatoes and exhausted grass land, the prevention of diseases in grain crops or the most suitable flax seed for a particular district. As well as this, a series of lectures was organised to help to educate the dairy farming community and those engaged in other agricultural activities. As one of the speakers I travelled North, South, East and West to lecture to large audiences in the well populated areas, and to small groups in the remote districts. With such assistance as I have mentioned, the education of the farmer made safe and rapid strides forward into the new century.

The complete lack of a general standard of cleanliness in the dairying industry, and the total lack of efficient standards for the proper production and sale of butter (so important an export in the Ireland of these days) was one of the chief obstacles with which we had to contend. Ordinary day clothes were worn by both men and women during their work in the creameries, overalls or aprons were a novelty. Spilt milk was often inadequately removed, and the sour smell from some of those creameries is best left to the imagination. In many cases the milk used to arrive at the creamery by donkey cart, driven by young children who, no doubt, sampled the contents of the cans whenever they felt thirsty, and who should have been at school. An unpleasantly revealing light is shed upon the social welfare of that day and upon the dairying industry, by this quotation from a notice displayed in a shop window in a Dublin street: - "Dirty butter for servants!"

As a contrast to the child and ass-cart mode of carrying milk, a unique vehicle made its appearance in County Waterford on the route from Bonmahon to Dunhill. This portable creamery (designed by W. J. Watts) was a large, closed wagon equipped with the latest dairying machinery and drawn by a traction engine. The shrill whistling of the engine, and the dense volumes of black smoke attending its progress, attracted a fascinated audience on its journeyings to and fro.

Co-operative dairying tackled the question of the milk supply to the creameries, of proper supervision and cleanliness there, of the pasteurisation of milk, and of the proper packing of first-class quality butter for export. It was about this time that Professor Robert Koch made his fatal mistake in believing that the tuberculosis germ in cattle could not be transferred to the human. The extent of infection by contaminated milk or meat, he declared, was hardly greater than the hereditary transmission: - "which is extremely rare".

"If all the dreadful things we are told about the transmission of T.B. disease by the flesh and milk of cattle be true," he wrote to a colleague, "how is it that any of us are left alive?" However, he agreed that this statement was not necessarily final. Unfortunately, his words were sufficient to discourage those faint-hearted disciples of cleanliness and pasteurisation, who immediately relaxed their efforts. If it had not been for the fear of a typhoid epidemic this state of affairs might have long continued, but the great dread of this disease, combined with the immediate closure of such dairies as were affected, and the subsequent 'out of work' condition of the employees, helped to combat Professor Koch's words of mistaken reassurance.

Meanwhile in the United States of America and Canada, great strides were being made towards the export of fam produce to Great Britain, which sounded a note of warning in the ears of those Irish farmers who were alert enough to listen. The high standard of Danish produce, and the care taken to pack it according to the wishes of the buyers, made them formidable rivals; this was particularly the case with butter.

Little encouragement or assistance had come from the Government to improve the standard of butter sold by grocers, and high were the hopes raised among the trade at the end of the century by the introduction of Walter Long's 'Food and Drugs Bill'. It was a common practice at that time to sell a mixture of butter and margarine under the name of butter, and occasionally this mess contained as much as 85% foreign fats. The dairying industry naturally hoped that the new Bill would forbid this completely, and great was their dissatisfaction when it was announced that only an admixture exceeding 10% was to be illegal. Notwithstanding this, grocers continually came up in courts for selling over-adulterated butter. In more than one instance in London the Irish creamery was blamed, from which they declared the butter had been obtained. Another fraudulent practice believed to exist at that time was the adding of water to the butter, supposed to be done for the grocers by certain persons on payment of a small sum.

I might add here that, parallel with these slurs on our trade, was the encouragement given to our co-operative creameries by their obtaining many first prizes in Dairy Shows throughout England, where the standard was of the highest order.

Improvement of the dairy industry depended very much on the speed with which we could obtain trained and competent managers. I remember one stormy meeting at a place called Croghan in Co. Roscommon where the local dairy society, abounding in wrath, were avid to suspend their manager for absence and inattention to duty. Had they done so, their case would have been far worse in the latter end. It took me four solid hours, most of my patience and all the tact and persuasion that I possessed to ride out the hurricane and humour its components into agreeing to retain the manager on a promise of competence to the shareholders of the Society. Although there was little or no excuse for his somewhat frequent neglect of duty, he had a doctor's certificate to account for his absence, and the meeting ended amicably enough with the compromise that a vigilant committee of four members be appointed to see that the manager did not suffer a relapse.

The conservatism of the Irish farmer was responsible for a prolonged war that was waged against the dairies, concerning separated milk. It was averred that such milk would cause great mortality among those calves fed upon it, not because of the nourishment subtracted from the milk, but because of the mysterious and highly dangerous substance added to it in the process of separation.

Talking of calf mortality reminds me of the man from Killarney who sought advice from the correspondence column of a current agricultural journal. "What would you recommend to cure a two and a half year old bullock?" he asked, "I have not one ill at present, but I would like to know what medicine I ought to give him."

Another objection to co-operative dairying was raised in the rather muddled statement of a farmer in Wicklow, at the end of a meeting at which I had been speaking. "This butter dairying and co-operation tends to take away the home work of our people," he declared angrily. "Instead of giving employment in the farmhouses to our girls and all that, the creamery seems to take away all the milk to a factory, thereby throwing the girls very much more or less idle."

One of the most successful creameries, and one of the most rapid to be established during my association with the I.A.O.S., was the co-operative society creamery promoted by Lord Emly. Only twenty-eight days elapsed from the time that the first meeting was held to consider the matter until Lord Emly performed the official opening. His energy and enthusiasm was rivalled only by his kindness, and I have such happy memories of my visits to Clarina, where I stayed with Lord Emly and his charming wife.

In a small country like Ireland, where agricultural products were the main exports, an efficient and co-ordinated system of railways should have been part of the country's organisation. This was not so, and as a one-time railwayman I was fully aware of the shortcomings of the system. The sale of agricultural produce was handicapped by high rates and defective facilities for loading and discharging. I have frequently seen perishable consignments such as eggs and butter awaiting transhipment at a railway junction, the eggs broken and cracked, the butter boxes torn, squashed and filthy. Where speed of transport was essential there were avoidable delays, and the exorbitant rates charged by the railway companies killed many a promising young industry. Indeed, there was widespread belief that railway rates and management had retarded the material progress of the country.

In April 1899, I was present at a conference held at the Mansion House, Dublin, on the railway question, where a resolution was passed to establish an Irish Railway Reform Association. We were still battling about it two or three years later, for the Government refused to appoint a Vice-Regal Commission to enquire into the workings of railways and canals. All we could do was to urge sympathetic M.P.s such as James McCann (who had long experience as a director of railways) to keep the matter of railway reform constantly before the public. He admitted that the rates were fifty per cent too high.

Travelling through the wilds of Ireland was certainly an experience in those days, whether one went by train, bicycle, or motorcar. My most amusing experiences were with a car man of the name of Patsy Coyle, who drove Magan and myself to the various and multitudinous meetings we attended together. Patsy was a tall man with a drawn face and cloudy eyes, and from whose mouth came a never-ceasing dribble of porter. He was always drunk and, to the best of my memory, he upset our car at least three times. However, these alarms and excursions did nothing to hinder the rapid growth of co-operative societies in the neighbourhood of Tisara, Co. Roscommon, where Shaen Magan and his beloved sisters, Rachel and Violet, worked with whole-hearted enthusiasm for the cause of the I.A.O.S. On their family estate we experimented with co-operative grazing, leasing one hundred and thirty acres of land to sixteen men for a period of five years. The importance of this scheme was that these small farmers, who individually could not have rented the grazing land direct, were now able to do so without the necessity of paying middlemen.

While Rachel Magan organised handicrafts throughout the district, Violet started a library at Tisara, which became an immediate attraction to the local people and a centre for self-education. Their favourite reading matter varied from the current novels of Conan Doyle, (Sherlock Holmes was much sought after), to works by those in the Irish Literary Revival. I remember a poor labourer informing me that he had sat up till three o'clock in the morning reading, in the dim light of his kitchen, the 'Literary Ideals of Ireland'.

Occasionally, after the opening of Village Halls or Libraries, and sometimes at the end of a particular meeting, we held some sort of musical entertainment; I well recall the concerts which we organised, and to which Magan and myself were sometimes prevailed upon to contribute.

That born entertainer, Percy French, I have mentioned elsewhere as the composer and singer of comical songs, but I have not spoken of the way he supported the I.A.O.S. movement by attending meetings in the village halls or National schools. The number of sketches which, with a few masterly strokes, he delineated on sheets of paper pinned to a blackboard, for the edification of the audience at co-operative meetings, would fill half the schools in the County of Roscommon. As soon as one picture had been appreciated, it would be torn from its moorings and flung crumpled into a corner of the room, and in a minute or two another would be in its place. Percy French had some amusing artistic tricks too, which he was often called upon to perform after dinner. His pictures made from candle smoke upon plates were always a fascination to his fellow diners, and he had a facile way of drawing one picture which, when turned upside down, would make another picture. No social occasion was dull if he was present.

In May 1900, I was appointed Assistant Secretary to the I.A.O.S., and from that time until I left Ireland my work was largely with the headquarters of the Movement in Dublin. By this I do not mean that my activities around the countryside were more or less ended, on the contrary, I suppose I travelled further and lectured to larger and more diverse audiences throughout Ireland than ever before.

But it was farewell to Clifden House, Loughrea, and to the many good friends in the surrounding district, whose acquaintance I could now renew only on 'flying visits'. My wife and I moved to a house in the Torquay Road, on the outskirts of Dublin, not very far from Horace Plunkett's beautiful home 'Kilteragh', which was later destroyed.

It had occurred to me on my frequent travels over the countryside that the purchase of a motor bicycle would add greatly to my convenience. They were somewhat of a novelty in those days, so it was with a certain pride and excitement that I obtained one from the Dublin agents, and had it sent out to my home at Foxrock. It so happened that there was a youngster in the neighbourhood who also acquired a new motor bicycle, and the next day he rode it along Torquay Road and turned left to cross the railway line. The poor fellow came a terrible cropper on the level crossing and was killed. The tragedy so affected my wife that she made me promise that I would never ride one, so back the machine had to go before ever I had the chance to try it out. All these long years I have kept my promise, and although I became a Director of the B.S.A. Company, I have not been able to experience the singular speed and thrill of riding a motor bicycle.

I remember Sir Horace Plunkett purchasing a pedal bicycle a year or two before this, and quite clearly recall his accident in London in which he broke a leg. Subsequently, I spent an afternoon with him at his bungalow at Birchington, discussing various co-operative projects. It was almost at the same time that Father Finlay was flung from his bicycle on a country road and rendered unconscious; a curious coincidence that both the President and Vice-President of the I.A.O.S. should be put out of action through the same cause in different Countries.

A wonderful scheme for helping the congested districts in Mayo was projected by Sir James Power, who lived nearby in Leopardstown Park, and I accompanied him on a tour of inspection to see if his plan was at all feasible. Along the wild Atlantic coast near Belmullet there were many inhabited stretches of land which turned into islands at high tide and were completely cut off from the mainland in stormy weather, on which occasions the poor people suffered great hardship. It was Power's idealistic concept to build bridges from each of these islands to the mainland, thus ensuring the safety of the inhabitants and providing employment for some years to come. How disappointed he was, when he was told that his enthusiastic scheme was too expensive to be put into operation. His amusing companionship helped to pass many a tedious mile, and I thoroughly enjoyed this somewhat unusual departure from lecturing on the joys and benefits of agricultural co-operation. I remember he used to boast that a letter addressed merely to 'Leopardstown Park' would find him from any part of the British Isles.

In the summer of 1899, the Agricultural and Technical Instruction Bill became an Act of Parliament, and the Department of Agriculture for Ireland was instituted. What a lot of fuss and difficulty there was to bring about such a necessary matter. Some years previously, when it seemed that it would be only a matter of weeks before the Bill would be passed, a complete change of policy towards Ireland's equivalent grant of money under the Agricultural Rating Act took place. The Government reconsidered the matter and withdrew the Bill.

John Dillon, so much against the agricultural policy of the I.A.O.S., rejoiced that he had been instrumental in killing the Bill. "We shattered that policy and we trampled on those Bills," he exulted. But when the matter came up again in July 1899, all Dillon's attacks upon it, supported by the Nationalists Flynn and Michael Davitt, came to naught and his amendment was defeated. The first Vice-President of the new Department was Horace Plunkett, who investigated a variety of schemes to help the farmer, including free instruction for students in the Royal College of Science, the inauguration of the Royal Veterinary College of Ireland and travelling lectures throughout the country. During the trouble with the cost of railway freightage, the Department was largely responsible for successfully opposing the claims made by the G.S.& W. Railway Company for an increase in their rates, an appeal made to the Railway and Canal Commission.

Only a few months after I came up to Dublin, an election was held in which Plunkett lost his parliamentary seat for South County Dublin, the upshot of which disaster was his proposed resignation from the Board of Agriculture. I attended a large and magnificent banquet that was given in his honour, and at which he was presented with an address signed by twenty thousand persons, expressing their desire that he should retain his agricultural position. Lord Dufferin, presenting the address, pointed out the greater benefits he could confer by remaining at home to help the agriculture of Ireland, rather than by his work as a politician in England. Plunkett, in an amusing reply, said how strange it was that in 1892 he should be the guest at a banquet to celebrate, among other Unionist victories, the winning of the seat for South County Dublin, and eight years later he should be an incomparably more honoured guest at a banquet in the same place, having lost the same seat for the same Party.

After considerable doubt and trepidation among Plunkett's supporters, great was the rejoicing when he retained his position as Vice-President of the Department of Agriculture and Technical Instruction. In contrast to the general pleasure felt by Plunkett's decision, I well remember the repercussions that took place when T.P. Gill was appointed Secretary of the Department. My recollection of Gill does not embody many pleasant features although, when I was in Parliament and his resignation was contemplated, I fought very hard to make his compensation on retirement as full as possible. Gill was also installed by Horace Plunkett as editor of a Dublin newspaper called 'The Daily Express', which had originated as a diehard Unionist organ. I was present on various occasions both at the I.A.O.S. offices and in the office of the 'Express' during the negotiations which brought that newspaper under Plunkett's control, and I distinctly remember the fall of the 'Express' for want of support.

It could not withstand the antagonism of the Church of Ireland, and the quality of its highbrow articles failed to make an appeal to common folk in Ireland. Gill gradually changed the Unionist paper into a Nationalist one, and finally Lord Ardilaun bought shares outvoting Plunkett's interest in it, and the editor and controller both withdrew. During the period of Gill's editorship, Marconi was making his memorable and far-reaching experiments with wireless telegraphy, and I can quite distinctly recall the incident in which one of these was exploited by the 'Daily Express'.

Years afterwards Harry Brittain and 1 were Marconi's guests at his original Broadcasting Station in Essex. I later took him to dinner at the House of Commons. During various visits to Rome, Marconi (whose headquarters were there) showed me very much friendship and consideration. My work in the I.A.O.S. headquarters in Dublin enabled me to take a wider view of the agricultural movement, and gave me an opportunity to encourage the spread of those industries which were almost the monopoly of one Province, adapting them to suit the different soil and situation of others. What was successful in Ulster might have had an equal success, if given careful thought and treatment, in the Province of Munster. The profitable industries of Leinster might have saved the homes and families of some Western town. I had been particularly anxious to bring the linen trade to the poor villages of Mayo, but knowing my own people so well, I feared they might lack the necessary qualities for the peculiar cultivation of flax. It was also difficult to find sufficient money in the poorer districts for the equipping and working of a scutching mill. The project was fairly successful, however, (at least for the first year) and encouraged us to continue the introduction of flax cultivation in various parts of Connaught, until it became clear that our efforts were useless.

From the headquarters of the I.A.O.S. I organised special conferences of the Societies all over the country. In the main they were very successful and gave members the opportunity to voice their difficulties or put forward original plans, but I recall with some amusement one meeting summoned in Londonderry. In this stronghold of the Orangemen, the special conference consisted of Hugh Law, myself, a large airy room full of empty chairs, a bedraggled parrot in a cage, and a pretty maidservant who paid us periodical visits of inspection.

The Annual General Meetings were occasions also of particular interest and occasional entertainment, at which a number of prominent personages were present. I remember one such meeting, with Lord Mounteagle in the Chair, which closed with a presentation to R. A. Anderson, the charming Secretary, who did such a lot to forward the Movement in Ireland. The presentation took the form of a cheque, and an illuminated address made in the shape of an album of bog oak bound with silver. This was followed by a most enjoyable banquet.

The officials of the I.A.O.S. with whom I worked in the office in Lincoln Place come before my mind as I send it back on its long journey down the years to the start of the century, and I see clearly the faces of Harry Norman (that impractical idealist), Father Tom Finlay (energetic and precise), dreamy AE (entrancing and entranced), R. A. Anderson (willing but weak) and a host of others. Now, in addition to the conferences and meetings throughout Ireland, I had to attend many congresses overseas in the towns of England, Scotland and Wales. One of the first which I attended as joint representative of the I.A.O.S. was in Liverpool, where I was accompanied by Captain Bryan. It was remarked to me on that occasion that the co-operative movement had done little for the Irish labourer, for it was not appreciated that the Irish farmer and the Irish labourer were practically one and the same, and a movement that incorporated some forty thousand farmers (as our numbers were at that time), considerably raised the status of the Irish labourer.

Another time that I recall, D.L. Roche of Limerick and I went as delegates to a congress in Cardiff, where we endeavoured to assure our audience that the co-operative movement in Ireland was directed towards providing them with the purest articles that money could buy. At first at these congresses, coming as I did from a country which boasted a certain spirituality in its character and traditions, and which participated to a large extent in those sentimental feelings which are a recognised characteristic of the Celt, I was somewhat inclined to regard the co-operative movement in England as being very materialistic in character, but, after I had talked to the leaders of the Labour Association, after I had visited several congresses and exhibitions, after I had met that venerable patriarch Mr. Holyoake, and had been warmed by the fire of his enthusiasm, I realised that the Saxon race had other desires than that of sordid money grubbing.

I remember so well the visit of Mr. Laurie from England, who accompanied me to the Aran Islands to teach the islanders the Cornish methods of gardening. He was amazed at the beautiful, sheltered nooks to be found all over those remote islands, and declared that they were far superior for vegetable production to any lands in Cornwall, and should make a small fortune for the people if properly cultivated. He came in December, bringing his young son with him for the holiday. With the approach of Christmas, the weather changed abruptly and a terrible gale lashed the shores of our little island. Laurie was in a fearful state in case he should not be able to reach his Cornish home by December 25th. His wife would never forgive him, he said, if he did not celebrate Christmas with her, and in any case his son would be heartbroken.

Time went by, and each day we watched out for the arrival of the vessel from Galway to take us back to the mainland, but we waited in vain. Eventually, as the storm seemed somewhat abated, I chartered a boat from a stalwart fisherman for the sum of £6, and he embarked with me for Galway, rejoicing in his good fortune. Not half way across, we met the gallant little ship steaming out to Aran after all. I think it was the following Christmas that an even more furious gale swept over the Alan Islands, in which one third of the fishing boats were lost, four men drowned, and damage of all kinds occurred which brought still greater hardship upon these unique people.

Father Farraghar did much to help the co-operative movement in Aranmore and Inishmaan, and, indeed, wherever we went on our tours through the islands we were enthusiastically received as we spoke of early potato growing, agricultural banks and home industries. How clearly the scene comes back to me, the women in their red petticoats and jackets stained with madder, the men-folk in pampooties and layer upon layer of waistcoats and woollen drawers, the home-made cradles and baskets and the tiny wooden vessels that took the place of earthenware, the salt tang of the Atlantic alive and dancing in the brilliance of a summer's day, and the blanket of mournful mist that blackened the sharp limestone rocks and brought a sombre feeling of exile and desolation.

My happiest memories of the west coast of Ireland are connected with my trips in the 'Granuaile', the ship owned by the Congested Districts, when I accompanied Horace Plunkett on a number of occasions all along that area. The crew were first class sailors, and we soon became old friends.

The I.A.O.S. had been interested in the cultivation of early potatoes for the market since the beginning of the Movement and were, in the main, successful. The difficulty was not so much in cultivation, as in marketing the crops, for the cost of transport from remote areas made the scheme impractical. I recall inspecting the district of Castlehaven in County Cork, and thinking it peculiarly adapted for the purpose, the soil was ideal and the position well sheltered from the cold winds. But the only available market was Skibbereen, where a very poor price was offered, and the freightage charge to large towns would have eaten up the profits.

In 1901 I represented the I.A.O.S. at the Scottish International Exhibition and for several months, on and off, I introduced deputations to the Irish section, demonstrating products of agriculture and home industries in Ireland. The Exhibition was opened in May by the Duke and Duchess of Fife, with a round of brilliant ceremonies. Thereafter, great crowds of people attended daily, not only to see the displays, but also to look at the exhibition of pictures, to listen to the first class foreign orchestra, or to idle in the amusement park. During that summer there were bad outbreaks of smallpox, and some cases of Bubonic plague in Glasgow, but this did not appear to frighten away the large attendance. Macartney-Filgate and I were staying at the Central Hotel in Glasgow when it was confirmed that an unfortunate fellow guest had contracted Bubonic plague, and naturally three was a tremendous uproar in the Hotel. I was going to and fro at the time, a week at the Exhibition and a-week at home, so I was able to leave before the Hotel was segregated, thankfully removing myself to St. Enoch's Hotel. The others, however, including Macartney-Filgate, had to remain in quarantine, but none of them, I am thankful to say, contracted that dread infection.

While I was in Glasgow, the freedom of the city was conferred upon Andrew Carnegie. He had just given £100,000 to defray the city's recent scheme for municipal branch libraries, and had, incidentally, visited the exhibition. I well remember the ceremony that marked this occasion, first at the University and later at the City Hall. From the time that I became a resident of County Dublin, I was frequently called upon to give lectures upon subjects only remotely connected with the functions of the I.A.O. S. Some of these took place overseas. One that I remember as an incident of pleasant variety was given to the Oxford Reform Club, where I spoke on 'Ireland at the Present Time'. Various societies in Dublin, statistical, social, literary and educational were good enough to ask me to stand on their platforms and speak to them on such subjects as befitted their particular association, and I must admit that, busy though I was, the experience of addressing such a variety of audiences was of peculiar benefit in my later years, I remember travelling down to Limerick to speak to the Foynes Social Improvement Society on the historic subject of the Desmonds, using their story to preach an ideal, virile nationality, so clearly defined by that great Irishman, Thomas Davis. We met on that occasion in a shed, made as comfortable as the weather permitted on a November day, and most of the audience were members of the Working men's Club. Lord Monteagle, who presided, in apologising for the somewhat incommodious meeting place, explained to us that he had promised to build the Society a hall, and had actually arranged for an architect to begin upon it the following week. The Hall was to be erected in memory of his son Stephen, who had died a few years previously. What a delightfully warm-hearted man was Lord Monteagle, and how much I enjoyed his generous friendship and that of his wife and their daughter, the Hon. Mary Spring-Rice. He had founded the Foynes Social Improvement Society with the aims of encouraging the study of Irish folklore, antiquities, music and language. Lectures were given in home gardening and regular shows were held.

Consequently, the Society was a model for all others that were set up in that part of the country. The following autumn they held a splendid flower and vegetable show, where there were numerous exhibits of a really high standard and I was delighted to be one of the judges. Mary Spring-Rice attended all the meetings and shows, and was keenly interested in encouraging the local home industries, particularly lacework. She was a lady of headstrong enthusiasms, which a great friend of hers (a Miss Knox) did a lot to curb. Nevertheless, it was rather a surprise to find, a decade later, that she had turned into a rebel and had thrown in her lot with Sir Roger Casement. Mary was a vigorous and forceful young lady, who gave immense time and thought to the subject of Irish history and, in process of time, became an active supporter of the Sinn Fein Movement and the close personal friend of Maud Gonne. I was sorry for Mary, and I think, she was sorry for me, because when I at long last entered the House of Commons, she bitterly reproached me as having sold my Country to the Saxon invaders, as she always regarded the English in Ireland. All I can say now is, in the fullness of my heart, may her soul, and the souls of all those devoted people in those far off golden days, enjoy eternal happiness in the Kingdom of Heaven.

The benevolent work of the Monteagle family, not merely in Co. Limerick, but to a variety of Christian organisations throughout the country, will long be recalled as a shining example of the happier relations which existed between certain Landlords and tenants, in the prolonged period of Irish recovery from the disastrous effects of famine, and the cruelties of vindictive Landlordism. It was my great joy to drive with Lady Monteagle in her two-horse carriage round various districts, where in her charitable work she rendered help and spiritual inspiration. It was in those days that I was brought into contact for the first time with the Anglican community, who settled in an area of County Clare. I made a host of friends of the Anglican Church of Ireland with whom, afterwards, many frequent contacts made my life bright and cheerful.

One of the most interesting recollections of those early years is of my repeated interviews with Lord Monteagle's Aunt, the Hon. Alice Spring-Rice. She lived in a small cottage at Foynes and, unhappily, in her old age was completely deaf. Our conversations were conducted in a rather amusing way, written by me on an old school slate, and responded to by that wonderful old lady in brilliant and memorable phrases recounting her romantic and adventurous story. In the Famine years when universal starvation afflicted the Irish people, and emigrant ships were employed to take thousands of starving men and women to the United States, Miss Spring-Rice volunteered to, accompany these poor emigrants and to plead for them with American charitable organisations, for such methods of employment as could then be brought into action to save these miserable emigrants from starvation and death.

When I enjoyed her hospitality at her little cottage at Foynes she was bright and talkative, despite her deafness. The pitiful account she gave me of the tragic situation of the emigrants, their sufferings on the Emigrant ships, their bitter experiences in finding menial jobs in the States, was given me in touching language which (even in my old age) I can never forget.

This, I think, was of all the incidents of my young life in Ireland the only real contact I made with the Potato Famine of '47, during which the Irish population fell by two and a half million.

It is true of course that my Father and Mother, who were born during the famine years, received stories of those times from my Grandfathers and Grandmothers, and all had doleful memories of those grim years during the most terrible affliction in the melancholy story of my beloved old Country.

Many of the emigrants of those terrible times steadily rose in the States through their intelligence and hard work and, under-going long periods of misery, gradually crept up in the situations which brought them settled conditions and enabled them to exercise all their faculties to struggle through the thorny way to their steady advancement in the social, business, and political life of the United States.

Talking again of rebel Irishwomen, I have already mentioned Maud Gonne, who came to Loughrea in 1895/96. She became a close and affectionate friend of my wife (we first met her on April 15th 1893), was happy and beautiful and, accompanied by her great Irish boarhound, devoted herself to the cause which was then vaguely interpreted as Irish Freedom. She addressed meetings in the Hall of the Carmelite Fathers at Loughrea, at one of which I presided, and I saw her from time to time afterwards during her stormy career in Dublin, including the historic meeting at which Edward Martyn played a conspicuous but very uncomfortable part.

This was the famous Rotunda meeting, which began with stage fright and ended with a free fight. The Dromahair Society was another splendid and nourishing branch of the I.A.O.S., and won the competition (inaugurated by Horace Plunkett), for the co-operative society which, during six months, did the most to make their parish a place from which no Irishman would wish to emigrate. There were a large number of entries for this competition from all over Ireland, and the variety of attractions designed to keep the men and women in their own district were a credit to the imaginations of the committees concerned. In the case of Dromahair the Curate in charge of the parish, Father Meehan, organised farming lectures, night schools, domestic training for girls, carpentry classes and demonstration plots. The social activities included concerts, cinematograph

64

exhibitions and entertainments for children, cattle shows and athletic contests were held, add the curious local industry of fishscale work was revived. The keen and healthy rivalry existing between the various societies caused a great blast of enthusiasm for the I.A.O.S. which, for a time, did much to hinder the incessant emigration in their own localities.

James McCann once said that the actual cost of rearing an emigrant on the east coast of Ireland was £100, and using this figure as a basis for calculation, a very considerable financial loss must have been suffered by the country. Migration, rather than emigration, was an equally difficult factor to circumvent, and among the many tasks undertaken by the I.A.O.S. was that of the official who was detailed to look after the employment, housing, and moral welfare of the migratory labourers who left their turf bogs and stony fields (to the accompaniment of the heartbroken sobs of their women-folk) for the pleasant pastures of the English and Scottish countryside to help with the harvesting. At one time the figure for the migratory labourer from County Mayo was as high as 46 per 1,000 population. Certainly it could be said that the I.A.O.S. had achieved nothing if they enabled the farmer to extract a greater income from his land, yet failed to raise his standard of living, The first means by which the worker's position could be made happier was, beyond question, the spread of education. I would like to repeat here the advice I gave in a speech many years ago: -

"Those who have had the good fortune to acquire a good education, should remember it is neither a couch on which to rest, nor a cloister in which to promenade alone, nor a mere workshop for gain and merchandise, but a rich treasury for the glory of the Creator and the ennoblement of life."

As a first step we encouraged the cultivation of cottage gardens, so sadly neglected, mainly through ignorance. In the West of Ireland, the small farmer was usually content with a few potatoes and a plot of cabbage. Carrots, broccoli, lettuce, cauliflowers; these were unknown to him, and the idea of using any part of his small portion of land for flowers was, to his way of thinking, downright foolishness. In the lectures on gardening which I gave to the people, and the articles I wrote on the subject, I had to use the elementary point of view, such as urging that the gardens should have an entrance gate or stile, a path wide enough to take a wheelbarrow, and that rubbish should not be flung haphazardly upon the ground. We held as many small shows as possible, which spread the knowledge of what such strange vegetables as peas and beans should look like when properly grown.

Miss Fitzgerald Kenny was one of the many ladies who were keenly anxious to improve the homes of the people, and she devoted much of her energy to this purpose, which was for her a life-long interest. Indeed, it was many years later that I heard from her about some work she was doing for the people of Ballintubber. At one time it was her great scheme to install a district nurse in a certain remote part of Connemara, where there was much sickness, and no one knew how to relieve the distress. An appeal was opened in the spring for £100 to finance and equip a nurse, but winter came before the subscriptions were sufficient to justify engaging one of the new Jubilee nurses and, alas, she did not stay the course for more than six months. Who could blame her? Cycling up and down mountain tracks in all sorts of weather, worn out from hard work and drenched with driving rain from which there was no shelter, she soon gave up the unequal struggle and, slightly shattered in health, she reluctantly left the district. In addition to her efforts to raise the standard of living for the poor around her, Amelia Fitzgerald Kenny acted as Secretary to the local agricultural bank, and also spent some of her abounding energy on the improvement of the egg trade.

I wonder if Ireland is still as full of philanthropists as it was at that time. So very many names spring to mind when I think of all the branches of minor industries that were founded, financed, and managed by private individuals, not for personal profit but for purely philanthropic purposes. R.H.F. Wandesforde of Castlecomer was one of this generous band. He started a basket factory for which he grew several acres of willows on his charming estate, and he paid for a skilled worker from Austria to come over and teach the trade to the local inhabitants. He was a member of the Carlton Club, and there we used to meet each other in later years, when I had left Ireland.

Fruit growing was another industry favoured by certain people, and one which was largely neglected. In 1902 the actual acreage under fruit was only one twelfth that of Great Britain, and the export trade was sadly affected by the cute habit of packers to put their best produce on top only. Consequently, a complete re-organisation of the trade, and constant supervision was necessary.

Of course, there was Irish tobacco. The first few crops sold at a sufficient price to forecast that the industry might be a profitable one. Colonel Nugent Everard was a pioneer in tobacco growing, and J. Willington of Parsonstown conducted many experiments with the crop. Colonel Everard also fought for the reconsideration of the duties on home-grown tobacco, on which subject William Redmond constantly urged the Government's attention.

Redmond used to declare that Irish tobacco was really quite smokeable, but he played a prominent part in an amusing incident which was jocularly supposed to prove otherwise. It happened that the Duke of York (later King George V) visited Ireland, and William Redmond solemnly presented him with a gift of Irish tobacco, part pipe, part cigarette. Much fuss was made of this in the current newspapers which supported the industry. Alas! A couple of days afterwards, it was regretfully announced in the social columns that:- *"His Royal Highness, the Duke of York, has been indisposed for the last two days."* Poor Redmond got horribly teased for this.

Those industries better fitted for women and girls to work in, were usually organised by a religious Order, outstanding among these being the "Providence" woollen Mills at Foxford under the guidance of Mother Morrogh Bernard, who thus guided the agricultural destinies of some fifty-two townlands. What an object lesson was this wonderful industry to other parts of Ireland where, if co-operative principles could have been applied among the toilers of homespuns in remote districts, how much more valuable would their work have been to them.

Lady Fingall, that delightful and vivacious personality, who had so much to do with the I.A.O.S. in those days, showed an especial interest in the Foxford Mills. Her lively spirits never flagged on the many uncomfortable and exhausting journeys that she made in the service of the I.A.O.S. in those days, and I recall with an abiding warmth of memory the frequent occasions on which we opened shows and exhibitions together. She was one of the three wonderful women who greatly influenced Horace Plunkett's life and work. The other two ladies were (as was well known by all his contemporaries) Lady Betty Balfour and Miss Emily Lawless.

Lady Betty Balfour, the wife of Mr. Gerald Balfour (then Chief Secretary), was one of the most loveable women of my time in the old days of the Government of Ireland. She was a charming personality, using the expression in its most delicate sense. She opened bazaars, flower shows, local agricultural societies, women's home industries, various classes and, in fact, touched the cultural and economic side of Irish life at every point where a gracious lady could encourage the finer side of home and family life.

It was my unforgettable privilege to attend many of those functions, and I recited from time to time some account of the vagaries of my fellow countrymen, which Lady Betty enjoyed. I have written elsewhere about poteen, and have quoted one instance in which it might have compromised a priest's reputation. I now turn to a happier episode concerning this exhilarating stimulant.

Among other stories with which I regaled Lady Betty, was some account of the influence of poteen on the backward districts of Donegal and Connemara, and she was much interested in securing samples of the forbidden product for the various guests who frequently stayed at the Chief Secretary's Lodge in Phoenix Park. So, on one particular occasion, Lady Betty though it would be something novel, notwithstanding its adventurous quality, to give her distinguished guests a wee drop of poteen, and she got in touch with me. The I.A.O.S, was then housed at 22, Lincoln Place, and I was politely called Chief Organiser. On hearing from Lady Betty, I telegraphed to the Parish Priest in Galway, whose wine cupboard included some finely matured poteen, asking him to send me by post two bottles of 'Altar Wine'. The bottles duly arrived at Lincoln Place (by messenger from the Chief Secretary's Lodge) and the 'Altar Wine' no doubt spread predictable enjoyment around the Chief Secretary's table.

I may add here that in years long after, I sat on the Board of the Westminster Electricity Corporation of which I was Vice-Chairman, with Mr. Gerald Balfour (as he was at that time), one of my co-directors. On the death of his great brother, Arthur James, he became Lord Balfour, and we exchanged friendly greetings up to the time of his death.

The year 1902 is memorable to me for the large and important Exhibition held in Cork, which it was my job to organise and administrate, and at which I represented the I.A.O.S. The Exhibition opened in the early Summer and did not close until November, and it was my duty to receive the visitors, numbering over 200,000, who came as delegations from co-operative societies and agricultural centres not only in Ireland, but from the U. S. A. and all parts of Europe. The Department of Agriculture was represented by Macartney-Filgate, and a visit of inspection was paid by representatives of the Board. The sixty guests were entertained to lunch, among them Horace Plunkett and the Bishop of Clonfert.

Two of the most popular displays in this enormous show were the 'Daffodil Dairy' (where the most modern methods of dairying were on view) and the 'Bee Skep' (a giant erection faithfully copied from the original, containing all the particulars of a beehive, complete with honey in various stages).

Of the many series of visitors whom I conducted round the Exhibition, I remember best the party consisting of the Lord Lieutenant and representatives of the Irish Government. Another party, not so important, but vastly larger, consisting in fact of twelve hundred persons, was brought by Canon Power of Emly. Normally I had to receive these delegations at the station, and pile them into buses en-route for the Exhibition, where I would then conduct them from stall to stall, explaining each exhibit and answering their numerous and, generally intelligent, questions. But, in Canon Power's case, we marched like an army through the streets of the city, headed by the Canon and myself, to the wonder and excitement of the citizens of Cork.

Another of the exhibits was a model cottage, with a pretty, well-kept patch of garden in front, designed to raise the social life of the poor countryman. In front of this I organised a ceilidh, where a huge audience was soon attracted by the singing and dancing and, I hope, encouraged to use this ideal dwelling place as a model for their own homes. When the Exhibition was over,

MacCartney Filgate was presented with a silver cup by the Department of Agriculture, and the I.A.O.S. Committee, with all round eloquent flourishes, made me a gift of £100 in recognition of my Exhibition work. Incidentally, the Lord Mayor, Edward Fitzgerald, was made a Baronet as a result of the Cork Exhibition.

The following year is memorable for George Wyndham's Land Act, which originated from a letter written by a Galway landlord, Mr. Stuwe-Taylor. The Land Conference, from which the Act was born, was held in the Standard Hotel, Dublin, under the Chairmanship of Lord Dunraven. Among those who had interested themselves in the question was George Moore, the novelist. He was present on this occasion, but so far had been a silent onlooker. Different viewpoints had been illustrated and the discussion was in full swing, when someone turned to George Moore and asked for his opinion. There was silence as he rose to give his reply, which was this: - *"A lot has been said which would have been better unsaid. The house is on fire, the landlord is trying to get out of the window, and the devil is coming in at the door."* The words roused such a storm of comment that the meeting then broke up. The transference of land from landlord to tenant was certainly epoch making and it entailed, for the I.A.O.S., much reorganisation within the Society.

One of the important industries which I have not yet mentioned was bacon curing, which was of great consequence both in Munster (famous for its Limerick Ham) and in County Mayo, more my earlier concern, where I organised a series of conferences dealing with the pig trade. After one of my trips to Denmark at the beginning of this century, the farmers became enthusiastic after reading the pamphlets and articles on this subject, which were produced as a result of my visit. They clamoured for the erection of bacon factories, often in the most unsuitable places. Far from having to encourage them I had, in several cases, to damp their enthusiasm and suppress their wild schemes.

At one meeting in Tipperary town for instance, at which Lord Ikerrin, R. A. Anderson and myself represented the I.A.O.S., we were strongly criticised for our excessive caution by most of the local agriculturalists, including Count Moore. One of the most powerful trade combines in the country was the bacon and pig industry, and a cooperative bacon society would have been of immense advantage to the farmer, but the financial perils of such a venture, coupled with the fact that the cost of building and equipping such a factory could not be less than £10,000, were grave drawbacks. This meeting however, would not listen to our advice and, having deplored our attitude, decided to go ahead with their plans.

At a Sligo Co-operative conference, with Sir Josslyn Gore-Booth as Chairman, the same question came up, but in this case the members appreciated the difficulties of having such a powerful ring arrayed against them, and I had little trouble in advising them to go slow. Sir Josslyn was brother of the beautiful Constance and Eva Gore-Booth, both of whom I knew well. Eva with her gentle and poetic nature, and Constance with her burning patriotic fervour and glowing militantism. I was staying with the Gore-Booths some years before Constance married the Polish Count Markiewicz, and lent a sympathetic ear to the worried confidences of their father, who was most uneasy about his somewhat spoiled elder daughter.

At that time a young fellow in the militia called Wynn was madly in love with her, and Sir Henry did not at all approve. Some days later I was travelling in the North and met Wynn on the platform at Enniskillen. We went to the Refreshment Room and had a drink together and it was obvious that he was very much upset. We were bound for the same destination, and when the train came in we were able to get a carriage to ourselves. All the way to Armagh he told me, with tears in his eyes, of the sad break that had just occurred between Connie and himself. He was fearfully cut-up about it. I have often wondered if Countess Markiewicz would have played so prominent a part in the Easter Rising, or indeed, participated in it at all, if she had married young Wynn.

In the Year of Grace 1903, His Majesty King Edward VII, accompanied by his fascinating and unforgettable gentle Queen, decided to visit Ireland, and it is somewhat strange in these days to remember the enthusiastic scenes which greeted them. Having spent some days in Dublin, they sailed in their yacht (the 'Victoria and Albert') around the North of Ireland, calling in at several towns on their way, and arrived in Galway on a sunny day at the end of July.

An enterprising man named Colonel Courtney, who occupied the rather singular position of Master of the King's Bench in the High Court of Justice in Ireland, induced the friends of the King to bring him to the marble quarries as an incentive to the development of Irish industry. The Hon. John Ward (brother to the Earl of Dudley), was A.D.C., and an intimate friend of the King and, in response to an urgent request from Col. Courtney, the King agreed to perform the ceremony of opening the Serpentine marble quarries, which were already more than one hundred years old.

The royal party landed at Leenane, were promptly conducted by Sir Horace Plunkett to their motorcar, and the party drove off to Recess preceded by Sir Horace as guide. At every inhabited spot along this beautiful route, the people gathered to cheer and wave as the motorcars passed by. A striking feature of their reception at Recess was a band of forty men, riding on bare-backed Connemara ponies and flaunting 'favours'. His Majesty and the Queen were met by an immense concourse of the somewhat primitive inhabitants of Connemara. The actual quarry was situated some hundreds of feet higher than the main road, and arrangements were made to convey the King and Queen up the rough and tumble way. A somewhat crude carriage drawn by two horses awaited their Majesties at the foot of the hill, but the local' peasantry took the horses away from the carriage and decided to draw their Majesties up the slope by the vigorous manual labour of Connemara peasants.

The crowds of cheering people pushed the carriage up the steepest parts of that steep and difficult road, and I recall vividly the curious contrast between the affluence of royalty and their retinue, and the barefooted children who scrambled agilely from rock to rock. It was a wonderful performance. I was at the side of Her Majesty the Queen who, to say the least of it, was quite a little naturally nervous in her extraordinary surroundings in a scene which, while enthusiastic and affectionate in the Irish way, would be difficult to regard as appropriate for the reception of their Majesties.

We reached the top of the ascent, where the Chairman of the Quarries Project, with hat in hand, bowed low and begged their Majesties: - "... to declare this immense project for the expansion of the industrial life of Ireland Open."

With all that grace and charm which always enveloped His Majesty, the King, in a few pleasant words, and with his slight touch of German accent, said:- "How proud I am to have the opportunity of doing a service for my Irish subjects, and wish the scheme with which I have been made familiar, a continuous, abounding success." There. were wild cheers, and the next part of the proceedings had to be undertaken. This consisted of guiding the carriage with their Majesties backwards down the 'slope' of the hill where the ceremony had taken place. Stepping alongside, I said every kind thing which my imagination could suggest to assure Queen Alexandra that she brought a flood of happiness to the people of Connemara, and that her unique journey down the face of the hill would be accomplished in perfect safety. The windlass and wire chain, which was customarily used as a brake for heavily laden wagons from the quarry was, at King Edward's request, attached to the carriage, and no further incident befell.

At the foot of the hill we came to the public road, surrounded by masses of people, when out of the weird assembly an excited woman rushed forward and threw herself at the feet of the King as he prepared to board the Royal train. She said: - *Oh King. God will bless you for the whole of your life, if you will release my husband, who is serving a life sentence in Tullamore Gaol.* John Ward rushed to take the woman away from the King who said, in his gentle and touching way: - "Don't touch her, be kind to her; I would like to know her story." and "John, when we reach Galway, will you get in touch with Dudley, and find out whether, within all that is legal and correct from the point of view of the Law, her appeal can be regarded with sympathy."

The story was that a man named Connelly, the husband of the woman who fell on her knees before the King, had been imprisoned for life for the manslaughter of a cousin. On reaching Galway station, John Ward had received information from Dudley that the woman's appeal was worthy of His Gracious Majesty's consideration. The result: the life prisoner was at once restored to liberty. They travelled the next part of the journey by rail, and arrived in Galway late in the afternoon. Never before had the station been so splendidly decorated, and all the streets were gay with arches of colour and flags. A stand had been erected near the station entrance and immense crowds were waiting to cheer their Majesties. But something happened at Galway station that should be remembered in the records of the genial and benevolent quality of the King, a comical incident concerning one James O'Donohue, Chairman of the Galway Urban District Council.

The Town Council had for years been agitating for a Trans-Atlantic mail route from the United States to the Port of Galway. A deputation from the Council, led by O'Donohue, awaited the arrival of the King to submit a petition that His Majesty would graciously approve the Trans-Atlantic Mail project. As the special train drew into the platform, O'Donohue stepped forward and, refusing to hand the Address to the King's Equerry, John Ward, insisted on reading it aloud himself: -

"Recognising that your Majesty is raised high above all political questions, the City of Galway have very great pleasure in giving expression to the feelings of profound respect in which they hold Your Majesty."

The conventional sentences, read so unconventionally in O'Donaghue's breezy style and rich Galway voice, delighted the King, who thoroughly enjoyed the whole ridiculous affair and thereupon knighted O'Donaghue on the station platform. At the next meeting of the Council, the members of which were prominent Nationalists, O'Donaghue (replying to a resolution of congratulation) hastened to defend himself from the implication which he feared might be in everyone's mind: that of leaning towards England.

"There are some," he said, *"who might consider my action a cowardly and mean one, but in doing what I have done, I neither cringed, crawled, compromised, nor in any way demeaned my principals of Nationalism. I was the recipient of an unasked for and un-wished for title."* Naively, he spoiled this by adding proudly, *"I say that I alone, was the only recipient of a title in Connaught."*

The next day the Royal party travelled down to Cork by train from Galway. Originally, they had intended to continue the journey by yacht, but they had received such a terrible tossing corning round the North of Ireland that the Queen could not face the Atlantic again so soon.

Arrangements for this unpredicted alteration to their route were carried through smoothly, and the Royal Party left for the South, omitting the possibly rough sea passage from Galway to Kenmare. Their state arrival in Cork the next morning was a splendid affair, for they had spent the night aboard the yacht, and now, accompanied by a number of warships, were taken in a tender up the River Lee to the city. A number of us were lined up to receive their Majesties at Victoria Quay, and we waited in brilliant sunshine as the boom of guns announced the arrival of the Royal party. It was all a most pleasurable visit, and one that has long remained bright in my memory. The King conferred the title of Knight Commander of the Victorian Order on Horace Plunkett who, more than anyone else, deserved to be honoured by King Edward for his services to his country, and his Knighthood was warmly acclaimed by people of every rank all over Ireland.

I made quite a number of trips abroad that year, both lecturing and learning. Immediately after the royal visitors' departure, I set off for Denmark and Scandinavia for the second time in six months, accompanied by Hugh Law, A. T. S. Magan, T. M. Russell, The Very Rev. J. Daly and five or six other friends. I recall that on this occasion an editorial in the 'Irish Homestead' (the journal of the I. A.O. S.) had wondered where my 'exploring mind' would lead me next; and had suggested that when I had exhausted Europe, the communal system of agriculture among the tribes in Africa might lead me to follow in the track of Stanley and Livingstone. The Editor was not so very far wrong.

Denmark was a fascinating place of study for the agriculturist, and a very simple object lesson for the Irish farmer and his family. In 1839 Denmark had been the poorest country, per head of population, in Europe. By the end of the century it was one of the richest, due primarily to the surge of patriotic feeling which united the people, educated them and brought them to work in one large unit for the good of their country. That wonderful institution, the People's High Schools (founded by Bishop Grundtvig about one hundred years ago) enabled young men and women of the farming class, and of the 18 to 21 year age group, to obtain board and education for some months at a time, for the equivalent of about ten shillings a week. Technical instruction in agriculture was part of the curriculum, the pupils also being taught Geography, History and the legends of their own country, and the co-operative movement quickly spread through the farming communities, enabling them to produce and export the best merchandise in the best way possible.

The Danes boasted that they were now the happiest people on God's earth, and I am certain that my memory is not at fault when I look back on those trips around Denmark as being most delightful and happy events. What struck me most about those people was a complete lack of class distinction, and I noticed that in every village there was a hall where the neighbourhood gathered regularly for recreation. Artistic and sporting clubs were numerous, and there was an air of liveliness and well-being, contrasting painfully with the patient, philosophical outlook of so many of my own countrymen. At that time there was much enthusiasm for the peat industry, and the numerous bogs around Jutland were yielding peat for power fuel cut by special machinery.

Lord Ikerrin and I travelled to Denmark as delegates of the I.A.O.S. in the early spring. We were conducted on a tour of bacon factories, creameries and so on by the President of the Danish Export Society. The knowledge that I gained on that occasion enabled me to take charge of the party of my colleagues that I mentioned earlier, and at the conclusion of that second trip they presented me with a copy of Morley's 'Life of Gladstone', a silver cigarette case and a signed Address, which I still treasure. I believe it was in that busy and crowded year that I managed to spend a week or so giving lectures on agricultural co-operation in France, where I also studied the system of viticulture. Over seven hundred and sixty co-operative societies were registered in Ireland by 1903, and such rapid growth was made, it seemed almost impossible for us in the Dublin Headquarters to keep in constant touch with them. We would not have been able to meet the requirements of all the localities without the secondary form of organisation which existed in the shape of district conferences, more or less regulating the requirements of each separate district. The country was divided into twenty-five Conference Districts, and in the first ten weeks of 1903 I attended twenty-three meetings.

This multiplicity of organisation, where they actually over-lapped, constituted a grave danger to the I.A.O.S., and was actually the ruin of the Movement in some places. Obviously, co-operation had reached the point where it must pass beyond the parochial stage, and at the Annual General Conference (which for the first time had to be held separately to the General Meeting owing to the amount of business to be discussed) two lengthy papers dealing with re-organisation were read. One of these was read by H.de F. Montgomery, who had studied agricultural co-operation in Germany and Switzerland, and urged that their methods should be followed in Ireland. He specialised in co-operative credit, and had suggested the establishment of a central co-operative bank helped by a grant from the Department of Agriculture. The Irish farmer, being of very different character to the German farmer, made such policy unsuitable.

Such was the state of affairs fourteen years after the foundation of the I.A.O.S. So rapid had been the growth of societies, particularly during the previous five years, that the situation was getting out of hand. I remember how, at one of the District Meetings held shortly after the Annual Conference, a belligerent gentleman called General Clifford, who never found himself short of words, declared that he was not in favour of mending the I.A.O.S., but of ending it.

The generous gifts that had helped the finances of the Society in its earlier stages were now of little use to swell the funds in the face of this explosive growth, and once again the Movement was in dire need of money. It was ironic that some people actually believed that the I.A.O.S. was making a profit out of the work. To get rid of this fallacy, arrangements were made to convert the Movement into a Friendly Society. The response to our appeal for subscriptions (which met with some rebuffs from the usual quarters, such as the 'Freeman's Journal and the 'Sligo Champion') was not sufficiently great to enable the Organisation to carry on its work, and we had to look further afield.

When an Irishman looks for help, he turns naturally towards the United States of America, where so many of his friends, relations and acquaintances have already settled and are living in very different circumstances to their fellow countrymen in Ireland. So it was that Father Finlay, accompanied by Anderson and Father O'Donovan of Loughrea, was sent to the States to see if it was likely that practical help would be forthcoming. Sir Horace Plunkett had been a rancher in the Far West, and had made many lasting friendships in the political and business world of the U.S. A., for which reason we had greater hope of success. I might interject here that my interest in Tariff Reform, which was later to take possession of my life for a small number of years, had naturally been roused with the question of marketing our agricultural produce, and I followed with some enthusiasm the speeches made in Parliament upon this vital matter. The protectionist policy urged by Joseph Chamberlain was one which was much debated among the I.A.O.S officials, and the possibilities for good and evil were much discussed. At the beginning of the year 1904, Winston Churchill came over to Dublin and spoke in the Rotunda on 'Ireland and the Fiscal Question'. I recall the Earl of Mayo remarking on Churchill's pluck in coming to Ireland as an apostle of Free Trade, when we had suffered more than any other part of the United Kingdom from Free Trade.

The deputation to the States had now returned with the report that much sympathy for Plunkett's projected reforms had been expressed in the American Press. A wider and personal appeal for funds seemed desirable to enable the I.A.O.S. to strengthen and enlarge its activities. For this purpose, I was chosen to represent the Organisation, my visit being arranged by the Executive Committee in consultation with a body of leading American citizens, who were interested in economic development in Ireland.

Early in 1904 I sailed from Queenstown (Cobh), greatly encouraged in my mission by the good wishes of the people I was leaving behind me. I received over six hundred letters from all parts of the country and, most heartening of all, the blessing of two Archbishops and ten Bishops. Among those many letters I should like to mention one I received from Douglas Hyde, who spoke of our efforts to produce a real Ireland instead of a shoddy, imitation, England.

The liner 'Oceanic' deposited me in New York, after a severe spell of rough weather. As I am fortunately a good sailor, it was not too unpleasant an experience, although the voyage was afterwards described as one of the worst during the whole of that winter. The leading Americans who were so anxious to assist the work in Ireland were Mr. James Byrne (one of the most prosperous Corporation lawyers in New York) and Mr. Wickersham (who was at that time Attorney General of the United States). The American movement to help the I.A.O.S. had a remarkable and generous leader in Byrne, who was supported by many leading Irishmen in New York. Although he took no interest in politics, he was on very friendly relations with Dan Cohalan and other of the Extremists in their attitude to the policy of the British Government in Ireland. It was my great good fortune to number James Byrne among my friends, and I can never forget the hospitality extended to me by him and by his delightful wife, that fascinating woman Helen McGrigor, who was so proud of her Scottish origin. During the Cork Exhibition of 1902, they had been my guests in Cork and Dublin. It was my privilege during the First World War to entertain him again, this time in London. He was visiting Great Britain as a representative of the American Red Cross, and rendered outstanding service in dealing with the wounded of the war. Mr. Wickersham also received me most graciously and I made the acquaintance of his wife, who was a charming person, full of wit and with a wide and intimate knowledge of society on both sides of the Atlantic.

The American Committee had arranged offices (where we were known as the Irish Development Society) on the twelfth floor of a building in Pine Street, in the heart of New York City. My secretary, who was a graduate from one of the Universities, met me on my arrival, and we proceeded forthwith to plan a series of meetings and lectures where, with the help of local sympathisers, our efforts should have some measure of result. Much of the groundwork of my American campaign had already been laid by the Rev. Gerald O'Donovan (whom I have already mentioned) an intimate friend of mine and an active supporter of the Plunkett regime. Yet to enter upon a programme which had been necessarily haphazard and dependent almost wholly on the support of friends in New York and various cities throughout the U. S. A. presented a pretty formidable task.

I was, however, fortunate in securing the friendly support of Dan Cohalan. He was one of the most attractive and aggressive advocates in the political life of New York, and he afterwards became a Judge. Dan brought me into touch with almost every phase of Irish life and tradition in America, taking me in hand with an enthusiasm that I have always recalled with affectionate gratitude. He was an outstanding force in Tammany Hall, and he brought me into contact with Mr. Charles Murphy (1858-1924) who was then, and for long afterwards, the 'boss' of that singular institution. I was fortunate also in the welcome extended to me by two brothers, Directors of a well-known Banking Corporation in New York. It is amazing how a chain of friendship can be developed suddenly in that city if one possesses the necessary introductions. It would be difficult to enumerate, after this long period of time, the number of Clubs, Institutions and what are called County Societies to which I was invited and at which I was allowed to present my case on behalf of my Movement at home, but one of my happiest recollections was the occasion of my being elected a member of the Knights of St. Columbus.

I took a two-fold line in making my appeal. In the first place I pointed out that the Plunkett movement in Ireland was entirely economic in character, and in no way whatever impeded or frustrated the great political objective which the great mass of the Irish people entertained in the ultimate triumph of Home Rule. Any funds raised in the U.S. A. would be employed solely in preaching the gospel of conjoint effort among farmers, in the improvement of their present methods of raising the quality of their products, and in the provision of skilled marketing direction in the disposal of butter, bacon, eggs and other articles in the British and European markets. In the second place, I emphasised the anxiety to establish a permanent relationship between the Home Industries, which were gradually coming to life in Ireland, and the households of the U.S. A. The variety of artistic products gradually being extended in Convent Schools and elsewhere throughout Ireland, and the continuous efforts being applied to homespun weaving and lace needed the American market if they were to flourish. I was a sort of missionary, for the two-fold purpose of raising money to encourage collective activity in every branch of enterprise in Ireland, and at the same time to invite the attention of the American people, particularly those of Irish origin, to the potential market which could be created for women workers where rural life needed inspiration. Under the auspices which I have related, people were exceedingly kind, and hospitality universal.

Agricultural co-operation in the United States was not in a healthy condition. There was no central organisation and no system, and I found that statistics were not available. Even in the prosperous regions there was unrest among the farmers, and all over the country there was a town-ward movement. They had a barren social life, much more so than their counterparts in Ireland, owing to the immense areas that were farmed and great distance of the nearest towns. Labour was scarce, and many of the farmers were not settlers in the long term sense of the word, but merely intended to make as much money out of the land as they could in the shortest time possible. This attitude accounted in some districts for great impoverishment of the land, and a lot of soil erosion.

Theodore Roosevelt (1858-1919) was much interested in agriculture, and all that the proper study of it entails. For a while he had ranched in the West, and had the reputation of being extremely tough with 'bad men'. Shortly after coming to office, he realised that the welfare of the rural population had been too long neglected, and he declared his famous message to Congress: -

"Better farming, better business, better living." But the man who did so much for agriculture there at the time of my visit to the States was Secretary Wilson.

On my visit to New York, I stayed with Judge Martin Jerome Keogh (1855-1928) at his charming house at New Rochelle, where Alice Roosevelt (the fascinating, volatile, unpredictable daughter of Theodore Roosevelt) was a guest. She had the most attractive and vivacious personality, and her vitality was abounding. One evening at a dinner party she challenged me to ride round the lawn of Judge Keogh's home on the children's donkey. Naturally I accepted the challenge, much to everyone's amusement, for my evening dress got completely messed up with donkey's hairs, and I was in a horrible state when I re-entered the house. I met her later at the World's Fair at St. Louis after her marriage to Longmore, who was subsequently a Senator. She possessed much of the spirit of her father who, when he was ordered by his doctor to go quietly because of his heart, went to Europe and climbed the Matterhorn. I recall another memorable day spent with Judge Keogh, when we enjoyed a visit to Burke Cochrane, at his almost fabulous place on the East River.

The publication of Plunkett's book 'Ireland in the New Century' appeared during my visit to the States, and it was a constant frustration to my efforts to secure financial support for our Irish Movement. The book was favourably received in some of the New York papers, but, certainly, received a smashing condemnation in Philadelphia and Chicago. Very unfairly, some of Plunkett's references were interpreted as offensive to the Catholic Church, and to the Nationalist Movement in Ireland, and several of the Irish Societies which I addressed used this criticism as a pretext to withhold contributions to our American Fund. It was my great privilege at this time, however, to be the guest of no less than three Catholic Archbishops, each of whom made a distinct mark in the spiritual life of the United States. Archbishop Patrick Ryan (1831-1911) of Philadelphia was almost unique in the Catholic hierarchy of America through his abounding energy, being tempered with a flood of wit and humour. I do not think I have met anybody throughout my life who told me so many stories, and told them so well, with such pregnant references to the times through which we were passing. It was also my good fortune to meet Archbishop John Ireland (1838-1918) of St. Paul, a man of forceful character who, in the course of the various controversies that arose from time to time, exhibited gracious logic in argument, softened by tolerant respect for his opponents. The third of these prelates was Archbishop Glennon of St. Louis, of whom I saw a good deal during the proceedings of the World's Fair in that city during 1904. He was quite different from those to whom I have just referred, in his gentle and kindly character, but was, at the same time, endowed with immense organising capacity. He was particularly effective on every aspect of Catholic education. The elevation of University and school life owes much to his inexhaustible enthusiasm.

I suppose there is no spectacle in New York more striking and more abundantly popular than the St. Patrick's Day Procession. On 17th March, the city blossoms with flags and bunting, while two persons out of three sport the green of the shamrock. Carriages form into line, the military units (each in splendid uniform) get into formation, the bandsmen take a deep preparatory breath and the lengthy procession moves away to Central Park via Fifth Avenue, to the cheering of a vast throng of New Yorkers. Flags fly from every window, hats are thrown into the air and martial music and the deafening din of human voices exulting 'en masse' fill the ear. Or so it all appeared to me more than half a century ago when I took part in the spectacle. Many friends of mine marvelled, having regard to the short time I had been in New York, that I was selected to ride in carriage number 'Five' in that great procession. It was an experience that I have never forgotten. Indeed, some elderly people said that not since the year 1852 had there been so large a parade, so enthusiastic an audience or so fine a day. A curious element in the procession that particular year was the Russian flag, carried in the Parade and waved on the sidewalk by sympathisers of Russia; for this was the year of the Russo-Japanese War, and the Nationalist section of New York strongly supported Russia.

In the evening I was brought to a banquet, held by the Friendly Sons of St. Patrick, at Delmonico's, to which President Roosevelt sent a telegram of good wishes. The famous Justice of the Supreme Court, Justice James Fitzgerald (who afterwards became a great friend of mine) was in the Chair, and I was requested to propose the toast of "Ireland Rejuvenated." The banquet was a mighty affair, and lengthy, and I was last on the toast list. My feelings can be imagined as the evening wore on and on, and my duty still lay ahead of me. Finally, the moment came, and my short and very bedraggled speech terminated at midnight. The flood of memories of that St. Patrick's Day demonstration, and that almost never-ending banquet, have followed me through life ever since. I have had a long trail of social functions in my career, but nothing has ever reached the heights of exaltation on the one hand, and long-awaited misery on the other, as that throbbing day in New York, and the exasperating evening that followed.

A large number of the emigrants fleeing from famine-stricken Ireland in mid-century had settled in New York, and within a generation they established political control there, through the agency of that extraordinary organisation, Tammany Hall, which, with calculating charity, continued to draw the American immigrant into its net, whether he was of Irish, Jewish, Italian or German origin. Tammany, the meeting place and club of the poor and voiceless, with its notorious 'bosses', was a dread and terrible institution, perhaps nothing like it arose in any other community under the sun. It dominated New York politics from the Mayor to the crossing-sweeper, and its ramifications were met with in every phase of local life. It is not extravagant to say that employment and promotion were intimately within the sphere of Tammany control and direction. Of course, the cleaning up of New York has long since taken place but, stirring up my memory, it could not have been brought about too soon.

My impression of the time was that the Government of the City of New York was divided between the Irish and the Jews, and I must admit that the shady side of political tactics and manoeuvres could have received equal credit from the leadership of one or the other. Indeed, in most of the big cities which had received the poor and oppressed from across the ocean, the Irish, with the Jews and a sprinkling of Germans in many instances, dominated political life.

My experience of the police of New York, and indeed of some of the other cities I visited, bore out the wide impression of the place which Irish men occupied in these great organisations. No doubt immense changes have taken place for improvement in the relations between the American police chiefs and the local liquor trade, and also other branches of business that came under the purview of the Municipal Authorities, but I saw more than one instance when they were under the implication that the exercise of their functions was not without special regard to their private profit. Theodore Roosevelt (who was made Commissioner of Police towards the end of the century) did much, in his honesty and independence, to reform the Force and free it from graft and corruption. But the process was long and tedious. The same in general terms applies to Chicago, of which I also saw a great deal, and which seemed to me the most horrible place in the world, although I was treated with great kindness by many of my fellow countrymen and was made a member of various Irish

Societies and Clubs there. But I found in almost every instance that these Societies had political objects in view, and were being used by 'bosses' for objectives which at that time, at all events, I could not regard as of high repute.

In all I saw a good deal of the Irishman in American politics, Republican and Democrat, sometimes attractive, sometimes most decidedly the reverse. Michael Davitt (1846-1906) was in the U.S. A. at the same time that I was, enlisting the aid of Irish Americans for the Nationalist cause, and his efforts slightly impeded mine. For Davitt, being intensely opposed to British Government, and certainly having no love for Sir Horace Plunkett, was very much averse to my mission. John Devoy and O'Donovan Rossa were there, too, and I met them and goodness knows how many others who claimed to have taken some part in the struggle for the freedom of Ireland.

The World's Fair at St. Louis took place while I was in the States, and presented many episodes which I still recall. The Irish Department of Agriculture was represented by a group of very interesting Irishmen, including among their number Mr. T. W. H. Rolleston (1857-1920), with whom I had a happy and interesting time. The Irish Section of the World's Fair, which opened on June 11th, contained samples of an extraordinary variety of Irish architecture, jumbled in the most incongruous way. The front portion with its Georgian pillars, for example, represented the old Parliament House in College Green, Dublin, and behind it lay the ruins of Muckross Abbey, Killarney. The Manager, Mr. M. J. Murphy, was a theatrical manager in America, which accounted for this dramatic representation. Included in his many original activities was a party of Irish players, whom Mr. Murphy had invited to attend the Fair, and they gave continuous trouble throughout the whole of their visit.

Murphy was keen on presenting the 'stage Irishman', and the Irish players quite properly resented anything of the sort. I was drawn into the negotiations as a sort of peacemaker, but a certain Miss Quinn (who was the embodiment of the most virulent of the Furies, and of whom we used to say "From the fury of the Quinns, good Lord deliver us") made any adjustment impossible. Among her other castigations, she denounced me as the destroyer of the Nationalism of the Irish race.

Also at St. Louis, I met Major McBride who was extremely pleasant and agreeable. He was, of course, the husband of Maud Gonne, and suffered execution in the terrible Easter Rising in Dublin. Buffalo was another city that I visited on that occasion; I accompanied Cardinal Gibbons on his way to Canada, getting out of the train at Buffalo, the city where President McKinley had been shot. I recall thinking of this horrible event, which had happened but a few years previously.

One final observation I must make with regard to my American trip, and that is that the Catholic Church there, and indeed American society by and large, owes an immense debt to the Irish girl immigrants scattered far and wide, but more especially in the Eastern States. Against the many temptations that surround them, they maintained the purity and sanctity of the home life (which was sometimes indescribably miserable) that they brought from their peasant mothers in Ireland. It is no exaggeration to state that literally thousands of Catholic Churches, throughout the United States, achieved their present development on the support, in large measure, of these splendid young women. They divided their earnings between contributions to their Irish homes and the support of the churches to which they had become so warmly attached.

Directly I got home to Ireland, I once more plunged into my busy life as Organiser and Assistant Secretary of the I.A.O.S. at the Headquarters in Dublin. But this was only for a few more months. My work under Horace Plunkett was gradually coming to an end. In South Africa, the Jameson Government was in power, and attention was directed towards the attempts of the officials both to keep the recently restored peace between Boer and Englishman and to bring prosperity to the war-torn land. So much needed to be done, and there were so many difficulties to be faced. The situation was intriguing, but so far removed from Ireland, that it seemed to be. almost a waste of time to interest oneself in the problems of Africa. But Dr. Jameson, looking towards Great Britain for advice and example, was directed towards Ireland, where somewhat similar problems were in the process of being solved. Thus it came about that Owen Lewis, a Senator in the Upper House in Cape Colony, was sent by Dr. Jameson to Ireland to investigate our agricultural progress. He came to my meetings and we talked on various occasions, where I found him to be a delightful fellow. On his return to Africa he recommended me to the Jameson Government as a person who might stimulate agriculture in the Cape, with the result that I received an offer to inaugurate agricultural co-operation there, an offer which I joyfully accepted. In the middle of August 1905, the I.A.O.S. gave me a farewell dinner, with R. A. Anderson in the Chair, and on September 2nd I set sail from Southampton to begin a new chapter of my life.

CHAPTER 3

With the signing of the Treaty of Vereeniging, peace came once more to South Africa, and Boer and British farmer alike set themselves to the task of remaking their impoverished farms, tilling a neglected soil and building up their devastated flocks and herds. It is a mighty task indeed to bring order out of disorder, but the instinct of self preservation ingrained in the Boer through generations of struggle with life in a somewhat impoverished and uncivilised land, which was ever broadening its frontiers and inviting the adventurous to till its virgin soil, helped him to overcome his incredulous dismay at having lost the War, and sent him sullenly back to work in order to feed and protect his numerous family.

Up in Kimberley in the diamond mines, and in the 'golden' town of Johannesburg (where fortunes were made in a day) the land of Africa was giving up its riches with embarrassing generosity. But where man toiled on the fields and open veldt, expending his energy and brains, the reward was grudgingly given. His sheep produced a wool which fetched but a small price, the wines from his grapes found little sale and ostrich feathers brought him little profit. In a country such as this, where men of different races eyed each other with distrust and bitterness, where one farmstead was parted from another by great distance, the need for co-operation was very urgent.

It was a deplorable fact that where the country should have been able to export a large surplus of her produce, she imported foreign produce instead. Butter, maize, flour, cheese, oats and wheat were imported in great quantity and at much expense, and it seemed that nothing would be done to alter this state of affairs until new life was infused into the farmers and new methods enabled them to increase production. First, South Africa must learn to feed herself and then swiftly enter the world's markets.

In 1904, the Cape Parliament, with Dr. Leander Starr Jameson (1835-1917) as Prime Minister, decided to raise a loan of £150,000 with which to make advances in aid of all kinds to co-operative enterprise in agriculture. First, however, it was necessary to carry out a certain amount of educational work which, at the insistence of Dr. Jameson, and with Parliament's permission, was entrusted to me. And here I feel constrained to make a few observations relating to one of the best friends, and most loveable and honourable men I have ever met, a man who hated publicity, and loathed all kinds of compliments and eulogy, Leander Jameson. On New Year's Day 1896, he held Her Majesty's commission as Administrator of Rhodesia, the next afternoon he was a proclaimed outlaw, his life and the lives of his followers wholly at the mercy of Paul Kruger. The facts of the sequel should never be forgotten. A prisoner in Pretoria, a prisoner in England, the pathetic but ever fascinating, ever heroic central figure in the most remarkable trial 'at Bar' of those times.

Sentenced to fifteen months imprisonment, it seemed as if all his noble achievements in the cause of civilisation and humanity, his brilliant services to Queen and Empire, his heroism, his self-sacrifice, his enthusiasm for the great ideals of his great friend and leader Cecil Rhodes, was all to be silenced and forgotten in the grim isolation of a prison cell. But the spirit of the man raised him triumphant above all the tortures of prejudice, reproach and defeat, and he emerged from the ashes of apparent obloquy to become, in a few years, the most illustrious personality in South African life. When he took over the Government in 1904 his ministry was beset by a condition of political, social and economic chaos, calculated to stagger even his own abounding courage. But he threw himself with all his old energy and wide sympathy into the maze of problems that confronted him, so that in less than two years the dawn of a new era of hope and prosperity for Cape Colony arose. And when, shortly after, myriad difficulties presented themselves to those who were working for the Union of South Africa, their rapid and happy solution was largely due to Dr. Jameson's genius, zeal, and moderation.

The co-operative movement had originated in Bloemfontein at the beginning of 1905, while down in the Cape, the Hon. A. J. Fuller was initiating the work preparatory to the arrival of the 'co-operative expert' (as I was termed). I arrived in Cape Town in September, the South African springtime, filled with eagerness at this opportunity to guide a war-torn despondent country towards confidence and prosperity. Mr. Arthur Fuller had arranged a series of meetings extending over a period of more than three months, and with the assistance of a Mr. French, who was delegated to me as secretary, I plunged immediately and enthusiastically into my work. My itinerary included all the principal towns and districts of the Cape, beginning some 50 miles north of Cape Town at Malmesbury and ending with Caledon, about one hundred miles to the South-east, incorporated in a gigantic loop of several thousand miles extent. The South Africans, above all the Boer farmers, regarded my visit with some suspicion.

"Why," they asked, "should a foreigner be sent to teach us how to farm? What can such a man possibly know about our country? We who have tamed the South African veldt, and borne the brunt of many years' experience, are not going to submit ourselves to the advice of one who has never set foot in the country."

They were conservative and cautious to a fault, and the only way to persuade them was by showing them how bad their farming techniques were. Not until they were forced to contemplate some successful project, would they grudgingly give it their interest and attention. I was prepared for the farmer, where he was not completely indifferent to the idea of agricultural co-operation, to be somewhat critical of it. I was prepared for an amount of hard work with little success. What I was not prepared for was the immediate and rapid growth of the Movement. John X. Merriman came to my first meeting in Stellenbosch, prepared to dislike me on sight, but he quickly realised the advantages of co-operation in agriculture, and I am glad to say we soon became good friends.

The result of my first lecture in the Cape came in the form of a poem, a 'stage-Irish' poem by one 'Rip van Winkle', which occupied a portion of space in the 'Cape Times'. In spite of the 'iligant' language in which it was written, it afforded me some amusement, and I think a few verses are worth quoting. The poem was entitled "A Broth of a Boy", and began in this way:-

"Oh, begorra, Mr. Hannon
You're from County Clare or Shannon
You've kissed the Blayney stone, of that I will be sworn.
When I heard your lovely spache,
Irish methods for to tache,
Faith, I said, this is an Irishman iver I was born."

The verses then go on to mention certain Irishmen then prominent in South African affairs, and continues:-

"Now along of these and others
We have always fought like brothers
In the ardour of the battle confusing friend with foe.
And we've shouted federation
And we've cried conciliation
But this new co-operation is a thing we do not know."

The author speaks of the money advanced by the Treasury toward the Movement, and refers to Merriman thus:-

"Then John X. began to jibe,
And he said this is a bribe,
You want to buy our loyalty with your ill-begotten self.
But I know the Dutchman's nature
He's an independent crayture
And he never will co-operate wid no-one but himself."

The last quoted line of the poem made me all the more determined to win the Afrikaner over to agricultural co-operation with his neighbours, whether they were Boer or British. My ideal, as a preacher of co-operative agriculture, was to have a self-centred, self-respecting colony, neither British nor Dutch, but South African. This seemed to me to be of the first importance, and I think that I achieved my purpose.

Even before I had left Ireland, I had been advised not to go to South Africa because of the almost insuperable difficulties that (my friends declared) I would meet in the Cape when trying to establish co-operation there. Naturally some districts were more difficult than others; Burghersdorp, for instance, was a very bitter town. But I recall my slight surprise and satisfaction at the town of Worcester where I spoke in the second week of my tour, when I attended a banquet at which men of widely different political creeds sat side by side. I spoke to them of Holland where the Liberal and Catholic parties were in bitter disagreement yet, when collaborating over butter, bacon and pork, they forgot that each man would like to poke his fingers in his neighbour's eyes. From the applause that this remark created, and the heightened attention that I was given, it was evident that it had caught the Dutchmen's fancy.

One thing was clear to me, that as soon as possible I must master the language, and speak to the Boer in his mother tongue. If the problem of friendliness between the two nationalities (and also between native and white man) was not at first as insurmountable as I had anticipated, there were other problems to face of a nature vastly different from anything to which I had been accustomed in Ireland.

Firstly, there was the peculiar and drastic weather conditions, which alternated between torrential rainfall and drought that caked the ground to iron, so that as many as ten oxen had to be employed to drag the plough. Devastating hailstorms, with stones that killed the animals and birds and destroyed the crops in the fields and on the trees, were not infrequent in certain districts. Then there were the locusts, another abominable plague that was used in Biblical times to intimidate the ruthless Pharaoh. I saw these creatures in every stage, and there are few more threatening sights than their black advancing clouds of destruction. The Kimberley district was particularly attacked during my first year in the Cape.

I was shown a dairy farm on Schmidt's Drift where, in another week, scarcely anything would be left for the stock to subsist on. Experiments were being made by research workers in the culture of locust disease, but the trouble was that even if the creatures were completely eliminated by the ordinary methods of the farmer (who was able to destroy them at a certain stage of their development) they bred unhindered in the great unoccupied areas of the northwest and came down upon the good land with the surprise attack and ferocity of the Assyrians of old. A Mr. Christie who, I learned, had 'been the Resident Magistrate at Vrysberg, told us how he had seen a quantity of insect deposits unearthed during excavation for a water supply, which the inhabitants declared to be locusts' eggs, although no locust had been seen in the vicinity for sixteen years. Being, as it was thought, harmless, they were allowed to lie there, unmolested. A month or two later came those weather conditions appropriate to their growth, and soon the locusts once more had infested this area. It was disheartening for the farmer to deal with such long-lived insects.

Another raider was the jackal, which did great destruction among the sheep and young animals. No amount of shooting or trapping could entirely safeguard the farmer from the ravages of this cunning animal. In my preliminary lectures I explained the way in which agricultural co-operation brought prosperity to Denmark and, in a lesser extent, to my own country. I pointed out that the Colony was unable to feed its own population and quoted the value of the food imported: butter £250,000, cheese £100,000, meat £1,000,000 etc. When these facts had penetrated the somewhat sceptical minds of my farming audience, I suggested the remedies: co-operative credit societies, co-operative creameries, co-operative wineries and so on, stressing that the position of the Government with respect to agricultural organisation was purely educational, and that the people must realise that the success of the movement depended absolutely upon themselves.

The cartoonists found plenty of scope in the new Movement and myself for their jokes. I remember one particular cartoon that appeared at the beginning of my tour, a 'stage Irishman' (myself) complete with shillelagh, dancing a jig over the caption: - "Share it's aisy enough. Ye've just got to do as we do in Ireland." But there were many who began to take the new Movement seriously. At Stellenbosch, for instance, the dairy farmers began immediately to organise a co-operative creamery, and Klipheuval was quick to follow in their footsteps. Alas, perhaps too quick! I remember well the opening of the Klipheuval Creamery, for which a Government loan had been procured. A Scotsman was installed as Manager, and the foreman himself came to open the building. Great interest was expressed at the sight of semi-tiled walls, the floor of coloured cement, the steam driven churns and the refrigerating chamber with walls three feet thick. Dairy farmers from other districts who had been invited to the ceremony went away with inflated ideas of what the Government were willing to do for the asking.

Where the South African's method of cattle keeping in certain districts was merely foolish, his method of retailing milk in the large towns was shocking. In the neighbourhood of Kimberley, for instance, he had the foolish and lazy habit of allowing the calves to run with the cows. A large percentage of the milk was lost, so that in the towns the demand far exceeded the supply. As for the retail of milk, in the average large town of the Cape, old whisky bottles were filled by the retailer every day and exchanged for empties. Obviously, it was practically impossible to clean whisky bottles thoroughly, and when I say that the death rate for children under one year old in Bloemfontein in 1903 was 220 per 1,000, and in Johannesburg the previous year was 262 per 1,000, the cause is not hard to see. The immense distance between the farms was a great handicap in co-operation among the dairies, and the hot weather increased the difficulties of carriage and the storage of butter.

The typical Boer farmstead consisted of solid, whitewashed buildings, the living house being a long one storey building, and thatched, with perhaps two or three gables, and the outhouses conveniently arranged beside it. Nearby stood a tall, whitewashed arch, underneath which hung a bell that was used to call the men to work or meals, and to summon them in cases of fire in the bushveldt or danger from native attacks. I saw so many thousands of homes like this on my first tour of the Cape.

Some of the incidents of that tour are still vividly engraved on my memory. In Swellendam, for instance, heavy rains had caused the flooding of many rivers, and the attendance at my meeting was limited to those farmers who could cross the fords or bridges with safety; and these were not many. Whereas, about a week later, when I had travelled across the Cape towards Basutoland and arrived at the town of Dordrecht, the conditions were such that the crops were a failure owing to severe drought. Swellendam was a very English town, but in Malmesbury, where the Boer farmers predominated, I had to speak through an interpreter, which inevitably impedes one's enthusiasm, and I determined there and then to master the Taal as quickly as I could.

A special coach with a dining car attached had been allotted to our party, which consisted of Mr. Fuller, our secretaries and myself. In districts to which the railway lines did not extend, we were provided with a covered wagon drawn by four horses. I recall the trouble we had to get to the town of Bathurst on the south-east corner of Cape Colony. We had to cancel the date of our meeting because the train did not run on that day. Later, arrangements had to be made for a special train, provided most happily by the manager of the Kowie railway. This was a particularly pleasant journey. The country was looking beautifully green, and our train stopped at certain vantage points to allow us to alight and admire the wild beasts of the distant Kloof, in contrast to the quiet pastoral land and farms surrounded by orange groves. There were pineapples, too, large acreages of them growing in well-kept formation.

On arrival at the town we were met by a detachment of Mounted Police, and a deputation of influential citizens. After our meeting I was driven down to Port Alfred where the Indian Ocean, in all its romantic reality, pounded steadily outside the lagoon. Our special train then carried us back to the nearest railway junction, where we were attached to an express and brought to our next destination, the town of Uitenhage, where we spent the night. But of all the spectacular views which abounded throughout this preliminary tour, the one with which I was most enchanted was the glorious scenery around George and the Montague Pass. And how could I forget my inspection of the diamond mines at Kimberley, and my first sight of a diamond in its natural state. Our party on the trip was augmented by Mrs. Fuller and her daughter, who exclaimed in amazement at the lengthy processes (the pulverising, sieving and washing of the earth) which produced the jewel so significant of romantic attachment. I descended one of these deep tunnels and was shown the miners at work, cutting the earth and shovelling it into the tubs that came rumbling past me from time to time. In contrast to the badly planned, haphazard layout of this mining town, was Aliwal North, most remarkable for its state of advancement and its well laid out streets. In this town our biggest meeting was held. Situated as it was at the junction of the Cape with the Orange River Colony and Basutoland, it was practically the intermediary of trade, and, therefore, of great importance to the co-operative movement. I remember how tactful we had to be with our audience at Caledon. Some of the members were indignant because their important district had been left to last on our campaign. A. J. Fuller assured them that it was because of Caledon's importance that it held this position in our itinerary, we were now able to devote more time to the study of its particular problems. I had listed these towns in the order of their productive importance, and Caledon came about third in the production of cereals, but was also rich in wool.

So much re-organisation was needed in the wool industry. Cape wool was packed in a mixture of fleece, tails and locks which usually contained a certain quantity of sand. Naturally, it did not fetch so much on the London market as New Zealand or Australian wool. Yet, I interviewed numbers of farmers who invariably informed me that time and again they had tried to introduce methods to improve the value of their wool, but had given up the attempt in disgust because they obtained so little extra money for their time and trouble. The government had engaged an English wool expert, a Mr. Moore from Bradford, to teach the farmers how to shear and how to grade the wool. He was touring the Cape at the same time as I was, and declared unreservedly that South Africa was the most backward wool-producing country in the world so far as the 'get-up' of the wool was concerned. One manufacturer had told him he would shoot the first wool merchant who offered him South African wool again.

Some of the better clips went to American buyers direct, and a certain quantity was sold to Germany. In some cases, merchants bought the farmers wool only in order to sell their own goods to him, and therefore were not dependant on the quality of the product but would take it however poor it was. Over and over again I was told that energy and hard work were of no avail, there was no encouragement to wash or grade it properly. Swellendam was the first town in the Cape to introduce the classification of wool, but others followed in ever increasing numbers. The mohair industry, which was of importance in certain districts, depended (like the ostrich feather trade) on the vagaries of fashion, and I made every effort to extend the export of this commodity to Germany, America and Japan. Sheep and goat breeders were, on the whole, the most likely class to benefit greatly from co-operation, and they were anxious to try new methods, though at the same time somewhat sceptical of the result. As a matter of fact, it was at a large gathering of wool and mohair merchants held in Port Elizabeth at the beginning of the New Year that trouble first arose.

Towards the end of my preliminary tour, I received an invitation from the Irish inhabitants of Cape Town to give a lecture to them on my return. Fearing the division that might be caused in the co-operative movement if I allowed myself to become embroiled in Irish politics (even in a place as remote from my country as South Africa) I made it clearly understood that I would address them only if their meeting was held entirely apart from politics, either in the Cape or at home, and that my subject would not touch the political or religious differences that divided both peoples. This the Committee fully agreed upon, and I spent a most pleasurable evening in the Hall of the Dutch Reformed Church, which had been decorated with greenery of all kinds and thronged with harps and shamrocks. A Mr. Upington presided, introducing me to various men whose familiar names soon discovered them to be related to people with whom I was well acquainted in Ireland. 'Outsiders', with no Irish in their blood, were also welcomed to the meeting, and the Hall was packed to capacity. When the audience joined in the singing of some favourite Irish melodies as the evening drew to a close, I felt that Ireland could not be so many thousands of miles away, and in a different hemisphere.

The previous month I had heard of the death of the Hon. C. A. Owen Lewis (an Irishman), in England. Shortly after our last meeting in Dublin, and after I had left for the Cape, he caught pneumonia, from which he never recovered. His father had been M.P. for Carlow, and he was born and brought up in Ireland. Through Rhodes' agency, he had been brought out to South Africa in 1898 to organise the Progressive Party. He was famous there for an exploit during the Boer War when he rode out alone to address a Boer commando unit in the Transvaal and succeeded in inducing them to surrender.

The co-operative movement was now going ahead rapidly, and seemed to have fired the imagination of the farmers. Indeed, from every part of the Cape I was being inundated with requests and questions, so much so that I had to appeal to the farmers to have patience and bear with me a little. Many of these requests were for Government aid, money for buying stock, erecting jackal-proof fencing, for water excavation or for restocking a depleted fruit farm. Everywhere the Movement seemed to be going grand by leaps and bounds, and so far there were no failures to be recorded.

In December I was officially appointed Superintendent of Co-operative Agriculture in Cape Colony, whereby it was arranged that I should serve a term of five years there. It was with high hopes that I made the journey to Ireland, at the beginning of 1906, to bring my wife and family out to South Africa. There were such enormous possibilities of agricultural development in the Cape, the resources seemed to be limitless. One of my first duties on arrival in London was to attend the wool sales in England, and to make elaborate inspection of Cape wool in the London Docks. I was invited to speak at meetings in Bradford, Leeds and other cities in the North concerned with the industry, where a deep interest was aroused by our proposals for the improvement of Cape wools.

At this time the Royal Horticultural Show was taking place in London, which included an exhibition of produce from the Cape. Captain Bam was organising this, helped by Mr. Charles du Plessis Chiappini (a prominent Bondsman, and largely interested in the fruit trade). Both were men of energy and capability, and succeeded in getting a large quantity of first-class fruit shipped to the Show, which turned out to be an unqualified success. The fruit industry, as regards exports, was then in an elementary stage, somewhat of a curiosity and addicted to freakish fluctuations in quality. I remember suggesting to one of my audience in one of the Cape fruit farming districts that they should try canning pineapples and other fruit for export, a scheme which I thought should work out satisfactorily. There was also a need for a central fruit depot where the produce could be stored in correct temperature while waiting for shipment.

During the middle of April, I addressed members of the London Chamber of Commerce in Oxford Court, Cannon Street, on the condition of agriculture in the Cape. Mr. T.F. Blackwell, the President, was in the Chair. Mr. Chiappini also spoke, and we were listened to with great attention. In addition to this, we convened in London a public meeting of people interested in South Africa, which we hoped might lead to a better reception of imports from that country.

Shortly before my return to the Cape, I was entertained to dinner by the I.A.O.S., at which Col. Nugent Everard (the President), Father Finlay, Sir Henry Grattan-Bellew, ' A.E.' and others spoke, and at which I was presented with a cigar-box as a testimony of my seven years activities in the Movement. At the same time there was a formal presentation of my portrait, which was painted by Mr. Dermod O'Brien,

President of the Royal Irish Academy, and which is still a treasured possession. Let me say here what a delight it is to me now, after so many years, to recall the friendship and gentle kindness of Mr. Dermod O'Brien and his very charming wife. I saw a good deal of them at Mountjoy Square, their Dublin home, and I also stayed with them in County Limerick where they resided and farmed at Adare.

On my return to South Africa it was late autumn, and the great heat of the summer was over. The grapes had been gathered for the wine presses, and the harvest gathered from the fields. In the wine trade there was great depression. The farmers took little trouble with the fermentation, and their standard of cleanliness was poor. If it turned out well, they sold it to their local merchant. If it turned out badly, they sent it to the distiller to be mixed with the 'dop' brandy (a vile drink, which used to be largely drunk by the natives) and which, along with Kaffir beer, was still obtained surreptitiously, although the sale to the natives was illegal. It had a rank and powerful smell, and could not satisfactorily be used even for blending in small proportion with better branches.

Before I had left for England two co-operative wineries had been established, one at Stellenbosch, the other at Wellington. Both were anxious to procure the best vines and inaugurate new methods of winemaking. A viticultural expert, Professor Hahn, was sent to Europe to find suitable places where the South African might study the art, and I arranged for him to visit Frankfurt-on-Maine. While I was away from the Cape, Mr. Chiappini and myself had spent some days at the largest and best-equipped cellars in the Rhine district, and had visited the German Viticultural College at Geisenheim. Incidentally, Franz MaIan (editor of the South African Press) was one of those politicians who greatly encouraged European viticultural education for young South Africans at that time.

The wine industry has certainly blossomed since those days, greatly to the credit of all concerned when one considers the amount of competition, and the experience of their rivals, whereas the industry peculiar to South Africa (that of ostrich feathers) has declined, owing to the change in ladies' millinery from enormous, softly curving creations, difficult to keep in place no doubt (but intensely becoming), to the more practical fashions of today. I went to Paris during my trip home to interview the French feather merchants, and tried to revive a fashion that was already on the wane, but there is little a man can do to influence a lady's taste in dress.

At Oudtshoorn, ostrich feathers were the staple industry, and I learned that the buyers were making handsome profits, the ostrich breeders obtaining only a very poor price for the feathers. In London, I saw feathers marked in the shop windows which showed a ridiculously high profit over the two shillings and sixpence paid for the farmer's best product. In most cases the ostrich farmer sold direct to a peddler (so like the higglers at home) who wandered from farm to farm, amassing a small fortune. At one of the meetings in my original tour, in a district abounding with these strange and foolish birds, I got into hot water by my outspoken comments on these peddlers. They were not usually South Africans, but invaders from Poland, Russia or Germany, well versed in the ability to look after themselves. My reference to these speculative dealings incensed the Jewish element in the feather trade, who complained that the inference would rest upon them. They wrote furious letters to the newspapers and protested vehemently whenever the occasion offered. One gentleman, apparently jealous of the Government loans, added the question: -

"... why could not someone in the Ministry obtain loans to help the struggling shop-keepers? The only people who got all the money they wanted were the farmers."

I think it was during the British winter of 1906 (South Africa's summer season), that reports came through from the lovely island of Tristan da Cunha that the inhabitants were in grave straits. The remote state of that island was almost unbelievable. Little more than a barren rock in the centre of the South Atlantic, and out of the way of all regular traffic, it sometimes did not receive a visit from the outside world for as long as two or three years.

Occasionally, a ship would set out from Cape Town for South America with the intention of calling in at Tristan da Cunha and dispensing some cargo and mail, but would find that the ocean conditions would not allow a landing. The feelings of these storm-bound people, watching the emissary from the outside world sailing westward again without any communication of value, must have been most bitter. It is a very small island, holding a hardy and, indeed, long-lived people numbering about one hundred at that time, and possessing a climate that rendered the growth of foodstuff somewhat precarious. Apart from the import of cereals, potatoes were the main diet, augmented with the eggs of wildfowl, the flesh of sea birds, an occasional dish of beef and some unappetising fish. The months from June to September were the most perilous for fishing was impossible because of storms, the egg season was still to come and the potato stock would be falling low.

The winter of 1906 found many of the inhabitants starving, and all badly in need of clothing and other necessities. I was, therefore, commissioned to take out an expedition to their relief. How splendidly the people of the Cape co-operated! I got tremendous quantities of food, medical supplies, clothing and those articles of civilisation which we take so much for granted (such as tools, cooking utensils, cutters, china and so on) and also arranged for their immediate shipment to the lonely island. For a number of years, the inhabitants had been without a clergyman. Incidentally, I believe that their former pastor was a brother of the author of 'Alice in Wonderland', but he had to return to civilisation before the close of the century. Hearing that this ship was leaving for Tristan da Cunha, the Rev. J.G. Barrow volunteered to leave with it, so we sent to those isolated people both spiritual and physical comfort. I did not visit the island myself at that time, but many years later (in the middle 'thirties') my second wife and I made a delightful cruise which included that lonely island.

Meanwhile I was on tour again round the Cape, renewing my acquaintance with those Societies that had adopted co-operation and finding new districts to address. The Bond Party were very much averse to my plan, but I recall the just remarks of Mr. Malan when he declared that he wished me well and would be prepared to judge me by results. "If those results are good, no-one will be better pleased than I." he said. At one period, however, he was advising the farmers to hold aloof from co-operation, until further protection by tariffs would ensure the worthwhile sale of their products. I remember reading a paper in Dutch at the Bond Congress which had an excellent reception due,

I suspect, more to the fact that I was taking the trouble to learn their language than to the contents of my address. Certainly, I found oddly contrasting opinions about agricultural co-operation which had sprung up in the interval of my journey home, one of which was a strong rumour that I was about to become Director of Agriculture in the Cape, a rumour which had to be strongly refuted.

Towards the end of the year I made a special tour of the native territories, a somewhat disheartening trip. Near Mafeking, for instance, there were complaints that the large native reserves were lying idle, and thus impeding the development of the district. It was the same, or much the same, in other territories. The natives would not learn the proper methods of cultivation, rotation of crops and so on, nor would they care for their stock as the law designed. The result was bad soil erosion, spread of disease, and poverty. Raids were occasionally made on the white man's cattle, which would be killed and left lying on the veldt with a small choice portion cut off the beast for meat. Yet the game near these regions was practically eliminated because the native would not respect the breeding season. The districts consigned to the Negroes may have originally been in good heart, but it was pathetic to see their state in 1906 and '07. The Karoo in particular could never have been a prosperous region, and the unfortunate inhabitants could do little in the way of agriculture, co-operative or not, without the water which they needed so badly.

On several occasions I had spoken scathingly about the handling of colonial produce for export, for which remarks I was severely castigated by the produce brokers, and now, in the South African winter of 1906, I had appointed to me as commercial adviser a Mr. Hartley, who was what one might call a government official middleman to bring farmers into direct contact with the retailer and consumer. The object of this new departure was to do away with the jobber and secure good prices for the farmers. Hartley was President of the Grocers and Provision Merchants Association, and advised me regularly on the sale of produce in the Cape. The produce brokers declared that I was actually setting up a monopoly in Hartley, and that it was my averred intention to abolish them all. Their bitterness made wide publicity against the campaign, and increased the difficulties that were beginning to loom up over my horizon.

How I disliked the 'stage Irishman' so popular among comedians in those days, even in South Africa. After celebrating my first St. Patrick's Day in the Cape, I read an article that suggested I might occasionally impart a little variety to political life by going on tour in 'knee breeches and a green tailcoat'. There was a goodly proportion of my fellow countrymen in South Africa at that time, many of whom were prominent in their different professions. I am proud to recall that at the inaugural meeting of the Cape Town All-Ireland Association I was the President. A month or two previously we had held a meeting to consider the formation of this society, and I had proposed that it should be an association of Irishmen with no political discrimination, and non-sectarian, but one of my listeners jumped to his feet protesting that an Irish Society without politics was no society at all. He was, however, over-ruled. Our membership numbered over two hundred, and included many distinguished men.

Incidentally, Mrs. Botha had been a Miss Emmett, and was very proud to be related to the famous Irish patriot, Robert Emmett. Botha lived a good deal away from Pretoria, but I met him before the Union when he represented the Cape Colony and the Inter-Colonial Committee. I recall Mrs. Smuts sending me the message that I would be very welcome at her home in Pretoria because I was an Irishman. At that period no Englishman would have been welcomed at her house. She was a very charming woman, highly cultured, and spoke about half a dozen languages. At one time she was bitterly disappointed with her husband's attitude towards their conquerors and hated the word 'English'. In later years, however, she changed her somewhat rigid views.

The experience of a year's active and constant touch with the Colony, without abating in any way my earlier hopes in the future of South Africa had, at the same time, brought about a fuller realisation of local conditions and, consequently, a more cautious treatment of many of the projects contemplated on behalf of agriculture and industry. For instance, I had somewhat gloomy forebodings regarding the construction of the new co-operative wineries, and the co-operative creameries were tending to oscillate between feast and famine. The difficulties of the dairy industry were more serious and irritating than I had expected, but at least we had the satisfaction of having reduced the quantity of imported butter by 20%. The lack of competent managers and skilled hands had been responsible for a good deal of trouble. In this organisation, as in most new Movements, the danger was that where it had an enthusiastic following there might subsequently be a certain reaction, and cases where something unsatisfactory or unfortunate had occurred were apt to be grossly exaggerated to the discouragement of others.

I was to have gone to Natal, but the Prime Minister came to see me on his way to London and suggested that I should postpone my visit until his return. When he returned from London however, it was decided that my proposed visit to Natal be cancelled altogether. I was invited by the Government of Rhodesia to visit that Colony, and make a report on the possibility of introducing co-operative methods in agricultural development. Accompanied by my secretary, Mr. Hofmeyer, I arrived in Bulawayo and was immediately in consultation with the local Magistrate and leading personalities, and the settlers there gave me the benefit of their experience and arranged visits to various settlement centres between there and Salisbury, including the settlement established by Colonel Raleigh Gray, who treated me with great hospitality and consideration. I visited the battlement where the settlers had made their last stand and where, unfortunately, they had all been wiped out by Lobengula. This was a dreadful battle, one of the tragedies of Rhodesia.

During my time in Bulawayo, I visited the headquarters established by Lobengula in the days of his tyrannical rule, and sat in the chair from which he issued his deadly commands before the advent of the British South Africa Company. I visited the Matopas Hills to see and venerate the grave of Cecil Rhodes, and also the Shangani monument which stood nearby, erected to the memory of the men who were wiped out at the Battle of Shangani. I addressed various conferences with settlers, and when I returned to the Cape I prepared my report, which afterwards was published by the Rhodesian Government. I have forgotten the number of lectures that I gave to schools, clubs and other institutions on the duties of citizenship and like topics, impressing upon the youth of South Africa that national ideal which had so helped the Danes in their efforts to rebuild their country. I told them, again and again: - "You are South Africans ... Independent of the race from which you sprang. You are South Africans, not British or Dutch."

So, some of these young people were prepared in their minds for the Union of South Africa which was shortly to take place. But for me, the storm clouds were rapidly gathering. A special meeting of the Produce Association of Port Elizabeth was held in the Chamber of Commerce, in which my scheme for bringing the farmer into direct contact with the retailer was bitterly commented upon. I was likened to Napoleon after Waterloo, and was told that I ought to go back to the place from which I had come. Their ire seemed to raise a storm of protests against me in the Press, and elsewhere I was held responsible for every misfortune, important or trivial, that had befallen those engaged in the agricultural industry, some of which had occurred months before I had ever reached the shores of Africa.

In parliament, Mr, Pretorius asked the Secretary of Agriculture to make a full statement of my duties, and here I was ably upheld by many of the speakers. Then I brought out my full report for 1907 (which was issued as a Parliamentary paper) in which I suggested that a complete reconstruction of the methods of agricultural co-operation should take place. I pointed out that it was impossible for one single man to keep in touch with the whole farming community; also that certain principles should be brought into operation to limit the too rapid extension of the Societies and to encourage self-help. And now the storm broke! In the House of Assembly, the Prime Minister made a provocative and somewhat ill-informed speech upon my report and the state of agriculture in general, although he admitted that had my advice been more strictly followed, the experiment would have been a pronounced financial success, and he quoted an utterance made in Port Elizabeth by the Governor of Cape Colony to a farming audience: - "You talk a lot about co-operation, but why don't you co-operate?"

My staunch supporters, in opposing him, declared that they were sure that the co-operative principle would eventually lead to South Africa's becoming a large exporting country, and suggested that the Prime Minister should move about the country a little more and learn the facts for himself. Mr. Cronwright-Schreiner pointed out that it was too early yet to expect success, and that I was giving the farmers valuable education. But only a few weeks afterwards there was further criticism of my work which, someone declared, had caused a scandalous waste of money. From then on my days in South Africa were numbered. I shall always think kindly of Mr. Cronwright-Schreiner and his wife Olive Schreiner, the celebrated South African authoress who wrote many books, the most well-known of which was ' The Story of an African Farm', and which still survives as a fascinating account of South African life.

As I think of those South African days I catch glimpses of the scenes impressed on my memory: the arum lilies blooming at the roadside; a native wrapped in a blanket plodding along a dusty red track; a blue mountain; a white thatched group of buildings with some ostriches in the foreground; a dull brown landscape spiked with numerous ant-hills; a pleasant, broad street with water gurgling along the roadside; and the Table Mountain, so fantastically flat, as though a giant hand had cut it with a knife, as it disappears into the remote distance.

The voyage home was the prelude to an amusing interlude, for I became acquainted with a fellow passenger on board ship by the name of Harry Piers. He had just retired from his job in Nyasaland where he was something like an Assistant Administrator, and he was very friendly indeed toward me. A few weeks later he became engaged to a cousin of the same name, a daughter of Sir Edmund Piers, an impoverished Baronet with an estate near Mullingar in Westmeath. To my astonishment, Piers wrote to me asking me to be his Best Man, and although I remonstrated with him and told him, that as a married man it was impossible (married with family) and that he should get some bright unattached young man. He wrote to me a pathetic letter declaring that unless I was his Best Man, he would not get married. Well, I agreed and was invited to an evening party to meet his fiancée who must then have been very well on in the fifties, but very nice, and very capable. She drew me aside into an alcove, and privately wanted to know what I knew about Harry. I, of course, told her that had she asked me to pick for her the most perfect, ideal husband, I would have picked Harry! They were married at Holy Trinity Church in Chelsea, and I went as Best Man. There were crowds of people at the wedding and never in my life have I been so nervous. All through the service I kept fingering my pocket to make sure I had the ring, and when eventually the moment arrived and my vigil was at an end, in my most sheepish manner I presented it. The reception was held at the Hans Crescent Hotel, where I was again involved. A paper should have been signed before the wedding ceremony (it was Harry Piers' settlement on his wife), but this had not been done. The blushing bride came up to me and said: - "Mr. Hannon, I rely on you, you must get Harry to sign this document. I don't leave the place until it is signed."

Champagne flowed, and there was much merry-making. But she came to me again, singled me out in the midst of it all, and hissed: - "The paper has not yet been signed. You must see to it." I managed at last to get the couple to accompany me to a private room where Harry was made to sign the paper with appropriation to his wife.

Many indeed were the letters that I received on my resignation from the Cape, both from the British and South African inhabitants, all of which cheered me on my way. One of a number of these letters, which I have kept all these years, is beside me now as I write. It was from a most charming man, Mr. Alfred Maleig of Cradock, who wrote to me thus: -

"Dear Mr. Hannon,

I have read with much interest and very great pleasure the account of your farewell banquet, and also of the several other functions at which your friends and representatives of the public were afforded the opportunity of expressing their appreciation of you, and their feelings of goodwill. May I take the liberty of also offering you my most sincere good wishes and of saying how I, a South African born, with all my interests in this country, have appreciated your efforts on our behalf, and how very certain I am that in good time your work will prove as fruitful as you in your earnestness have ever wished to see it. That your leaving us without yourself ever seeing the fulfilment of your hopes, is no surprise to me. I had not been with you ten minutes (when we first met in

London) before I felt that you were ages ahead of times out here, and that it was a case of 'casting pearls before swine'. I think that you will admit that we, or the bulk of those about whom you concerned yourself, are a peculiar people. I, who have known them all my life, don't pretend to understand them even yet, and don't think I ever shall. At any rate I don't think that for a generation at least an Angel from Heaven would succeed in working them up to an earnest attempt to carry out your Gospel. But you have sown good seed, which has not fallen amiss; rest assured of that. I am sure great numbers of us out here will follow your future career with very deep interest. That you and those near you and dear to you may be richly blessed is the sincere wish of

Yours very truly,
Alfred Maleig.
P.S. I was quite relieved to hear that Malan had the grace to be there."

The postscript referred to the farewell banquet given for me at the Royal Hotel, Capetown, at which about 400 people were present. I recall sitting on the right of the Mayor, and I think Mr. Hofmeyer was on his left, while a number of important personages in the life of the Colony were seated at the top table. A couple of days previously, on the night of a severe storm, the Catholic Association had honoured me in the same manner, and presented me with an illuminated address and a tantalus. In all I received, I think, seven public addresses. These gracious acts I look back on with much pleasure and gratitude.

Despite my disappointment and irritations, Africa, that great continent, had exercised its fascinating influence upon me, as indeed it does upon every soul I have met who has been there. It would be difficult to quote any example of a people where abounding hospitality more strongly manifested itself than among the people of the Cape Colony. During my short time there I had truly witnessed a remarkable change. I had seen the dividing chasm of the European races bridged over and finally obliterated altogether, thus forming, as I believed, a roadway to a democratic multi-racial Union of South Africa.

CHAPTER 4

When one is placed somewhat askew by the 'giddy turn of fortune's wheel', there is much consolation to be found in the encouragement and advice of friends, even when the advice is more well-meant than practical. Some of my acquaintances expressed surprise that I did not intend returning to the work of the Irish Agricultural Organisation Society. It appeared to me, however, that this decisive curtailment of my South African career was giving me the opportunity I required to forward the case of the agricultural worker from a somewhat wider and more far-reaching point. The expansion of Empire trade was being hindered by the policy of those in power in London, therefore to London I would go to fight the adherents of Free Trade on their own ground. Before I left Cape Town, I became a member of the Imperial Colonial Club which, upon landing in England, I immediately made my headquarters.

Among the letters of introduction that I brought with me across the oceans was a valuable and generous tribute from Dr Jameson, which played no small part in my immediate affairs. Viscount Milner, the former High Commissioner for South Africa and Governor General of Cape Colony, wrote to me on my arrival in London, saying: - "I am leaving tonight, not tomorrow, as the papers say. Not to waste your time, will you communicate with Mr. L.S. Amery of 2, Temple Gardens, sending him Dr. Jameson's letter and this letter, asking him if he can put you in touch with people who might enable you to work. Mr. Amery is himself one of the leading Tariff Reformers among the younger men. I shall be happy to see you myself on my return about Easter time."

I should like to add here that Mr. Amery became one of my closest friends in the arduous, but rewarding, campaign in which we were both involved. In addition to drawing me within the circle of those devoted to the cause of Tariff Reform, he assisted me in more personal ways by writing letters of recommendation to the Editors of 'The Times', the 'Morning Post' and the ' Standard' on my telling him of my desire to write articles on Tariff Reform and other matters for the leading newspapers.

At the beginning of March 1909, I received a

communication from the Secretary of the Liberal Unionist Council asking me to make an appointment with him, and stating that he was acting on the suggestion of Mr. Austen Chamberlain. After this interview I was embroiled in certain political meetings throughout the country, where I supported the Unionist candidates in their bye-elections, and attempted to establish myself on the political Scene.

It was about this time that Henry Page-Croft, M.P. a very young fellow in those Days, and Basil Peto founded a body called the Imperial Pioneers. This was created with the object of stimulating public interest here in the progress of, and closer relationship with, our overseas Dominions. Every part of the Empire was represented, and I was included as representing South Africa. The average Briton did not realise to the full the meaning of Empire, nor comprehend that we had in those days the complete means of self-support within our own territories. The exports to our Colonies had not increased in proportion with the enormous increase of manufactured goods exported elsewhere and I realised, from general experience, the abiding benefits that would accrue from a closer tie with the Empire. At any rate, a series of meetings was started, urging the necessity for Empire preference. It was a terrible series, and I shall never forget those meetings. Our chief handicap was that despite our speakers stressing that the Imperial Pioneers were strictly non-party political, there was no getting over the fact that they, and the promoters, were largely Tariff Reformers and Unionists.

At one of the earlier meetings, I recall that one of the speakers was the Hon. Dan O'Connor (for 30 years an Australian Parliamentarian, and now representing that country in the imperial Pioneers, together with Frank Fox). There were a certain number of Irishmen in the audience, and the cries of "Home Rule for Ireland" and "Bravo Dan" did something to liven the meeting. But only too soon we needed a pacifying, not enlivening element. The newspapers reported our activities according to their own political trend and, do what we could, there was nothing that would keep out the 'party' element. We were told that the Colonial Pioneers were meeting with success in their attempt to stir up the people of the mother country to a sense of responsibility as citizens of a great Empire. We were also told that to go about calling oneself an Imperial Pioneer was to invite ridicule.

The meetings grew more and more out of hand, and I shall never forget one disastrous affair in which the late Major Archer-Shee almost created a riot by bringing a pugilist to the meeting as 'chucker-out'. The Free Traders and Socialists stormed the Hall

and continually interrupted the proceedings. I don't believe I was heard speaking more than ten words during the whole evening. The unfortunate Chairman, constantly jumping to his feet to remonstrate and cry 'Order', was told by one of the gang below him: - "If you keep on interrupting, I shall call upon the stewards to chuck you out." But even this sparkling wit failed to move the crowd to good humour. Every time there was an interruption, the boxer brought by Archer-Shee attempted, and in most cases succeeded, in man-handling the heckler out of the Hall. At last, the crowd set upon him and free fights started all over the place. We were booed, of course, and it seemed as though the platform was about to be stormed, for the audience was getting very ugly. Someone sent for the Police. Pond, the Australian representative, and myself slipped through a back door and raced down the road. One of the old horse-drawn buses was trotting by, and we jumped aboard to escape the toughs who had noticed us. The bus-conductor regarded us somewhat with indignation and no small amount of suspicion as we flung ourselves abruptly on to the seats, saying: - "We've just escaped with our lives."

It is generally acknowledged that Alexander Hamilton (the famous American who established a permanent Government in the United States of America, and was dramatically killed in a duel with the Vice-President) was the Father of the of the Protectionist School. My interest in the theory of Protection, already awakened by what I had observed during my term in Ireland with the I.A.O.S., was kindled on attending a lecture upon this subject at the World's Fair in 1904. I kept in touch with the Tariff Reform movement in Great Britain as far as it was reported in the papers. Indeed, since 1896 (the year that I had the good fortune to become associated with Sir Horace Plunkett) I had it constantly borne upon me that a reasonable measure of protection was an essential consideration for the solution of the rural problem, which yearly grew more acute in Great Britain. My frequent tours through Northern Europe convinced me that it was absolutely necessary to give the farmer some preference in his own market if the prosperity of the agricultural industry was to be established.

There was no doubt in my mind at all that any permanent prosperity depended upon the measure in which the creation of small-holdings might secure the economic independence of their owners. This was impossible so long as the small cultivator was at the mercy of foreign competition, too often State fostered and subsidised. The small cultivator was not alone in being thus affected, but thousands of manufacturers suffered through this appalling economic tragedy. The lessons of the growth of all our sister states was, to me, eloquent of the advisability of imitating their example in the old country.

So, upon my arrival in England, I sent out a circular letter to two hundred and forty large manufacturing firms, enquiring in what way they were being undersold by foreign competition in British markets and the reply, in the majority of cases, could be summed up in the word 'dumping'. It became my purpose then, to free the British merchant from this terrible evil. But it needed more than an active part in the Tariff Reform movement and in the Imperial Pioneers to pay my household accounts and my children's school fees. I had to look for a paid job. Among the gifts which fortune has bestowed upon me is a somewhat persuasive manner, and a knack of getting on with strangers. I wanted to be able to move about the countryside, and yet have time to further the causes which I had adopted as my own. The solution, of course, was to become a commercial traveller, and I applied for this position to Messrs. Arthur Morris and Co, the hop merchants. My confidence in my own persuasive powers received a sad setback. To sell hops to some brewers is like trying to get into Heaven without passing through the needle's eye. But I enjoyed it all, and it gave me the wherewithal to support my family, and the opportunity to address meetings on behalf of Tariff Reform as often as I desired.

Early in 1910, having established my family and myself in a temporary home in Clifton, Bristol, I addressed a large meeting at Portishead on the subject dearest to my heart. Lord Rosebery had just made a statement that the Tariff Reform movement should be dropped, and that the next Election should be fought on the House of Lords question. Naturally, I wanted to contest this proposition. Lancashire and Yorkshire were the weak spots in the Tariff Reform question, because a tax on raw materials was greatly feared by the manufacturers there. But in Somerset our supporters had been greatly on the increase, although the majority of them scarcely understood the Movement. The words 'Free Trade' have a romantic ring, suggesting an abundance of movement and business in the commercial world, and if universal Free Trade could have been adopted there would have been no grounds to complain. But the difficulty had rarely arisen, because as a Free Trade country we stood alone. While we were able to buy freely, we were restricted with regard to our sales. Tariff Reform would enable us to have at least equality of opportunity in the markets of our own country, preference as far as we could secure it in our own Colonies, bargaining power with foreign countries and fair competition in the neutral market. Where other countries had made their Colonies an ever-increasing market for their productions we, under Free -Trade, had not increased the proportion of goods sold to our Colonies beyond what they were in 1854, and during the previous eight years these Colonies had increased their imports from foreign countries by £20,000,00 0. That the Tariff Reform movement should be shelved in favour of reform of the House of Lords seemed to me particularly dangerous.

How difficult it is to influence people who do not comprehend one's subjects. I recall one instance among many others when, in order to draw the Socialist Party away from Free Trade, we held a debate on Tariff Reform versus Socialism. Although the Hall was crowded with our opponents, I was given a good hearing, but I fear made very little headway, for the majority of the audience left at the end of the meeting singing, "Keep the Red flag flying." I was growing very fond of Bristol and the surrounding countryside by this time, and was accordingly delighted when the opportunity presented itself to become a Unionist candidate for a certain Division of that City. Walter Long, with whom I was already on very friendly terms, brought me down from London, where I had been busily engaged, and proposed me for membership of the Clifton Club (a very exclusive institution). We arrived on Saturday, and I was elected on Monday. I owe much to Walter Long's kindness and trouble.

But to become a member of this exclusive Club was ridiculously simple compared with my adoption as political candidate, although Walter was my sponsor. First of all, I was proposed for South Bristol. There was a delightful fellow on the Executive Committee called Aubone Haire, but in spite of the fact that the Chairman of the selection Committee (who happened to belong to the same religion as myself, the Church of Rome) supported me, I was turned down by a large majority, and my candidature for South Bristol wiped off the slate. He came to me full of apologies, saying: - "I am awfully sorry, but it has never been known to have a Catholic candidate in Bristol, and so I am afraid you can't be adopted."

Bristol certainly is a non-conformist city; Wesley held one of his biggest meetings there. Having recovered from this blow, I was advised to try for the constituency of North Bristol. Somewhat doubtful, I explained that I had not been accepted for South Bristol because of my religion. "Would not this," I asked, "be the same case?" The reply was an emphatic, "Oh, no. Not at all." I went to North Bristol, everybody shouting tremendously to get me as a candidate, but I was turned down. This was defeat No.2 in Bristol.

At the end of June I stood before the Executive Committee as candidate for East Bristol, and the following week I was most fortunate in being able to attend a banquet (presided over by the Duke of Marlborough) to celebrate Joseph Chamberlain's seventy-fourth birthday. It was held at Prince's Restaurant, where I beheld a galaxy of Members of Parliament and prominent Unionist supporters, many of whom, I am proud to say, were later to become good friends of mine. Ned Carson, I remember, was there, and Lord Charles Beresford, not to mention Walter Long, L. S. Amery and Joynson Hicks. We sent a telegram to Chamberlain, which declared: -

"... that 90 ardent Tariff Reformers, dining together to celebrate your birthday, express their unalterable devotion to you, and their confidence you will see your Imperial ideal soon realised."

About 90% of the voters of East Bristol were composed of the working and industrial classes, and about four thousand had recorded their votes for Tariff Reform at the last election which, as a bye-election, had been held less than a year previously. There was an immense amount of social work to be done here, and, as Joseph Chamberlain had so forcefully put it: - "Tariff Reform is the beginning of Social Reform," a truism which was to me an article of political faith. My policy then agreed in almost every detail with that outlined by Mr. Arthur Balfour in a famous speech at Nottingham. Among other points of my programme, into which I shall enter later with some detail, I was in an unqualified opposition to Home Rule. A supreme Navy for the protection of our trade and commerce, and repeal of a recently imposed taxation upon the Licensed Trader, were other points.

One argument frequently raised against me during this political campaign was that the man whose shadow I served, namely Joseph Chamberlain, was inconsistent because during his political career he had declared variously for and against Free Trade. The answer I always gave was that it takes a great man to admit his error, and great men before Joseph Chamberlain had admitted their errors and changed their minds. I cited as example Lord John Russell who, as leader of the Radicals in early Victorian days, had repeatedly declared that his party could not accept a policy of Free Trade yet, in 1846, he had astonished the country by voting whole-heartedly for the introduction of Free Trade. Again, in 1880, Gladstone had come into power with a great majority who pledged him, yea or nay, to prevent the advancement of Home Rule for Ireland. Yet only six years later he and his Party were voted into power again on a pledge to advance, by any means possible, Home Rule for Ireland.

My opponent, Mr. Hobhouse, was a Liberal and a man of great political distinction, but he descended to abuse in his Election campaign, which was somewhat surprising. He accused me of being a traitor to my country and to my religion, and the enemy of every farmer in Ireland. Naturally, I challenged Mr. Hobhouse to prove his statement which, to anyone knowing anything about Ireland, must appear absurd. He replied by attempting to

115

evade the issue, suggesting that it was not myself but my policy that he was attacking. The policy of the Liberal Party was, of course, for Home Rule, but my expressed opinion was that Home Rule at that time would re-open strife between the religions, a matter too terrible to contemplate. It was because I did not want to see race opposed to race, creed opposed to creed and class opposed to class, that I consistently opposed Home Rule. Sir Pieter Bam (the South African, whom I have mentioned previously) believed that since a Convention and a united settlement of racial and party difficulties had been possible in South Africa, it should be equally possible in Ireland. He had now acquired an estate in Co. Donegal, and was staying there with his wife. The political position in Great Britain at that time was both extraordinary and anomalous. A particularly small force, the Irish Party, was directing the entire policy of the Liberal Government. For out of every £100 of taxation, £88.15s.0d was contributed by England, £10.13s.0d by Scotland, and only £00.13s.4d by Ireland, whose Party at Westminster dictated to the Empire. It was my opinion that if the regime established by Arthur Balfour and George Wyndham was given full opportunity of working, the Irish people would be perfectly contented, and lose interest in any agitation to separate themselves from Britain.

I have before me a series of articles which I wrote for the 'Bristol Times', one of which referred to Birrell's treatment of the Irish question. I said: - *"Mr. Birrell's Government of Ireland would be fairly described as a series of blunders and jokes. His bubbling witticisms have alike done duty in exercising the antagonist Unionist demon who recognised that he concedes too much, and the friendly Nationalist demon who persists in seeking more and more favours... Mr. Birrell has lamentably failed to understand that his Irish policy has made him the laughing stock of all classes in Ireland, where, thank Heaven, some sense of humour still survives."*

One of his greater blunders was in dismissing Sir Horace Plunkett from the Department of Agriculture (the man who did more for his country than any Irishman of the nineteenth century, and who continued to devote his life to her service) and appointing in his place the many-sided T. W. Russell. Mr. Hobhouse, however, understood nothing of all this, but duly followed his Party leader with zeal and devotion.

To counter any ignorant opinion on the Irish question, the Irish Unionist Alliance sent over some gentlemen from Dublin to support me at my meetings. Among these came Mr. Tyrrell (the son of Professor Tyrrell of Trinity College) and several other good friends. Incidentally, Mr. S.R. Lysaght, to whose energetic offices I was largely indebted for my candidature to East Bristol, was an Irishman. All through the campaign he was my constant adviser, and whenever there was work to be done, or responsibility to be undertaken, he was always ready. He was a type whom you meet only rarely, but when you do you ought, as the poet says, "to bind him to your soul with hoops of steel." I was more than fortunate to find him as my colleague.

Taxation on products of the licensed trade was a point which naturally raised interest in me as a commercial traveller in hops, and to the working classes to whom I was making my appeal. Some of the electorate belonged to the St. George's Club for working men in Bristol East, which was in flourishing condition, but somewhat excited by this new imposition. An example was quoted in the Licensing Bill debate of about that time, stating that the receipts of the Club bar in "X" totalled more than £2,200, while the receipts in the Club reading-room totalled 10/9d. The Licensed Trade of the Kingdom provided considerably more than one quarter of the total produce of our entire taxation, and it seemed to me unnecessary to strain the taxable capacity of the Brewer, or force him to increase the wholesale price of his products. Those, alas, were the good old days, and it is hard to realise now the amount of liquid refreshment that could be obtained for a matter of a few pence.

However, in spite of these appealing points in my political programme, it was generally presumed that I would suffer defeat in this Liberal stronghold, and the most that I could be expected to do was to strengthen the Unionist vote. Nomination Day came, December 2nd 1910, and I handed in six nomination papers, to my opponent's eight (four of whose papers, however, were refused). Election procedure in those far-off days differed considerably from that to which we are now accustomed. Among other changes, the polling of districts was spread over a period of several days, and Nomination Day immediately preceded Polling Day. For the ten days previous to Election Day, I had spoken at so many meetings that I was unable to produce my voice to its proper extent across the Hall on that final occasion, and had to ask for indulgence from my audience. There was such a crush and crowd at some of those final meetings that it became necessary for me to mount the table and answer hecklers from this elevated position in a voice which, alas, croaked hoarsely in their ears. On December 2nd (my wife having accompanied me to the Higher Grade School building, where a crowd awaited us) I read aloud, to the accompaniment of much cheering, telegrams from Arthur Balfour and from Joseph Chamberlain. The latter was worded thus: - *"I wish you success in your uphill fight. I am glad that someone should put the Irish case for us."*

I shall never forget the thrill of that first Election contest, for although I had no abiding hope of beating my opponent, there was always the possibility that the people of England might show a swing towards the Unionist policy, and I knew that I was fortunate in having some very strong supporters.

A curious incident occurred on Polling Day, which was seized upon by the local newspapers. Women suffrage was then at its height, and the ladies of Great Britain let no opportunity slip for the furtherance of their cause. Having had as colleagues (in the old I.A.O.S. days) some of the most brilliant women in Ireland, I could understand the feminine urge for a greater measure of independence and wider recognition of their undoubted brains and ability, but I had no sympathy with some of their tactics. In Bristol, however, there were no aggressive manifestations of feeling for Women's Suffrage, no great public meetings, or picturesque processions. They played their part in the election campaign in many valuable and un-ostentatious ways, working behind the scenes in support of their men-folk or of the Party which they believed to be most in favour of allowing them the Vote. I calculated at that time that the womanpower in Elections would be twelve to eleven against manpower in deciding political advantage, and on the whole this thought was somewhat alarming. Yet, as the politicians accepted their very influential help, should they not be considered worthy of some measure of trust and confidence in national administration? It was a peculiarly difficult question, and one in which I was somewhat wary of getting involved.

At any rate, at this particular election, a Mrs. Jessie Eastman appeared at the Polling Station and tried to record her vote, declaring that she was entitled to do this because her name was on the register. The bewildered officials found that indeed her name was recorded, but spelled Jesse, an error that saved their faces and legally aided the police on duty there in preventing her entry. How the mistake arose is a mystery. The lady was a widow, but the name could not have referred to her late husband, for he had been called Alfred. Whether her vote would have been in my favour or not, I cannot say, but the result would have been unaltered.

Hobhouse was elected with 7,229 votes, and I polled 4,263 (incidentally, the highest Unionist vote ever polled in East Bristol to that date). It was quite a satisfactory result, for the Liberal vote had been decreased by some 1,240 votes since the previous General Election in 1906, although admittedly it had been slightly higher in a recent bye-election where a Labour candidate had also gone to the polls (over two thousand votes being recorded in his favour).

The general election as a whole was a sorry defeat for the Tory Party, and many prominent members of Parliament lost their seats, including Bonar Law, Mr. Philip QuedaIIa and even Tim Healy, the nationalist. It was warming to receive a vociferous welcome on my entering the Constitutional Club in Bristol for the first time since my defeat, where on my calling out: - "Are we down-hearted?" I was answered by cries of, "No, never!"

Although the actual Election was over, there was still much work for me to do, and I spent a busy time until Christmas addressing meetings throughout the West Country. In addition there were certain social occasions which demanded my attention. These. included a small presentation to our chief Agent in Bristol, Mr. Morton Pask, and a farewell luncheon given by me to my Irish colleagues. On New Year's Eve, the gratifying resolution was passed by the Bristol East Conservative Association that I be earnestly requested to stand for them again. But more gratifying still was the wonderful reception accorded me by the citizens of Bristol. At first they had planned to hold the reception in the Higher Grade School, but so many people wished to be present that the meeting place was changed to the Assembly Rooms. Yet again, it had to be altered to find space for my good friends, and we ended up in the Colston Hall which, strictly speaking, was outside the East Bristol Division. Accordingly, on the 24th February I went to Colston Hall to find the place adorned with flowers, and a huge placard over my chair on the platform which read: - "Long life and prosperity to P. J. Hannon."

Sidney Lysaght presided, supported by Walter Long. My entry was the signal for a burst of, "For he's a jolly good fellow." To my astonishment I received a magnificent presentation of plate, consisting of a canteen of ivory handled table cutlery with sterling silver rat-tailed spoons and forks (for twelve persons), together with a tea and coffee service and a silver tea-tray. The total weight of silver must have been about three hundred ounces. The tray was engraved:- *"Presented to P.J. Hannon Esq. by his friends and admirers, as a mark of appreciation of his gallant fight as Parliamentary candidate for Bristol East, December 3rd 1910."*

It was one of the proudest moments of my life, although we were all, ironically enough, celebrating a defeat. The beautiful testimonial and address bore the names of nearly two thousand Bristol citizens, and the words: - "… In asking you to accept our gift, we all join in expressing a hope that at no distant date, you may have an opportunity in the House of Commons of exercising your abilities in support of the cause for which you have already done so much in the country."

Austen Chamberlain's message, which was read to the assembly, was typical of his magnificent fighting spirit: - *"The Unionists of East Bristol have had a hard fight against long odds. I am glad to learn from you that they are going to recognise the services rendered to the Party by Mr. Hannon. I trust that both he and they will continue the fight until they can bring it to a successful issue."*

There was at this time a Movement to awaken interest in the Conservative Party (called the Reveille Movement) and I attended one of its earliest meetings, which was presided over by the Earl of Malmesbury. Rumour had suggested a split in the Unionist Party, and this Movement did much to combat this suggestion. Our main points of policy were the Reform of Trade, Land and Poor Law, closer union with the Empire and better Defence of the Realm. Apart from the Reveille Movement, the local Conservative landowners helped greatly to rouse interest in the Party. Carnivals, sporting events, and dancing were held at the Manor House. And then there was the Primrose League, whose energetic Committee arranged splendid attractions. I remember one outdoor Fete held in Bathford on a glorious August day, which was a tremendous social attraction. Across the lawn beautiful young ladies in flowing dresses danced in line, carrying garlands of flowers. There was some comedy too, I recollect, supplied by a group of rustics wearing the picturesque smock frocks (which have so nearly vanished from the English scene) and smoking churchwarden pipes.

On another occasion there was a Conservative Association outing to beautiful Longleat House, near Frome, with its stately beech trees so perfectly grown and its costly treasures on view inside the house. What pleasant times those were in 1910, and how little the average person realised the imminence of danger... Four years to the holocaust.

It was during the month of August that the Kaiser made a startling speech in which, astoundingly clear, unequivocally and unambiguously, he declared his martial policy. Whether viewed from the economic, social, educational or military standpoint, German internal policy was virile, forceful, aggressive and definite, as the Kaiser's message demonstrated with reckless emphasis. "We should always be ready to keep our armour without flaw," he said. Yet his words meant little or nothing to the gentlemen reading them disinterestedly behind the shelter of the morning paper while he consumed ham and eggs. They raised no qualms in his wife, fondly regarding her schoolboy sons quarrelling over the silver dishes on the laden sideboard.

The working man regarded Germany as a land of fat musicians blowing brass instruments. The better educated classes had a vaguely sentimental feeling towards the jolly Bavarian puffing his pipe outside his hut in a forest clearing, and regarded the Prussian with his pear-shaped head and his inability to speak the King's English as nothing more, or less, than a joke. There was too much of the 'don't care a damn' and 'let some other silly fool do it' feeling among our people, and particularly among the young men who were to be the first to go down in destruction. They rushed in their

121

thousands to stand shivering at a football match, but howled their indignation if they were asked to spend a few hours a week in learning how to handle a rifle. German sentiment was being built up by the fires of patriotism, whilst some here regarded as absurd ideas of having to defend our mighty Empire. But in 1910 and 1911 Lord Roberts' voice spoke alone, or almost alone, and his warnings went unheeded.

About this time I attended a meeting of those of us who were interested in the Imperial Exhibition scheduled for the portentous year of 1915 to be held in London. Lord Strathcona presided, and Sir Pieter Stuart Barn and Hamar Greenwood were present. The assurance of full co-operation of all the High Commissioners of the Empire had been given to the organisers, and it was proposed that any profit should be used to further the interests of the Empire. At that meeting, I was made joint Honorary Secretary of the provisional organising committee, along with Cecil Beck M.P. A few months earlier the Royal Society of Arts had awarded me their medal for my paper on 'Commercial Expansion within the Empire', and this honour no doubt helped my progress in Empire Affairs.

I have as yet made no reference to an institution which was to play a vitally important part in the next decade of my life, and in which I became interested immediately after settling in Bristol. This was the Navy League, whose aims and objects attracted my keen attention and ultimately drew me to London. Briefly, these were to promote public interest in the activities of the British Navy, to urge upon the Government the need for an adequate naval defence force as a means of protection from the enemy in times of warfare, and to provide boys of the working classes with every facility to join the Royal Navy or the Merchant Service (provided they were of good character). The League was founded in January 1895 by a group of patriotic gentlemen. The Bristol Branch, which was opened one month later, has the distinction of being the oldest branch of the League now in existence.

During the summer of 1910 I was elected Vice-Chairman of the Executive Committee of the Bristol Branch of the Navy League. Admiral Close was the Chairman in those days, and I well remember General O'Dwyer, an invaluable member of the committee. At one of these meetings it was proposed that I should confer with the originator of the Naval Volunteer Force in the Kingdom, Mr. C.S. Strettell (at that time Manager of the Bristol Branch of the Bank of England), with the object of establishing a Naval Veteran Volunteer Force in Bristol from the numerous citizens who had served with the Royal Naval Artillery Volunteers. Strettell had proposed a military scheme for the organisation of a Veteran Military Reserve, which the government had already adopted, and it was felt that through his efforts a similar naval scheme might be laid before the Admiralty. I felt very strongly that wherever it was possible to arouse or hold the interest of seamen in national defence, it should be done.

It was both exasperating and saddening that the Government paid so little attention to the Navy League's constant demands for a large efficient and well-paid Navy, and their obtuseness stiffened all the more my desire to serve the League in whatever capacity when I was elected.

Here is one point among several, which early on indicated the Government's attitude. I was a member of a deputation from the Bristol branch of the Navy League to the Board of Trade, our object being to secure Governmental aid in the establishment of a National Committee to train British boys to be seamen. The President, Mr. Sydney Burton, regretted that he could hold out little hope of the grant being given. Such short-sightedness was deplorable.

The first Annual Meeting of the Bristol branch that I attended was held on the one hundred and fifth anniversary of Trafalgar, at the Grand Spa, Clifton. The Duchess of Beaufort, I remember, presided at that Meeting. This was one of the occasions on which my dear wife was able to accompany me. She suffered greatly from asthma, and this infinitely distressing complaint frequently made it impossible for her to be at my side on these public occasions, although she followed and supported all my activities with the keenest interest. It was a great joy to me whenever she was able to be present.

Within a few months of the General Election, Mr. Hobhouse resigned from the East Bristol constituency, owing to his accepting the Duchy of Lancaster. So deeply had I become involved in the Navy League, I declined the invitation of the East Bristol Unionists to contest the seat once again, feeling that I could do better service in my present position.

CHAPTER 5

A gentleman writing to the Times in January 1894 about naval matters, and signing himself 'Civis', ended his letter thus: - "If my suggestion for a National Navy League takes root it will soon grow into goodly shape, and the collective wisdom of my countrymen will give it a better form than any I can suggest." This is probably the first time that the term 'Navy League' was used, and it is interesting to see how firmly the root was planted and how strongly it grew. The Navy League has always endeavoured to impress upon popular thought the transcendent importance of our sea power, as compared with all other considerations affecting our national and Imperial life. From time to time it used to offer strong criticisms upon what it regarded as defects in our naval policy, and it carefully watched for, and immediately pointed out to the proper authorities, anything in its judgement constituted a want or indicated a danger or discrepancy.

On February 16th 1911, a meeting of the Grand Council of the League was held in London, which I attended as representative of the Bristol Branch. Mr. Robert Armstrong Yerburgh M.P., Conservative M.P. for Chester, 1886-1906 and 1910-1916, presided (I shall have more to say about this delightful man later), and afterwards I was elected to serve as a member of the executive Council. In August I was appointed Secretary of the Navy League, upon the resignation of Lieut. Brian Hewitt R.N. This meant that the greater part of my time had to be spent in London or travelling round Britain, and it was only at weekends that I was able to return to Bristol to my family. We decided not to move, however, until 1913. The children had had enough disturbance in their education with our change of continent, and the climate suited my wife.

Following my appointment I made arrangements to tour the British Isles, explaining and propounding the work of the Navy League. A most interesting part of this publicity campaign was my tour in Scotland, where I visited Edinburgh, Aberdeen, Glasgow, Dundee and a host of other engaging towns, The Declaration of London and the Naval Prize Bill occupied my attention at once, and for a considerable period thereafter. The Declaration of London was arrived at on December 4th 1908, and we had no fault to find with the greater number of its provisions as they were reiterations of well-known principles of international law. However, any international agreement that would prejudice the free coming and going of our merchant ships in time of war seemed monstrous to us who, in those halcyon days, thought of warfare in terms of lawful fighting and 'fair play'. In the Bristol Branch there had been the feeling that the policy of the central authorities of the League was not vigorous enough, particularly in regard to the Declaration of London, where they were inclined to let matters take their course. This subject, then, engaged much of my time, and during September we issued a manifesto concerning it. I think a statement that we published in August had something of prophesy in its wording, though so far as the great public were concerned it went unregarded: - *"... The urgency of giving effect to such recommendations of the Royal Commission as will tend to safeguard the public against a panic rise in prices due to the ... outbreak of a great war."*

In January 1916, the Naval executive sent a letter to the Prime Minister, Mr. Asquith, begging him to urge the Government that the terms of the Declaration of London should now be totally abandoned. With regard to the Naval Prize Bill, in the December 1911 issue of the Navy League's journal ,'The Navy', we signed a manifesto explaining our opposition to it. The Germans had their objections too. They declined absolutely to agree to a clause, which it had been proposed to insert, prohibiting the arming of merchant seamen.

Nearly half the Great War had been fought before the Government agreed to a measure of protection for these gallant sailors. But, in 1911 the Bill was rejected by the House of Lords, by 145 votes to 43. Our great campaign of the time was 'Two Keels to One'. In 1911, we had twelve ships of the Dreadnought class against five of Germany's. But by 1915, the increased rate of ship-building in both countries would have been so much less in our favour that we would then have had but thirty-two ships to twenty-three. This miserable and inadequate superiority in naval ships over other powers was the subject of an article I wrote to the 'London Evening News', appealing to Churchill not to neglect this golden opportunity for additional ship building.

I was convinced of the very real danger of a war. Also, I was exasperated with those whose misplaced confidence in what they believed to be our overwhelming naval superiority, and in the friendliness of other nations which had led them by their naive belief into such drastic policy errors.

Early in 1912 a contingent of cadets from Australia visited this country, and a large reception was held for them, through the kindness of Mr. and Mrs. Yerburgh, at Kensington Gore. It was good to see these lads from overseas and to feel that our Dominions at least were alive to the possibility of having to defend themselves against enemy attack. The Chief Justice of South Africa was present, I remember, and several members of Parliament (including Shirley Benn and Page Croft). It was a splendid gathering of distinguished people interested in Naval and Empire affairs.

One of the great aims of my colleagues and myself was to secure a naval career for suitable boys, and I took great delight in explaining the work of the Navy League and expounding naval history to school audiences. Valuable prizes were offered both to boys and girls for essays on naval subjects, and this undoubtedly helped the education of our youth in seamanship. I recall with some amusement that, apropos of our lectures to girls' schools, the question was asked in Parliament whether the First Lord of the Admiralty considered it a fit and proper thing that young ladies should be encouraged to interest themselves in Naval matters. When one thinks of the marvellous works that were accomplished by women in two great wars, the question seems to have been completely ludicrous.

In 1911 I became the Chairman of the Central Committee of the Boys Naval Brigade, an immense movement now, which I had the honour of helping to create. One of the most famous leaders of youth whom I came across at that time (mostly in connection with the Sea Scouts) was Lord Baden-Powell, a charming personality. Perhaps the earliest institution connected with the Navy League in the training of boys for a maritime career was the Liscard Boys Home, near Liverpool. Captain Thomas, secretary of the Liverpool Branch of the Navy League at one time, is believed to have suggested its origination. In October 1902, the foundation stone was laid by the High

Commissioner for Canada, Lord Strathcona, and in less than twelve months the first boys were being received. One of principles of our Training Homes was: - "No boy or destitute is refused admission, and the poorer he may be the better his recommendation." (Of course, providing he is physically fit for naval life).

I visited Liscard in the summer of 1912, when it was under the guidance of Captain Garnons Williams. There were one hundred and fifty boys in training, and a new wing had just been added to the building, which was designed to accommodate a further one hundred boys. Captain Williams resigned shortly afterwards and died during the Great War. He was a magnificent youth leader and dearly beloved by members of the Navy League. It is largely due to his devoted service that the Liscard Home produced so many fine examples of seamen.

In 1912, I also had much to do with that well-known training ship, 'The Stork', a vessel of some four hundred and fifty tons hired from the Admiralty in February of that year, and moored off Hammersmith the following December, fully fitted and equipped for the training of boys. It has always been of the greatest interest to me, and I am proud to have served on the committee of management at its foundation. The work was carried out by the Kensington Branch. Miss Amy Gordon Barrett (much later to become my second wife) was largely instrumental in its formation. Miss Gordon Barrett served on the executive committee of the Ladies Council of the Navy League from 1910 onwards, and was as keenly interested in the work- as I was. 'The Stork' particularly was her especial delight. It is a tragic honour that ninety-three of the boys who trained in this ship fell during the Great War.

These recollections recall to my mind a celebration in Glasgow for the centenary of the launching of the 'Comet', the first steam-propelled vessel to run regularly on this side of the Atlantic. She was wrecked in 1830 off the Scottish coast. Representatives of the Navy League were invited, and I went on a most interesting excursion, arranged by the Glasgow Branch, with about eight hundred members and friends of the League. To go back somewhat further into the dim depths of our glorious naval history, back in fact to the man who so largely was responsible for the Navy as she is today, Sir Francis Drake; for some- time it had been felt that a memorial should be erected in London to him, and the 'London Budget' (a newspaper long since defunct) formulated a scheme for public subscription. This journal proposed to subscribe one thousand pounds, if fifty thousand pounds was given by other subscribers. A special committee of the League was formed, on which I served, and we decided to give the project our support in every possible way. A design for the memorial was submitted by Frank Brangwyn R. A., in his peculiarly beautiful style.

At this period (and indeed for most of my public life) my time was so fully occupied with meetings and committees, in addition to my general business, that I had little or no time I could call my own. Although I would not have had it otherwise, I sometimes regard with admiration those who manage to indulge in hobbies of one sort or another. Most of my interests outside my work have been in the service of public institutions, among them Aston Villa Association Football Club.

I was in somewhat of a dilemma at that time. The journeys that I had to make so frequently, in the interests of the League, could so easily impair the progress of my work in London. At the Grand Council meeting in February 1913, however, a good friend of mine, Colonel Walter G. Webb, declared that since it was impossible to spare me from my campaigning labours, he proposed that I should be given a personal assistant upon whom the Navy League could depend in my absence. The assistant chosen was Miss Dalrymple-Hay, daughter of the famous Admiral Hay. A most competent lady she was, in whose hands I could leave my business matters without the smallest qualm. There was, in addition, a most competent assistant-secretary in the person of Lieut. Knox, who was a splendid public speaker. He resigned, much to our regret, that summer in order to undertake some work with the Railways.

The question of aerial defence was being raised by those who at that time were considered scaremongers. For three years, from 1912, I was the Honorary Secretary of the National Aerial Defence Association. Representing the Navy League, I attended a meeting of the National Defence Committee in the spring of 1913 having, in fact, arranged this conference. Every association identified with the progress of aviation had been invited to take part in the organisation of the meeting, and the greatest care was taken to avoid 'party' divisions, but as usual there were critics who accused us of belonging to a stereotyped division, and I had to publicly refute this. At that time 'water-plane' tests were going on at Monte Carlo, which had not only turned out to be rather disappointing from the engineering point of view, but had resulted in the death of at least one gallant fellow whilst attempting to take his ill-balanced craft off the water. Generalisations about the capacities and potentialities of the various types of aircraft were extremely dangerous, yet so many people then expressed their opinions in most dogmatic terms.

Lord Montagu of Beaulieu most shrewdly remarked that if we did not do something about aerial defence as soon as possible, we might some day have a terrible awakening, for no one could tell what course a war conducted by air-machines might take. Certainly, it was becoming increasingly obvious that the scouting activities of aircraft (flimsy as they all were in those days), and the bombing ability of airships (dirigibles, we used to call them) constituted a real danger, The agitation in favour of serious development of Aerial Organisation of Defence was brought to public attention by a mass meeting at the Mansion House, presided over by the Lord Mayor, at which a strong appeal was made to the Government to give serious consideration to the whole series of problems involved in the establishment of aerial defence.

But our most immediate concern was with the question of naval defence, and our standard of 'Two keels to one' was accused of not being sufficiently precise. To me this seemed simple and comprehensive, that a naval strength in completed capital ships, at any given date, of two keels to one possessed by the next strongest power, should leave us a reasonable margin of strength to divert units to any quarter of the globe where necessity arose. As for the manpower of our increasing fleet, we were doing all we could in the training of youths and in making a naval career attractive. One of the speakers at a Trafalgar Day meeting of that time remarked that grants were given in London for the training of hotel waiters, and it seemed a thousand pities that there was not the same desire to give assistance to enable us to become a nation of seamen as there was that we should be a nation of waiters. Incidentally, on the occasion of the Kaiser's Jubilee, the Navy League politely sent him a telegram of congratulation.

Talking of Jubilees, I recall a very pleasant occasion shortly before the Great War when the Navy League presented a piece of plate to the President (Mr. Yerburgh) and his wife on the silver jubilee of their wedding. The names of all the chief officers of the League were inscribed upon it, including the Duke of Somerset, the Marchioness of Bute and my dear old friend the Baroness de Goldsmid. She and I used to alternate as Chairman and Speaker at all kinds of Charity meetings. Through her hospitality I met many interesting people, and remember so well her 'At Homes' at Chesham Place. It was in Chesham Place that I first met Owen Seaman (the editor of 'Punch') and we became great friends. What a delightful man he was.

To give the number of meetings which our League members addressed in the first ten weeks of the year 1914 may give a faint idea of our activeness, and of the foolproof organisation required. The meetings numbered nine hundred all in all.

The Navy League, like most organisations of one kind or another had (as I have already mentioned) its opponents and critics, and I was called upon from time to time to defend our policy. In addition to the inevitable accusation of being a party organisation shielding ourselves under the cloak of patriotism, we were also accused of being in the pay and service of some of the leading armament firms in this country; the accusation actually appearing in print. Both these statements were emphatically and truthfully denied, and the writers silenced.

The journal of the Navy League, 'The Navy' (of which I became Editor, actively assisted by Alan Burgoyne, M.P.), had for some years before the outbreak of war been pointing out the danger of curtailing our naval plans, and noting at the same time Germany's efforts to build up the largest and finest fleet afloat. On the memorable visit of our Navy to Kiel in July 1914, the President of the German Navy League, Admiral von Koster said: - *"Germany has a powerful Navy which must be made more powerful still, but we drain our glasses sincerely when Hoch's' for the British Navy are called for."*

In a matter of weeks, they had the opportunity to practise respecting 'The greatest Navy in the world, and second to none in virtue of valour'. The August edition of 'The Navy' dealt at length with the position of the German fleet, ending with these ominous words: - "The German fleet may well be said to be 'all set for war'." In the same number appeared an article on the test mobilisation of our own Fleet at Spithead, in which the opportunity was taken once again to impress upon the Government the necessity for a superiority of 50% in ships of the Dreadnought class.

CHAPTER 6

On August 4th 1914, it was too late to waste any further time in criticism of what the Admiralty's policy ought to have been. War was upon Great Britain, and the call to arms had come. Those who had the Navy League at heart sent immediate and inspiring messages, urging the co-operation of all members to the utmost degree. Sir Edward Carson was among those whose words of encouragement were published. Jellicoe was at that time First Sea Lord, and we were on very intimate terms. He afterwards became Commander of the Home Fleet and fought the Battle of Jutland. The issue of 'The Navy' for September contained a manifesto signed by Mr. Yerburgh, Rear-Admiral Lionel Grant Tufnell (1857-1930), Colonel Alfred Welby (1849-1937, created K.B.E. 1918) and myself, the substance of which was to urge members to keep calm and brave in facing this tremendous crisis. Yerburgh was actually in Germany when war broke out and was placed in captivity. After great difficulty and some weary months of suspense, he was released early in 1915, but he returned in such poor health that he was unable to continue his work. Week after week I had sought to induce the Foreign Office officials to put their machinery into working for his immediate repatriation, but if it had not been for the assistance of the American Ambassador, Walter Page, his ultimate release would have been even further delayed.

One of the earliest of our Navy League officials to join the fighting forces was Lieut. Hanson, R.N., who had successfully run many boys' camps. Indeed, my own sons enjoyed a few weeks at one of his Camps in 1913. When his death was announced there must have been many thousands of youths, in every part of the globe, who mourned his loss. This gallant officer and dear friend was captured in October 1914 at the siege of Antwerp. For a tide he was believed to have died at Halle. We learned later that while he was being marched (along with other prisoners) to a P.O.W. Camp on October 10th, in a state of delirium he imagined he saw a small party of British troops advancing, unaware of the German's proximity. He shouted warnings again and again, seeing in his feverish mind his countrymen walking innocently into a trap. The German guards closed round him, and he was effectually silenced. Next morning he was shot.

The annual Trafalgar Day dinner, usually our most important social event of the year, was cancelled during the war. We took the opportunity, instead, of combining recruitment with the heightening of public morale. On the first occasion we held a patriotic demonstration, nobly attended, which was followed by a concert at the London Opera House. This pattern was followed for the succeeding four years.

All the lady members of the Navy League and its branches responded with one accord, instantly and nobly, to every call made upon them by myself and other Executives. It would be impracticable and invidious to mention by name all those who opened their houses to soldiers and sailors, and organised entertainment for the wounded. Miss Gordon-Barrett and other generous ladies organised groups of workers into knitting comforts for the troops, tirelessly and without complaint. Personally, she knitted over five hundred pairs of socks during the war period, placing in each pair a packet of cigarettes or tobacco. It fell to my lot to form and run a Social Workers Committee so that these splendid ladies might have a systematic means of ensuring that the result of their work reached the men for whom it was intended in the shortest time possible. There was a large depot house at a corner in Grosvenor Square, which was used when we received a tremendous amount of clothing, food etc., and from there we sent a vast quantity of parcels to the Front. I often think of the mounds of paper and great balls of twine in this place, and the sorting and the packing and the hours of standing for many splendid women who had probably never before tied up a parcel for an overseas destination. In the Dublin Branch depot at 47, Merrion Square, for which I was responsible, five hundred women were working all out, collecting all sorts of comforts for the Troops. It was a heartening sight.

The death early in the war, of Field Marshal Earl Roberts, touched us very deeply. He died on November 14th in the midst of his Army at the General Headquarters in France, where he was paying a visit to some Indian troops of which he was Colonel-in-Chief. He had constantly taken an interest in the League's work, and was in fact a Vice-President for many years, and President of the National Service League.

By the beginning of 1915 Germany had replaced the code of honour in warfare by a code of treachery, so that hospital ships and unarmed merchant ships were attacked and sunk with impunity. I saw to it that 'The Navy' played its part in awakening the public to the truth of these atrocities, and I published a clear rendering of the terms relevant to the Hague Convention, to illustrate the German Navy's utter disregard for international law. It was the new era in warfare gradually establishing itself, though mercifully we did not realise this at the time. We then believed this was the 'War to end Wars'.

As in the World War of 1939 (so to a lesser extent in the Great War) there was Fifth Column at work. Rumours and lies were spread abroad, some of them concerning the treatment of men in the Forces, and it became my duty vigorously to deny these attacks. In the summer of 1915 I signed the following manifesto sent to all members of the League: - "The nation is fighting for its life. The Empire is in the midst of a life and death struggle for our peoples' freedom. The subtle enemy and slobbering sentimentalist must have no toleration. Will members do their utmost to kill the pernicious propaganda of friends of the enemy, by arranging meetings and distributing pamphlets concerning the League and its work; and thus give the public the true facts."

I also wrote to the Home Secretary about this time, pointing out the abnormal number of fires in and around London, and asking for an investigation in case they should be the work of enemy agents. From the enquiry made, however, it appeared that the incidents were probably due to wartime carelessness. The Government did not issue precautions to the general public to the same extent which they found so necessary during the Second World War. Through the pages of 'The Navy' I cautioned Navy League members and their friends to be very circumspect in all their conversation relevant to naval matters.

Which reminds me of an embarrassing episode concerning a ferocious woman whom we nicknamed 'Mrs. Terrible'. We had organised a number of coastal watchers, among whom was a group of women led, alas, by 'Mrs. Terrible'. She must have got it into her head that an invasion was to be expected at any moment, for she managed to arm herself and her suffragette colleagues with fully loaded revolvers and they all set off for the north coast of Norfolk. Heaven knows what they thought they were going to do! And Heaven alone knows into what terrible mess they would have got themselves, and incidentally myself, if their alarming ideas on the defence of their country had not become known to the authorities!

Letters were exchanged with the Secretary to the Navy, while I felt my position to be an extremely delicate one in this extraordinary affair. The upshot was that Mrs. Terrible was given £100 on the understanding that she would never again organise a band of armed and warlike ladies.

At the end of the year, I had an interesting few days touring the Channel Islands, where I was given a splendid reception by the people of Jersey and Guernsey. Their geographical position made them particularly dependent upon the Navy, and they listened enthusiastically to everything I had to tell them about recruiting for the Navy and the Navy League. On leaving those gallant islands I brought with me messages of loyalty to His Majesty and to the First Lord of the Admiralty.

A stirring message on the first anniversary of the war from our President, Mr. Yerburgh, brought fresh enthusiasm to many League members. He was a man who firmly believed in the suspension of payment to M.P.s in wartime (barring exceptional cases) and, as long as the Government chose to pay salaries, he declared his justification in accepting his in order to hand it over to the Navy League. I remember his writing to me on this point after the question had been raised in Parliament. He expressed his intention to continue to give the whole of his salary to our cause. The treatment which he underwent whilst a prisoner had left its mark upon him, and his health had not recovered from the ordeal. In March 1916, he reluctantly resigned his seat in Chester for the strain of attending to his Parliamentary duties was too much for him. As the outspoken and forceful voice in Parliament for the policy of the Navy League, his resignation was real blow to us.

The trial and execution of Nurse Edith Cavell in October 1915 roused world-wide wrath and sympathy, and memorials were placed in many parts of the world. I was one of the Committee which organised the national memorial to her in England, and I was naturally very proud to feel that I should be partly responsible for perpetuating the memory of such a brave woman. Some people, I believe, felt that she was wrong and at fault to allow the medical community (which should stand apart in service to all mankind, regardless of race or creed) to become involved in the realities of partisanship in warfare, but no one would deny the courage of this gallant woman.

In 1916 I faced the citizens of Dublin once more at a Navy League demonstration in the Shelbourne Hotel. There was a very large gathering, under the chairmanship of Mr. G. Stewart (a Vice-President of the Navy League) and many of my friends were present. It was only three months afterwards that the Easter Rising broke out. I knew that a certain section of the people of Ireland would be interested to hear of the Navy's great work, and how the Navy League was helping, and from the interest which my speech immediately aroused I could see I had not been mistaken. It was as this time that Churchill was being subjected to bitter attacks, and I recall my defence of him, and my statement that when the history of the war came to be written he would be regarded as a hero.

In the first year and a half of the war the achievements of the Navy included the crippling of £130,000,000 of enemy trade. It was extraordinary that at this time no naval officer was included on the War Council. Kitchener represented the Army, but the 'Silent Service' had no representative, despite the tremendously important part they were playing in this grim struggle of the Nations. If I were to go into an extensive description of the many methods adopted by the Navy League to help war charities, I could fill numerous pages. One memorable effort I should like to recall. An anonymous donor gave a magnificent collection of plate, originally the personal property of Horatio Nelson, on the understanding that a presentation of a piece of this plate was to be made to each battleship specially distinguishing itself in action. The presentation could take place only if the Navy League raised on each occasion a sum of one hundred guineas for the Red Cross Funds. Twenty-three ships were the proud recipients of their hero's personal possessions. Altogether, with the extra money that was subscribed, we collected £2,500 for the Red Cross through this unusual method.

Various benefactors gave us their treasures which were

offered for sale through the League. A unique gift sold in this way was a cheque for £100 signed by Sir Walter Scott and dated January 31st 1824. How strange that the original owner, in refusing to cash the cheque, should have benefited his country nearly a century afterwards. We lost Lieut. Knox, our champion lecturer, early in 1916. He was an established favourite among us and a very good friend of mine. His resignation was announced at the annual meeting of the Grand Council. Another fine lecturer on behalf of the Navy League was Mr. Marshall Pike who, during a period of nine months, addressed over one hundred thousand people at a total of one hundred and eleven meetings. He had a particularly successful campaign, I remember, in South Wales. At that time there had been a most serious coal strike, and the mines were just recovering from the effect. Marshall Pike's campaign helped enormously to steady them down, and he induced the miners to work together from patriotic motives.

I believe it was at the conclusion of this Grand Council meeting that an Italian gentleman, the Baron di San Severino, addressed us on 'The Commercial relations between Italy and England'. He had come to England at the request of the Navy league and certain other interested organisations, and his visit provoked considerable attack from a section who claimed he was not behaving helpfully. This was another of the many occasions on which I wrote to the press to contradict ill-judged criticism. In the course of a two-months' visit, he addressed all the leading Chambers of Commerce and many organisations of varied kinds.

The Navy League was now greatly concerned with the advancement of aviation, and a mass meeting was held at the Queen's Hall (presided over by Mr. Yerburgh) to urge the necessity of having an adequate Air Force. A melancholy memory is the large number of gallant airmen whose lives were lost because their navigation instruments were inefficient. In those days, to fly a machine over the English countryside was almost as hazardous as a reconnaissance flight, in the same plane, over the German lines.

The famous Battle of Jutland remains one of the largest naval battles ever fought, and seldom has a naval engagement raised so much controversy. Our extensive losses were said to have turned victory into defeat, and the cranks and opponents of the Navy League seized upon this opportunity to declare the Navy incompetent and ineffective against Germany. On hearing the news of the Battle, and the public response, I sent an immediate message to Admiral Beatty congratulating him on the Navy's efforts under difficult conditions and assuring him of our loyal support. I then sent telegrams to the leading branches of the League all over the Empire, assuring them that the British Navy at Jutland had again vindicated its splendid tradition and secured a great naval triumph. In addition, I wrote to the press condemning the public for having judged the Battle before the official report was issued. This was actually made public in August, over two months later, and showed in truth that the Battle of Jutland had been a great British victory (although the casualty list was tragically large). Sorrow co-mingled with triumph as we contemplated that eventful action near the Skagerak.

Many valiant deeds have been recorded concerning the battle. One youthful hero was particularly admired and was posthumously awarded the V.C., John Travers Cornwall, of H.M.S. Chester. This ship was heavily shelled, and every man of the gun crew of which Cornwall was a member, now lay dead or dying. The boy (he was little more than sixteen years old) was mortally wounded, yet he continued to do his duty single-handed until he collapsed. His noble example was referred by Admiral Beatty in the official report, concluding thus: - "I recommend his case for special recognition, in justice to his memory and as an acknowledgement of this high example set by him."

A national committee was formed, with Mr. Yerburgh and myself representing the Navy League, to raise a fund to provide a memorial for this splendid lad. The money raised by school children alone, all over the country, totalled £21,000. About the same time as the Battle of Jutland, a gallant merchant seaman, named Captain Fryatt, saw directly in the path of his vessel an enemy submarine. With considerable courage and presence of mind he successfully rammed the submarine, but his action made him a marked man in German circles. Tragically, he was captured some months later, tried by court-martial and shot. The Navy League was largely responsible for the erection of a memorial to him, and one of the ways in which I personally helped to raise money for this project was a series of lantern lectures that I gave on the subject of the Navy.

The murder of Captain Fryatt once more stressed the obvious necessity for the arming of merchant ships. I did not cease my efforts until official recognition conceded the need to secure their self-defence. A deputation, of which I was a member, met the First Sea Lord in order to stress the extent to which submarine warfare had grown. We demanded a careful examination into the whole question, and were accorded an attentive hearing, which bore fruitful results.

On October 4th 1916, the institution of 'Sailors Day' took place, the existence of which the Navy League was responsible. With the war now beginning its third year, and showing signs of increasing ferocity, it was obvious that we must make still greater efforts to raise money for the various naval charities for which we were responsible and to find some new way to send further help to our sailors on active service. 'Sailors Day' met with a wonderful response throughout Great Britain, and the 13,000 flag sellers in various parts of the country brought in a magnificent sum of money. The following summer a journal called 'Sea Pie' was published, which we strongly supported, and which raised £1000 for comforts for prisoners of war.

Those of us who were in any way responsible for the youth of Great Britain (and who is not) became greatly alarmed at the appalling increase of juvenile crime during the war years. Adventure, boldness, and daring were in the air, and the unavoidable lack of parental discipline hindered the direction of youths' impetuous spirit into the right channels. I made the suggestion that a Committee should be appointed to investigate the matter, formed of representatives of organisations responsible for the welfare of boys, and during October this Committee (of which I became a member) held its first meeting, presided over by the Home Secretary, Mr. Herbert Samuel (later Viscount Samuel). Overwhelmed with work though I was, it was a joy to give this extra service to the youth of the country. Shortly before Christmas, on December 18th 1916, our beloved President Mr. Yerburgh died. It was a great loss to us all, and a personal and tragic blow to myself, and I missed him sorely. For sixteen years this fine and unselfish gentleman had put his whole heart into the progress and welfare of the League. He had given his energy, his money, his time, and at last his health, into making the League what it had now become. He never failed in his attendance at Navy League Executive Meetings, and was the ever-constant friend and champion of naval men.

Those members of the Navy League who can still recall his great personality, will remember him as a gentleman who was broad-minded, honourable, courteous and generous to a fault. He was beloved by all with whom he came into contact. Tributes poured into the Executive Offices from all parts of the world. I remember Lord Beresford saying of him, that if ever a man earned a peerage for loyal service to the Empire, that man was Mr. Yerburgh. His last message to the Navy League was to urge members to give their whole-hearted support to the Rt. Hon. David Lloyd George (the new Prime Minister). A window to his memory has been erected in the cloisters of Chester Cathedral, in which the badge of the Navy League and naval vessels of the Armada era are incorporated.

Before the next Grand Council Meeting, I was pressed to accept Presidency of the Navy League, but I refused, believing that I would be more useful as a humble and active Secretary. His Grace, The Duke of Buccleuch was, therefore, unanimously voted to fill the gap left by Mr. Yerburgh's death, an office which he filled with conspicuous success. One of the changes which Lloyd George made in the War Cabinet was the replacement of Lord Balfour by Sir Edward Carson, K.C. Almost immediately he proved himself a vigorous and able leader, who did much to restore confidence in the navy by his administration, but in June he was appointed to serve on the War Council, and Sir Eric Geddes took his place as First Sea Lord.

Having had such a dismal reception to my early recruiting campaign in Dublin, yet knowing what enormous numbers of Irishmen were fighting and dying for Great Britain, I still felt that there might be some means of inspiring their brothers to follow in their heroic footsteps. Accordingly, when Cardinal Davigh of Paris proposed that arrangements should be made to enlist Irish troops under the French flag, I undertook to submit this proposal to Cardinal Logue in Ireland. Shortt was then Chief Secretary for Ireland, and I went to the Castle to see him and explain this new scheme, but he would not commit himself one way or another. Cardinal Logue received me most kindly, so that I felt quite optimistic for the success of our proposal. But alas, the whole scheme was blown sky-high because recruitment could not be undertaken under the auspices of the Church.

I visited Dublin again, with Judge Meyer, at a very critical and dangerous period in the life of that city. Through various old friends I met Nationalist and Sinn Fein leaders, and exercised what influence I could through every possible channel. Especially did I plead for the stoppage of those disastrous Sinn Fein executions, and for the release of political prisoners. Besides being a most delicate and explosive situation to handle, it was a dread and terrible experience which has (and will) remain in my memory for my whole life.

Talking of Judge Meyer, he was one of the most dynamic people I have ever met. He was largely responsible for the conveyance of American troops and American supplies to the port of St. Nazaire after the United States came into the war, and he was immensely active in presenting the American point of view on the disturbed position in Ireland to leaders of both sides, Unionists and Nationalists alike.

The situation in Ireland was, of course, open to much speculation. Possibly the saddest chapter in the story of the British Commonwealth of Nations is the tragedy which Anglo-Irish relations underwent during, and after, the First World War. It would be difficult to imagine any more painful reading than the closing chapters in 'The Life of John Redmond' by Denis Gwynn. I could not, of course, agree with the policy of which Redmond was the most outstanding advocate, because I believed in the retention of Ireland in the British Empire, and it was one of the greatest sorrows in my life to speak in the final debate in the House of Commons when the Irish Republic was acknowledged. Redmond worked for Irish Home Rule during the whole of his public life. He was a man of the highest integrity, full of the spirit of self-sacrifice, and in every respect a great gentleman. No statesman or political leader, whom one can recall immediately, suffered a more harassing time than Redmond in the protracted negotiations which ultimately terminated in the exclusion of six counties (in Northern

141

Ireland) in the Irish Home Rule Act of 1917, and in the final establishment of an Irish Republic.

During 1913 and 1914 I became actively associated with various plans for the settlement of the Irish problem. I gave luncheons and conducted deputations to various Ministers and was in pretty constant contact with Colonel Maurice Moore, who was closely associated both with Sinn Fein and the Nationalists. He was a brother of George Moore, the novelist, and was just as vague and indefinite on political matters as George Moore was on the moral outlook of mankind. At one of my luncheons at St. Stephen's Club, a crowd of Irish representatives were present, and a great and serious row arose because of a 'Daily Mail' photographer who endeavoured to get a picture of our Meeting. It took me some time to emerge from this dose of hot water.

The Member for West Clare at this time was a retired British Colonel (Col. Lynch) who had been in the Irish Brigade (on the Boer side) during 1900-01. He was one of the most staggering humbugs I have encountered in my long acquaintance with that incompetent and politically sterile breed. It was my sad fate to bring this fellow over to Dublin on a recruiting campaign, along with Mr. James O'Grady (afterwards Governor of Tasmania and the Falkland Islands) shortly after the beginning of the war. Colonel Arthur Lynch was now enjoying his full freedom, restored to him sometime after being condemned to death as a rebel for his part in the South African war, and looked forward to curtailing the freedom of Dubliners (in the best possible cause) by outbursts of patriotic eloquence. Lynch, O'Grady and myself stayed at a small, second rate hotel (the Leinster Club, in Beresford Place) and the next day we held an open-air meeting. Never was there such a fiasco! Our audience consisted of eleven small boys who booed and jeered throughout the meeting, and no-one else. I was fairly well known in Dublin by a great many people on all sides of the political violence, but the introduction of my two colleagues made me a laughingstock wherever I appeared, and the whole expedition terminated in shouts of ironic laughter.

America's entry into the war gave us new heart to carry on our more tedious duties. Indeed, the tedium of routine was lightened by the various receptions and social events in connection with America's Navy League, functions I was by duty obliged to attend. Among other activities, we held a most successful recruiting campaign (lasting for one week from October 1881) in the Stratford-upon-Avon district which, in addition to its principal object of recruitment, also appealed for money to provide for the education of seamen's orphans.

During 1917, some distinguished Members of Parliament (who had seen much active service) took it upon themselves to form an association for Ex-Servicemen, and I became Organiser. After some preliminary talks, we decided upon the formation of the Society of 'The Comrades of the Great War', which later became (as most people know) the 'British Legion'. It is one of my happiest and proudest memories that I had the opportunity of founding and organising this community of men, who had suffered the misfortunes of warfare. The inaugural meeting took place at the Mansion House, on November 14th, with the Lord Mayor in the Chair. Sir Hamar Greenwood, M. P. (later Lord Greenwood) and Colonel Wilfred Ashley, M.P, were the principal speakers and I was with them on the platform. Here again, inevitably, came protests and criticisms. A Mr. Hoare wrote to 'The Times', contending that the organisation of 'The Comrades of the Great War' would interfere with the admirable work done by the Ministry of Pensions. He declared that an association such as this would involve complications, and implied that the sooner we abandoned the idea, the better for everyone. How very mistaken that gentleman was! My reply was published two days later, in which I pointed out that nothing was further from the Committee's mind than to hinder the Ministry of Pensions, and that 'The Comrades of the Great War' was formed to protect soldiers and sailors and to encourage 'esprit des corps' among them.

Dear old Sir John Norton-Griffiths made a sad 'faux pas' which (without consulting his colleagues on the Committee) invited contributions from a large number of people issued, without his consent, in the name of Lord Derby. His Lordship was furious, sent for me, and raged and fumed that I had not advised him of the action taken by Norton-Griffiths. I knew nothing whatever about it, and was then told that I should see Norton-Griffiths, make him apologise to Lord Derby, and at the next meeting of our Committee plead his enthusiasm as a pretext for taking Derby's name without consent. This action of 'Empire Jack' (as Norton Griffiths was always called) resulted in a cloudburst of cheques reaching Derby, amounting to several thousands of pounds. It took me a long time to throw oil on the troubled waters that arose, but we had the consolation of a substantial fund being created.

After a somewhat hectic existence, 'The Comrades' faded silently away, and the British Legion arose on the substructure which we had made. The beginning of 1918 was particularly notable for the Navy League, because of the change in the complement of Sea Lords. Admiral Sir Rosslyn Wemyss being appointed to the position of First Sea Lord in place of Admiral Jellicoe. We did not feel that this was a wise change, and we made it known that we believed Admiral Jellicoe to have been harshly treated, particularly by reports on the matter in the Press. In our defence of this great naval man, we stated that his service to the Nation was admirable, and that his conduct in leading the Fleet during these war years was magnificent, and he had maintained the noblest traditions of the Navy.

Early in the year, General Hubert Gough (commanding the Fifth Army) invited me to France to lecture to the troops on the immense' field of activity in which the Navy was engaged. I had a thrilling time, becoming a sort of liaison between the various fronts and being treated with great kindness by officers everywhere. In one of the sectors of the Front. I narrowly escaped sudden death from sharp-shooting, and got thoroughly 'wigged' for my indiscretion. The officer who had been put in charge of me was reprimanded for not having me under better control! But I was even luckier a short time later, for I left the Front just before the famous assault on the 21st of March, arriving home on March 22nd.

During those terrible four years of war, the tonnage of the Navy and Mercantile Fleets had increased from two and a half million tons to seven million tons, and the personnel from something over one hundred thousand to half a million. I can safely say that a large percentage of this increase in the personnel was due to the Navy League's recruiting campaigns. Over two hundred and fifty thousand men were secured by the League for the R.N., R.N.D.,

R.N.V.R. and Mercantile Marine. Out of a total of twenty million men conveyed across the seas to war areas, but three thousand, two hundred and sixty-two were lost. The figures speak for themselves.

I can never thank enough the generosity of all who responded so magnificently to our appeals for Funds. I myself was responsible for raising £600,000 in the various war charities for which I was organiser. It was a constant wonder and joy to me how, time and again, we received the money that we needed so badly from those who could least afford it. Rich and poor united in supporting the 'Ladies Emergency Fund', the 'Overseas Relief Fund', the 'Sailors Day Fund' and all the other charities for which appeals were raised by the Navy League.

My last public function as General Secretary to the Navy League was on October 26th 1918, when I opened the new headquarters of the Hackney Branch Naval Boys Brigade. Officially I had resigned in July, but I kept on with the work until the end of October to allow for the choice of my successor, who was Rear-Admiral Ross-Benson. For the last little while I had been attempting to carry on work in two entirely different organisations, the Navy League and the British Commonwealth Union (about which I shall have a good deal to say in the next chapter or two). I could not become officially attached to the B.C.U. in any active capacity because it was a political movement, and I did not wish to bring politics into the Navy League. This was a thing that had to be avoided at all costs. Nevertheless, I was connected with the Movement from the very start (behind the scenes so to speak) and the time had now come to concentrate on one rather than the other.

I was sorry indeed to relinquish my work with the League, it had become a part of my life. But I had accomplished that which I had set out to do, the war was nearly at an end and the 'Two keels to one' campaign had served its purpose. Intensive recruiting and energy expended on aiding war charities would soon be a thing of the past. England would need an industrial revival if her wounds were speedily to be healed, and it was with this in the forefront of my mind that I sent in my resignation.

On June 12th 1919, 1 was the honoured guest at a luncheon given at Prince's Restaurant by the Navy league, where I was profoundly moved by the very generous tributes paid to me and by the magnificent Presentation made by the Duke of Somerset. We were a very happy band that day, the war was over and we could look back upon the work we had achieved. Lord Ampthill was present, and Rear Admiral Benson, Wilfrid Ashley, Professor Pollard and a host of others also. I was presented with a cheque to cover the cost of purchasing a motorcar and, in addition, a magnificent gift of silver. It was a joy to me to learn that subscriptions had been sent from far-away overseas branches, and that I had so many unseen friends. In mentioning, The Duke of Somerset became President of the Navy League in 1919 upon the resignation of the Duke of Buccleuch. In resigning from the office of Secretary I remained, however, upon the Executive Committee for the space of three years.

The beginning of 1919 saw Great Britain (in an effort to restore financial stability) proposing to reduce the Cabinet by placing the War Office, the Admiralty and the Air Ministry under one head. The Executive of the Navy League took strong objection to this, for we claimed for the Navy the greatest share of glory in the Allies victory, and we deplored the suggested reconstruction of these Departments. I recall passing a resolution to this effect, in which I declared that to take such a step would tend towards a serious blow at the prestige of the British Empire among the nations of the world. To allow a decline in the full status and privileges of the Admiralty was tantamount to slighting the untarnished record and high traditions of the Navy, which must automatically lose the deep respect accorded her by the rest of the world. Of course, in most quarters the whole idea was very unpopular, and the Navy League was not by any means alone in its forthright criticism.

Mr. V. Tatton, who had devotedly and unsparingly given his time to the work of the Navy League, sent in his resignation some while later. Although in the latter part of my association with the League I did not subscribe to his views, he undoubtedly had done great work with the Imperial Service College, and subsequently with the Herts. Navy League. He came to the Head Office to take up the duties of Hon. Treasurer, and later attained the position of Chairman of the Executive Committee. My last year on the executive of the Navy League was an unhappy one, for circumstances arose that led ultimately to many resignations. The post-war policy of the League differed so much from the pre-war policy, and many of us could not see our way to supporting it. In vain we strove to prevent the League from committing suicide, as we saw it, and numerous were the Committee Meetings held in 1921 and 1922 to try to save the situation.

The Washington Naval Conference (to discuss the reduction in the building of ships of all nations) took place towards the end of the year 1921, and I asked the Executive Committee to pass a vote of confidence in the British Delegation attending it. My proposal was defeated by four votes to three whereupon, feeling that matters had now gone too far, I resigned from the Executive. At the next meeting of the Grand Council, Rear-Admiral Ingram proposed a vote of confidence in the Executive, endorsing the new policy of the Navy League. I hastily proposed an amendment: namely, that the Grand Council, although the governing body of the League, had not been convened or consulted as to the recent changes of policy, and therefore, it should be declared that: -

1. No change in the policy of the League as affecting British sea power (or its maintenance) shall in future take place, until such change has been definitely approved by the Grand Council of the Navy League.

2. The Navy League shall support with its whole organisation, the single power standard which in the view of H.M. Admiralty is the minimum consistent with national safety, and which has been approved as such by Act of Parliament.

3. The propagandist and educational works of the Navy League shall be devoted to the cultivation of public opinion, and to the efficiency and sufficiency of the Fleet, and to the history and traditions of the British Sea service.

4. The Navy League shall cease forthwith any association with the League of Nations Union, or any similar body.

I did not wish my remarks to be in any way injurious to the spirit of the old League, to which I was still devoted, but I very much resented the change of policy having been blatantly announced in two columns of 'The Times', when we were assured by Navy League Officers that no change whatever had been made. In all common sense this showed shocking inconsistency, and in any case, the publicity of the Manifesto was an act in excess of their powers. It amounted to a grotesque declaration to the public that, now the war was over, the Navy must be relegated to a position of obscurity. In view of the sweeping reductions suggested in the personnel of the Navy, the silence of the League on such a grave matter placed it in a position that could no longer be expected to retain the confidence of the British public.

A good many of us felt that the Executive had been making stealthy changes without consulting the Grand Council, and it was only reasonable and sensible to insist on the clause in my amendment, that no decision in regard to policy should be taken without the Council's approval. With regard to the Clause concerning the League of Nations, I felt it would be an indiscreet act for the Navy League to associate itself with this newly formed organisation, and might put us in a very delicate position. I had nothing against the League of Nations, but at that moment we were considering national, not international policy. Above all I urged that the Executive committee ginger up their activities, and let us have a policy of realism, not idealism. Considering that the executive of the Navy League had done nothing to identify themselves with the views of the Dominion delegates who had recently visited Great Britain, nor offered helpful suggestions towards the Washington Conference, this did not seem to me to be asking too much. Their actions (and lack of actions) in the past six months, had gone near to making the League a public jest. I'm glad to say that my amendment was carried.

However, this did not end the matter. Indeed, the worst was yet to come. The Chairman declared that my amendment was technically out of order, as he had received it only at a moment's notice, but he was good enough to propose that he should not make any decisions until he had conferred with his colleagues and reported to the Grand Council. At the Annual Meeting held two months later, Mr. Tritton accused me of being unfair to the Executive, and said that there was not a representative gathering on that occasion. I replied that this day we had come together not to condemn the Executive, but to help it to save and reconstruct the League. The financial position was extremely grave, indeed there was insufficient money in hand to pay staff salaries in full, and I suggested appealing once more for Funds. In April, the Executive Committee (which had been re-elected by 36 votes to 25) met again to continue their deliberations, but I was not present, my resignation from the Grand Council having now become effective. Among those who supported me in this unhappy controversy were Commander Salmond, Professor Bostock Hill, Colonel Gretton, M.P., Miss Gordon-Barrett, and a host of others (many of whom ultimately resigned from the League, including Admiral Fremantle and my old and valued friend, Arnold White). It was a sad way to end up my twelve years association with this great organisation.

CHAPTER 7

Under the arrangement of constituencies in 1918, the Mosely Division of Birmingham came into existence. It included a large area in the former East Worcestershire Division, which had been represented for many years by Sir Austen Chamberlain. For this new Division, Sir Hallewell Rogers was returned to the House of Commons by over 1200 votes.

Naturally, I took an active part in his campaign, for it may be remembered that he was the Chairman of the Executive Committee of the British Commonwealth Union. We became devoted friends. He had been Lord Mayor of Birmingham in 1902 and '03 and had been knighted by King Edward VII. He was largely instrumental in the building of the Gas Department, which was the largest municipal business of its kind in the world. In the closing months of 1920, Sir Hallewell felt the demands upon his time in the public service did not justify his continuance in Parliament. Although regularly in attendance in the House, he was not a very active Member from the point of view of either question or speech. So Sir Hallewell applied for the 'Stewardship of the Chiltern Hundreds' and resigned.

It was his particular anxiety that I should succeed him. A good deal of quiet negotiation took place, as I had no claim whatever for acceptance for a Birmingham constituency, and had to present myself in the frequently unenvious guise of a 'carpet-bagger'.

There were various potential contestants for so attractive a seat. The fortune of the 'carpet-bagger' was in the main dependent upon the support of the Conservative and Central Unionist Office. As a Unionist before the amalgamation of the Conservative and Unionist Parties, I enjoyed the particular friendship of John Boraston (the Chief Unionist Agent), a man of great charm and high personal character. After exchanges of views with the political leaders, I was adopted. I now recall with particular pleasure, gratitude and amusement, that the Selection Committee composed of three ladies and five gentlemen. Their function was to test my appearance and quality as a political exhibit, suited for recommendation to the general body of the local Executive Committee.

My previous career and experience implied some commodity value as a possible Member of Parliament. Following my selection by the smaller Committee, the Editor of 'The Birmingham Post' gave me a full-blooded advertisement with a catalogue of those activities in which I had played some part heretofore. The announcement of a new candidate for a safe Division of the city in this slapdash way excited considerable interest, not merely in the Moseley Division, but in Birmingham generally, and my life story became a topic of daily conversation, pending the meeting of the General Committee.

Two or three features of my preparation for this first contest may not be without interest. I had the great privilege (after my return from South Africa) of the enjoyment of the friendship and generous and kindly interest of the late Mr. Leo Amery. No man could have had a more loyal, kindly, or a more helpful friend. In offering myself for the Moseley Division I was given his full support and, more than that, he commended me to the friendly consideration of both Austen and Neville Chamberlain. In submitting my application as a candidate I had the support of these three statesmen. Mr. Amery signed a statement to which the names of some forty members of the House of Commons were attached, urging my acceptance upon the local Committee. Austen Chamberlain wrote to the local Chairman of the Moseley Division that he would be pleased to see me returned to the House of Commons, and Neville Chamberlain made clear to the Unionist leader in Birmingham that I could be regarded as an acceptable candidate.

The fateful day soon arrived and the meeting, under the presidency of Sir Cornelius Chambers, took place at the Grand Hotel. There was a crowded attendance, and I waited with somewhat mixed feelings for a considerable time in the lounge of the hotel before I was invited to face the gathering and vindicate the decision of the Selection Committee. I made a careful and, I hope, thoughtful speech, softened and simplified by full confession of my absence of substantial claim to represent the Moseley Division, but with a confident assurance that in the discharge of a great responsibility and the fulfilment of a great trust, I would give entire service. Among other matters, I spoke at some length upon the recent Budgets, analysing the spending of public departments and strongly protesting against the unfair and unjust attacks made upon Austen Chamberlain, who was then Chancellor of the Exchequer. On the whole, despite some opposition and a certain amount of bitter comment on the fact that a local candidate was not forthcoming, there was a sympathetic murmur of friendly feeling throughout the Meeting. And so I retired to await the momentous decision, to

be enthusiastically greeted on my re-entering the room and learning that the resolution of my adoption had been unanimously passed. Austen Chamberlain, in his letter to the Council, had written: -

"I feel a little delicacy in saying anything in my position as Honorary President of the Moseley Divisional Association which the Council might consider as an attempt to interfere with their free choice, but, they having decided to ratify the selection of Mr. Hannon, we shall have another active member added to our Birmingham team, a man who has taken a great and intelligent interest in political questions and whom all his Birmingham colleagues will welcome to the House."

Thus I entered, encouraged and exhilarated upon my election campaign.

Troubles, however, soon began to arise. Some members of the Ratepayers Association, who believed that the public money was being wasted, suggested Mr. Laurence Tipper (an anti-waste champion) as my opponent. He was a well-known Birmingham manufacturer of veterinary products, and President of the Chamber of Agriculture. He had previously fought twice as a candidate in Yorkshire constituencies, and now immediately put himself forward as an Independent. He was a forceful personality, full of great vitality, boundless energy, and an amazing faculty of speech. For the moment it appeared that a contest was inevitable, and I proceeded to develop the full machinery incidental to an election battle. Apart from an Election Address, this entailed a voluminous collection of what is called 'literature' in election times, with posters displaying my photograph, hoardings engaged for their exhibition, schools rented for evening meetings, and the varied details of expense which compose the financial burden attached to Parliamentary elections. As for Mr. Tipper, he declared that he had an organisation that would paralyse Mr. Hannon.

Seeing that I was not withering before his fire, he put forward an extraordinary proposal. He was, he announced, prepared to accept any two streets in Moseley (which we would mutually agree upon) in which two persons should enquire at every doorway for whom the occupiers would vote. These votes were to be duly recorded, and he was prepared to abide by the result. He hoped that I would feel that his proposal was a perfectly reasonable one and would accept it, thus avoiding a contest. Unfortunately for Mr. Tipper. I could not see that the political vote of the constituency could be 'perfectly reasonably' determined upon by the residents of two of its streets, and so I continued in my campaign.

On, the day of nomination, however, my original and forceful opponent did not appear, and I was declared 'returned unopposed' by the charming and kindly Lord Mayor of Birmingham, Mr. Cadbury (the returning officer) in one of the rooms of the City Council building. Mr. Laurence Tipper, now passed away, became afterwards a warm and fast friend, and we were associated in many interesting projects together. He had publicly stated that his reason for not handing in his nomination on the appropriate day was that the life of the present Parliament was so uncertain that it would be folly for him to incur the expenditure of thousands of pounds, only to have to repeat this within perhaps a few months. I used to venture to remind him, from time to time, of the hundreds of pounds which my first election contest placed upon my own limited resources, owing to the thunderous threats which he had poured forth against the impudence of a perfect stranger offering himself as a candidate for so fascinating a seat in Parliament as that provided by the Moseley constituency.

It may not perhaps be inopportune to say a word about the financial arrangements which were operative for the conduct of Parliamentary activity in Birmingham. In my early years in Parliament, each member made a yearly contribution of £250 to the central organisation, but in later years this was re-adjusted so that £150 was paid to the central body and £100 to the local constituency committee. Anyway, in Birmingham during the whole of my time the main burden of the finance of Conservative political vitality fell upon the Members of Parliament except, of course, at election times when special appeals were made by Mr. Neville Chamberlain, and substantial sums were contributed for the general purposes of the electoral campaign. It was a fact, however, that the election expenses in my case (and so far as I am aware, in that of the other members) had to be borne by the members themselves.

To close this account of this part of my life adventure, I was introduced into the House of Commons by the two Chamberlains (Austen and Neville), an incident which I don't think was repeated in the case of any other member either before or after I entered Parliament. That moment when I entered the House and walked up to the table carrying the blue paper certifying my election, was one which I have always remembered with humble pride.

Immediately upon my being made a Member of Parliament, I rather rashly advertised that I would be glad to meet any of my constituents who might need help. The result of this gesture was surprising. People came to me with the oddest requests. The object of my invitation had been to dispel the current apathy and disinterest of the people in those great questions that faced the country. But I found that my time was being wasted by those who came to give (rather than take) advice, or by people with personal problems. For example ... the woman who, left servant-less, wanted me to propose a Bill that factory girls be ordered to become domestic workers. I recall also an aggressive individual who enthusiastically advocated free football matches as a means of avoiding strikes. But among those who came to see me was a deputation concerning the Barnes Report Proposal, that ex-officers should secure work through the Labour exchanges, and to this naturally I could give full attention and sympathy, as the ordinary Labour exchange facilities were not adequate to meet the cases. I also entered into discussion with the leading commercial men of Birmingham, when the Key Industries and Collapsed Exchange Bill was introduced into the House, which was found to be very helpful.

I came into the house while Mr. Lloyd George was still basking in the full floodlight of popular favour. Seeing and hearing him speak (he made many admirable speeches before the collapse of the coalition) one can never forget his wonderful 'mans' vitality, and expressive oratorical faculty.

He was very kind to me personally. I remember him referring, more than once, to his adventurous night in Birmingham during his pro-Boer campaign!

Indeed, many years later, I had the privilege of presenting to him in Birmingham the late Sir Charles Rafter (Chief Constable) who played a prominent part in the Town Hall scenes from which Lloyd George emerged in the ill-fitting uniform of a policeman. During the course of a banquet in Birmingham, Lloyd George turned towards Rafter while making his speech and cried: - "I salute my Chief." In his bitterest moods Lloyd George was redeemed in public by his sense of humour.

Of the remaining Members of that Coalition Cabinet, and of ministers who were not included in the Cabinet, nearly all have passed away. Within a fortnight of my entry into the House, Mr. Bonar Law retired through ill-health, and there were several candidates for the position of leader of the Conservative Party. Austen Chamberlain had previously stood aside when the question of leadership was involved, but now (on the grounds of long experience and parliamentary distinction, and above all, of the loftiest conception of public life) his claim was foremost in our minds, and he was duly elected Leader. Sir Robert Home became Chancellor of the Exchequer, Mr. Balfour (later Earl) was Lord President of the Council, Viscount Birkenhead (later Earl) was Lord Chancellor, and of the others, Sir Winston Churchill is the sole survivor. Leslie Wilson (who was joint Chief Whip with Charles McCordy) shortly afterwards became Governor of Bombay and later continued his valuable Imperial service as Governor of Queensland. Freddie Guest, who was Secretary for Air, and a very loveable person, died all too soon.

Sir Alan Smith (who went to the House a year before me, and who was Chairman of the Engineering and National Employers Federation and the Chairman of my Executive Committee of the British Commonwealth Union) was my constant colleague and companion In the multitude of questions affecting trade and industry. The Industrial Group in the House of Commons, of which I have made mention in another chapter, ardently supported the 'Safeguarding of Industries Act' which was introduced by Mr. Stanley Baldwin, and it was on the second reading of this Bill that I made my maiden speech. I am bound to say here what has been said in thousands of instances by Members of their maiden speeches, that I approached the ordeal in a condition of mind difficult to understand or explain, but as near to mental trepidation and physical knocking of the knee as if I were arraigned for some grave violation of the law before a bench of Judges. To my surprise, the Member who spoke immediately after me was kind enough to declare (in referring to my speech) that I had already acquired what is known as the Parliamentary manner!

The experience of House of Commons procedure, and the cut and thrust of debate in Standing Committee affords valuable training in the early years of a Member in the House, and there are, of course, opportunities to make speeches on special features of a particular Bill. Sir Eric Geddes, the Minister of Transport, undertook the promotion of a great scheme of railway amalgamation, which was ultimately the creation of the four great railway groups which served the country so well for a full quarter of a century, until their nationalisation.

Eric Geddes had a virile character and was a glutton for work. He formed around him a small group of Members to steer the Railway Bill through the House. Private meetings and conferences took place almost daily, and my particular job was to assist in balancing the interests of industry and commerce in a fair and square deal with the railways. The Standing Committee on the Bill lasted for some months, and Lloyd George was so irritated by the obstruction in the Committee (on the part of the railways' representative) that the Committee was reconstituted in two parts, and I served on both. Indeed, 1921 was for me a year packed with continuous activity. For, apart from the several Committees on which I served, I gave a good deal of time to the Constituency and to constant attendance in the House.

The complex problem of the industrial situation perhaps overshadowed all other problems of the day, for the whole country was in the grip of a trade slump, which was in those days quite unprecedented. Pessimism seemed to be the prevailing fashion, and the prophets of ill surrounded us on every hand. The country held an enormous stock of manufactured goods, which had been produced at a time when all costs were abnormally high, and were consequently un-saleable owing to the state of the world's markets. Those countries that were in a position to produce goods, and could offer them at the cheapest terms, were naturally obtaining a very large proportion of the trade available. Germany happened to be in that particular position. She was, in plain fact, enjoying a comparative boom in trade. From the point of view of competition in the export trade, the cost of production in Germany was about a third of that in Birmingham. To add to the industrial difficulties came the coal strike, lasting from April to July 1921, which arose primarily from the governmental control of the industry. One of my earliest speeches to my constituents concerned this matter. Somehow or other we had to rouse the interest of the world's buyers to the fact that the quality of British goods should make a greater appeal than the quantity of cheap foreign productions, although the shortage of ready money was hampering us at every turn.

It was, therefore, with great boldness and optimism that a Conference, called in July, decided upon holding a British Empire Trade Exhibition throughout the summer months in a permanent place which, when the Exhibition was over, could become a home for other exhibitions and for athletics, the primary object being to demonstrate the possibilities of the future. So it was that, in 1923, the great British Empire Exhibition came before the public gaze in Wembley Park, and during the preceding year-and-a half I worked on its Executive Council on the many complex and peculiar problems of its organisation.

Another matter which engaged some proportion of my time concerned a scheme proposed by Neville Chamberlain for the reform of the House of Lords. Towards the end of March a discussion had arisen in the House of Lords upon that question (in reference to the King's speech), and Lord Selborne moved that the Government be urged to introduce their measure for reform in time for it to be dealt with adequately during the early summer. He was strongly supported in his proposal. Thus it came about that Chamberlain asked me to prepare the data for him, and sent me the following note: -

"Dear Paddy,
Herewith is the Schedule, and a note as to what I wanted.
Thanks so much for
undertaking the job.
Yours ever
Neville Chamberlain."

"Second Chamber Reform:
On the assumption that a reformed Second Chamber would
contain about 200 members directly elected, it is proposed that they
should sit for ten years, half their number retiring every five years.
In the First Chamber, half the number could only sit for five years.

It is further proposed that all constituencies should be either two
or four member constituencies, so that the representation of each
should not be entirely changed at any election, but half the number
only should retire. The problem is to arrange the constituencies, and
it is suggested that this should take two factors into account, viz:
population and territorial.

Large county boroughs such as Glasgow, Birmingham,
Manchester, Liverpool etc. would form two or four member
constituencies. Counties which do not contain the requisite
population to provide a double member constituency would have to
be grouped, but regard must be paid to the area which it is
reasonably possible to cover in one constituency. Sparsely populated
Districts in the North of Scotland might have to be somewhat over-
represented as regards population, in order to preserve the territorial
claim.

The accompanying schedule was proposed in connection with
another scheme involving proportional representation. P.R is not in
question now that the document contains useful information about
population, though compiled before the war.

Ireland need not be taken into account.
N. C."

The matter of far-reaching reform has, of course, cropped
up again and again in greater urgency as the years go on. It
was a year or so later, I believe, that the House of Lords spent
a considerable part of July in discussing resolutions for
Reform, during which it was pointed out that over a hundred
Members of the House had not bothered (or were unable
through youthfulness or infirmity) to take their places. When
Walter Bagehot wrote his 'English Constitution' he declared: -

"The danger of the House of Commons is, perhaps, that it may be reformed too rashly; the danger of the House of Lords certainly is that it may never be reformed. Nobody asks that it should be so; it is quite safe against rough destruction, but it is not safe against inward decay … Its danger is not in assassination, but atrophy; not abolition, but decline."

And here I may refer to a tragic matter which is brought to mind by Chamberlain's closing line: - "Ireland need not be taken into account." For this was 1921, and the Irish problem was uppermost in our minds, and Ireland had very much to be taken into account in matters relating to policy and trade. Indeed, the bitter situation of my country was very nearly responsible for bringing about a split in the Coalition government. The fear that Civil War there might not be averted was my constant unwelcome companion, But the influence of the Irish question extended far beyond Ireland. Our future prestige depended upon our policy in relation to that country. During the previous year, the Coalition government recognising (perhaps for the first time) that there were in Ireland two utterly opposing communities, framed the 'Government of Ireland Act', in which each of these communities was given local self-government.

The Act was passed, and the Coalition hoped that their effort might at last be successful in ending the controversy. But neither party was in the least satisfied, the Ulstermen declaring frankly that they could not accept any such measure, and the Sinn Fein Party denouncing the Act as one of Partition (which, indeed, it became). It has never been possible for England to solve Ireland's problems, and Ireland herself was in such a state of frustrated anger and ill-directed rage that she was being toppled over into the turmoil of Civil War by her revolutionary leaders.

The years 1921 and '22 were full of thrill and throb in Parliamentary life. A powerful section of the Conservative Party was determined to bring the Coalition administration to an end. As Secretary of the Industrial Group in the House, which was composed entirely of Conservatives, and all of whom resolved to extend the policy of Tariff Reform and Imperial unity, I became somewhat prominently identified with the political manoeuvres which were incidental to impending political clash.

Austen Chamberlain (as Leader of the House of Commons, and of the Conservative Coalition Members) was averse from an attack upon Lloyd George and the bulk of the Coalition Government. He was supported in this point of view by Lord Birkenhead and Mr. Walter Long. Walter Long (as he then was) wrote me a very full letter from Paris in which he reviewed in considerable detail the problems before the country, and the urgent need of National unity and, consequently, the importance of maintaining the Coalition. In consultation with several colleagues, I issued an invitation to a large number of Unionist members who were known to support the Coalition. Sir Edward Goulding (later Lord Wargrave) supported me in taking this course, at a meeting in Committee Room 14. He was one of my intimate friends, one to whom I owe much, and the man who played a dominant part in the political ups and downs of this testing time in the life of the Conservative Party.

In a difficult and embarrassing situation, I committed an ill-considered and thoughtless blunder. I decided that in addition to those eight or so M.P.s invited to attend the meeting (which was convened for the clear and definite purpose of supporting Lloyd George) I should invite the whole body of Conservative backbenchers. Accordingly, I left a note in the cloakroom indicating that all Members of the Conservative Party would be welcome at the meeting. The result was one of the most crowded meetings of the Tory Party held in the House of Commons in my time. I tried to get Ernest Pretyman to take the chair, but he declined, and after some difficulty the late, much respected Sir Samuel Roberts (Member for the Eccleshall Division of Sheffield) presided. Notwithstanding the great respect in which he was held by all sections of the House, he had much difficulty in the management of what (in plain, common fact) was a disorderly meeting, and there was little he could do to quell the outburst of a violent storm, during which it was quite clear that the majority of the Conservative Party desired to be freed from the shackles of the Coalition with Lloyd George.

The rumblings and grumblings of dissatisfaction with the method by which the meeting was convened, as well as by the object of the meeting itself, found expression in a tumultuous attack upon those responsible for the gathering, and upon myself in particular. Indeed, one of my secretary colleagues at the British Commonwealth Union, whom I had brought with me to make notes of the proceedings, was obliged to leave the meeting on cries of a 'stranger' being present. I read Walter Long's letter, not without continuous interruption, and, although of all the Conservative leaders Walter Long occupied an eminent place in confidence and esteem, the views to which he gave expression were received not merely coldly, but by a hum of resentment which spread over the greater part of those present.

The Resolution which I had hoped to have adopted was in fact defeated by a large majority, and Sir Samuel Roberts and I left the meeting fully convinced that the days of the Coalition were numbered. As for myself, I was indeed taking a thorny and obscure pathway in the world of politics, and I can never forget the atmosphere of misery in which I found myself having to face a barrage of newspaper men from the Gallery and Lobby, to whom the result of the meeting was, of course, front page news. I had a miserable time with Leslie Wilson (the Chief Whip) in the preparation of the somewhat colourless statement to the press, partly an apology and partly a lame summary of the proceedings, which satisfied nobody and which gave rise to a flood of comment and criticism in Parliament, as well as in the Press. This was a depressing, not to say painful incident, in my early years in the House, and although Lloyd George said some complimentary things to me afterwards, it was poor reward for a temporary loss of friendship with the majority of the Conservative Party. In my opinion the Coalition Government, despite its sins of omission and commission, had achieved great things and was the only one that had, so to speak, paid its way.

By October 1922, a general Election was obviously imminent. As a result of a meeting in the Carlton Club (at which a resolution was passed declaring that the Conservative Party would fight the pending election with its own leader and according to its own programme) the Prime Minister tendered his resignation and Bonar Law was invited to form a Ministry. For my own part I was again adopted for Moseley and carried on a pretty vigorous campaign to find myself returned unopposed for the second time. The Unionist Party were returned to power, with Bonar Law heading the new Government, yet the Labour Party had unexpectedly gained many victories.

Let me give some account of the Birmingham Group after the break-up of the Coalition. We were then twelve Unionists, four of whom were (or subsequently became) Cabinet Ministers. In pride of place stood Austen Chamberlain, who became Lord Privy Seal and who was regarded not merely by his colleagues, but by the whole House of Commons, as one of the great gentlemen of our time. His wisdom, judgement, and broad outlook on foreign and domestic politics commanded universal respect. I was indebted to him for many marks of kindly consideration, and I feel from time to time an acute pang of regret that I failed to adhere (at grave moments in my political career) to the gentle and wise counsel which I received from him. His brother Neville (who became Postmaster General, and of whom I shall say a great deal in the course of these recollections) was an outstanding example to us all in his industry, and in his maintenance of the highest conception of public service.

Mr. Leo Amery became First Lord of the Admiralty. I always regarded him as my political Godfather, combining great personal charm with singular intellectual power and political foresight of uncommon quality. Sir Arthur Steel-Maitland (who became Minister of Labour) had been a Member for the city and was returned unopposed. He was always a warm and helpful friend, and his early death caused profound regret in Birmingham, and in particular to his parliamentary colleagues. Then there was Sir Herbert Austin (who later became a peer) and whose generosity in the promotion of scientific research will be a lasting tribute to his memory. He was Member for Kings Norton, but owing to the exigencies of the great enterprise with which he was associated, he gave little time to the House of Commons (and was indeed unknown to many of its members). On one occasion our Chief Whip, Leslie Wilson, asked me if I would introduce Sir Herbert to him, when that honourable colleague made an appearance in the House.

Our senior Member was the Rt. Hon Sir Evan Cecil, an interesting and delightful personality who sat for the Aston Division for several years. He rendered a variety of valuable public service, both in the House and outside, in many capacities. We had that fine example of the Birmingham businessman and devoted friend of the ex-serviceman, Sir John Smedley-Crooke, who happily stayed with us, and whom it was a joy to meet from time to time after his retirement into the quiet enjoyment of his Worcestershire retreat. Sir Ernest Hiley became Member for Duddeston. He had formerly been Town Clerk of Birmingham, but, during the First World War, joined Mr. Dudley Docker's great industrial organisation, the Birmingham Small Arms Co., and rendered valuable service in the conversion of war production to peace.

Sir Francis Lowe (up to the time of his resignation in 1924) sat for Edgbaston, and had long been Member for that Unionist stronghold. He had been intimate friend of Mr. Joseph Chamberlain, and served the interests of the City with devoted zeal until his retirement. Then we had that gay and gallant champion of many great causes, Commander Locker-Lampson, a fascinating companion but sometimes, I fear, rather indifferent to his political responsibility. The team also included a vigorous and forceful representative of what, for want of a better term, may be called working-class Birmingham. This was Alderman Jephcott, self-educated and with a high sense of public duty, who had long rendered service on the City Council by which he gained experience of the problems affecting the relations between capital and labour, which was decidedly helpful in the constantly recurring labour questions which ever and anon arose in the House of Commons.

And thus we stood in 1922 after the General Election, facing the House (with the solitary exception to which I have referred with all the politeness that I can command). We were in constant consultation among ourselves on all matters which directly or indirectly affected the welfare of Birmingham. In slightly lighter vein we called ourselves the 'Birmingham Club', and met frequently for dinners together, to which we often invited the editors of some of the leading Provincial newspapers.

CHAPTER 8

In the early autumn of 1924 the British Commonwealth Union, in conjunction with the Federation of British Industries, sent my good friend Sir Philip Dawson and myself to central Europe to study the prevailing conditions. We spent thirty-five days touring Germany, Czechoslovakia, and Austria, examining the social and economic conditions of every leading centre. It was a most interesting and unforgettable trip, during which we were welcomed most kindly and given every co-operation in our work. In Austria we were received by the President, and had a long conversation with Dr Frank, the Chancellor. The economic situation of that country was in chaos. The old feudal system had been overthrown and no stabilising influence had risen to take its place, but we were given every facility for investigation, and in Vienna a splendid suite of rooms was put at our disposal by the Austrian Chamber of Commerce.

Our tour began in Cologne, however, and from there we went on to Dusseldorf and the other large manufacturing centres. We met leading manufactures in their Chambers of Commerce, and representatives of manufacturing organisations. We interviewed representatives of all the political parties including, if I remember rightly, the Chairman of the Communist group in the Reichstag. It was obvious to us that the whole industrial situation in Germany was unstable. At first glance one was aware of an absence of unemployment, but this gave quite a false impression of prosperity, for the public service had absorbed officials to the point of saturation, and every municipality was in a state of virtual bankruptcy. It was tragic to find that the splendid system of agricultural credit which, originating in Germany and helping agricultural co-operation in so many countries, had now been destroyed. Indeed, the system of saving money, however little, was now beyond the capabilities of ninety-nine per cent of the adult population.

We asked the leading German bankers the same question: - "Could they suggest a proposal to restore German currency to a stable basis preparatory to inspiring confidence abroad?" but inevitably received the same answer: - "No." In short, the industry of that country could not carry the weight of the people it employed, an extraordinary economic paradox. The Mark was, of course, a source of vast speculation and gambling, and everywhere the appalling situation gave rise to subdued political agitation, particularly from the Russians. We were glad to find that the majority of public men held a deep respect for Britain, and often a rather pathetic belief that she could help the country to rise from the slough of despond. In Czechoslovakia the situation was entirely different and far more cheerful. Their government had tackled the problem of organising a new nation in the most efficient and statesmanlike way. On our return, the observations we had presented to the B.C.U. were forwarded to the Prime Minister.

The following year I again visited Berlin during a tour which was chiefly devoted to the new republics on the Baltic, with whom we contemplated commencing trade negotiations. The economic collapse of Germany seemed imminent. I remember asking the price of certain articles in Berlin shops and being quoted a price in dollars, the shopkeepers refusing to sell when I offered them Marks. And not only shopkeepers, but also individuals of every class were graspingly eager to get possession of foreign currency from the tourists who were crowding into the country. A collapsed Germany would profoundly affect the economy of the whole continent, not excluding our own, and it was with great uneasiness that I returned to England. Part of the blame lay with the French who had (much against the British advice) occupied the Ruhr, thus cutting off the main source of Germany's industrial power. Germans, thus thrown out of employment, were being paid full Trade Union wages by the German government, but no money could be found to pay war reparations, either to France or ourselves, and we were already feeling the effects.

It was not until the late summer of the following year that the evacuation of the Ruhr was ordered, and this was not accomplished until halfway through 1925. I had a long discussion with Herr von Raumer (one of the most famous economists in the Germany of that date) in which the subject of reparations came up, and he had to admit that his country had not made one real sincere effort to pay. It seemed to me that when the Germans deflated the Mark they imagined that they were employing a 'safety razor' to rid themselves of difficulties, but this 'safety razor' was now cutting their own throats. The Industrial Group in the House of Commons met to consider the great question of international debts, and the memorandum that we prepared stressed the disruptive influence caused by them. The indebtedness of one nation to another was a source not only of economic insecurity, but even of war itself.

Our suggestions to deal with the matter included a World Conference to be summoned by the United States of America, at which certain debts should be ordered to be paid, and others cancelled. We in the Industrial Group were very worried about the rapidly growing number of unemployed persons in Great Britain, and a letter was sent to the Prime Minister urging that immediate work be started upon various transport schemes already proposed, such as the electrification of the London and South-West Railways. As is always the case in the black days of a country's life, numbers of skilled men were leaving the country to obtain work abroad, particularly in the U.S.A. The Imperial Economic Conference, convened by the Chamber of Commerce, was trying to deal with the unemployment situation through the means of expansion of Empire trade and Empire preference. Foreign competition in the home trade, which ought to have been relieved by the immediate imposition of import duties upon foreign goods, was largely the cause of this deplorable situation. The opening of the British Empire Exhibition (of whose Executive Council I was a member) took place in May 1923 at Wembley, and its vast display and grandeur in which the countries of our Empire were bound together greatly helped to foster interest in Empire trade. Which reminds me that during June of that year the Compatriots Club was revived, having lapsed after the death of its Founder and President, Joseph Chamberlain. The Club was formed by those interested in Imperial preference. The new President was Lord Selborne, and I was elected a member of the Committee.

In the early summer of 1925, Bonar Law concluded his painfully short period as Prime Minister, and Stanley Baldwin took over the Premiership. Less than six months later Parliament was dissolved, a General election decided upon, and for the first time I was opposed in the Moseley Division. The Liberal Party had selected Mrs. Clarkson as their candidate, a lady who had spent much of her life in public service, and was deservedly well-known and popular. The fortunes of a Parliamentary candidate are so intimately bound up with the character and quality of his Chairman, that I must pay my abounding tribute of gratitude to a Chairman whose loyalty to the Conservative cause and whose abiding personal interest in sustaining the efficiency of his Divisional organisation were beyond all praise. The late Sir Cornelius Chambers J.P. (widely known in Birmingham and the Midlands as 'Corney') was a man of high personal character, sound judgement and overflowing sense of humour. I was particularly fortunate during the greater part of my public career to have him as my guide, philosopher and friend. He was the head of a manufacturing firm with business connections scattered over the whole of Great Britain. He possessed inventive genius and secured patents for a variety of devises of acknowledged value in the brewing and allied trades. He possessed in a marked degree the faculty of making friends, although from time to time he became a little impatient when subjected to that peculiar process in life known as 'suffering fools gladly'.

He played an important part in Birmingham in the fusion of the Conservative and Liberal Unionist Parties which, up to the time of my election, had maintained separate organisations. His wise counsel, his generous sympathy and his foresight made a contribution to the political life of Birmingham freely and fully acknowledged by a generation now almost passed away. I enjoyed the further great happiness of the friendship and organising ability of Lady Chambers, Sir 'Corney's' charming and specially gifted wife. From my first acceptance as candidate until the end of her life, which came all too soon, she was President of my Women's Divisional Association. Under her directive influence and stimulating personality, I believe that during twenty years of my representation of Moseley I was supported by one of the most vigorous, most carefully balanced and most continuously active of any Women's Divisional-Organisation in Great Britain.

The size of my Division imposed a heavy task upon my various Women's Committees, extending right across the whole southern area of Birmingham and divided into nine sections, in each of which there was an active women's working committee. There were, of course, also general committees comprising of men and women, and also branches of our Junior Unionist movement, but the effective work of my Division, from the point of view of the political education of the electorate and the preparation of the electors for a parliamentary contest, rested largely upon my Women's Committees. The heavy burden of the maintenance of constant contact with this network of women's effort was cheerfully and effectively undertaken by Lady Chambers. Receptions from week to week at her delightful home, Monkspath Priory, meetings sometimes once and twice a week, whist drives, bazaars, country outings and every branch of social function large and small, were the constant concern of my Lady Divisional President I repeatedly said, in many public speeches, that the Conservative Party Organisation would indeed be in a hopeless condition of ineptitude if it were not for our enthusiastic and self-sacrificing women.

The experience of my own Division in this respect was, I think, characteristic of the Conservative machinery all over the country. Millions of men are no doubt interested in the continuance of Conservative principles and the maintenance of a strong Conservative Party, but the day to day work of spreading the principles, enlarging the educational outlook and focusing personal interest on the real substance and meaning of Conservatism rest with the women enthusiasts.

During my long association with Birmingham, I became more impressed from day to day by the immense influence which women exercised in the political life of the country. I was always an advocate of full particular and social equality between men and women, and I strongly supported the plea of 'equal work, equal pay', with the exception of those branches of industrial work in which it would be obviously inappropriate to employ women workers. As an act of gratitude for the devotion and loyalty of the two generations of women who were responsible for the Unionist organisation in Moseley and Acocks Green, it would give me particular pleasure in my declining years to see every right and privilege now enjoyed by men become, within fitting limitations, equally the rights and privileges of women.

I recall women's activities in politics from my first contested election in East Bristol, as I have previously mentioned. There I had two or three groups of women canvassers, and these ladies (in bitter weather, late and early) trudged from door to door urging support of my candidature. This is by the way, but most men who have seen as much of political life as I have (and particularly those of us who were attached to the Conservative Party) will gladly join with me in thanking God for the sympathy and the spirit of self-sacrifice of our women.

After which digression I must return to the year 1923 and the result of the General Election, including the Moseley Division vote. The Conservative Party was returned with a weak majority, but in my own minor way I had a small triumph, for I gained the third highest majority in my own Party and the seventh highest in Great Britain (beating Mrs. Clarkson by nearly twelve thousand votes). I think it was in this election that Alderman John Barman joined our team as Member for Duddeston and became a very valuable member of our group. His intimate knowledge of Birmingham administration was always at our disposal, and he performed constant parliamentary service till his defeat in the General Election of 1929.

Early in 1924 Stanley Baldwin resigned (the Government inevitably having suffered more than one defeat through the split in the Liberal Party, upon whom they depended for support) and His Majesty King George V called upon Ramsey MacDonald to form a Government. Of that first Labour Government little need be said. Much of our time in Parliament, and out of it, was spent in protesting against their acts of folly. I was particularly concerned with this Government's failure to carry on the work of the Singapore base, the abandonment of which greatly perturbed Australia and New Zealand. Mr. Snowden's cut in the Naval estimates was, I said at the time, tampering with the great silent force on which the efficiency of British diplomacy rested. Indeed, some of us were more distressed at this action than at any other of that ill-fated Government.

However, for a few weeks I was out of the country and away from its unhappy situation, examining with Sir Philip Dawson firstly, in April, the possibilities of developing trade with Austria and adjoining countries, and secondly, in

September, the industrial condition of Scandinavia and the Baltic States. Those were trips of the greatest immediate interest. In Austria we found vast opportunities for British trade, chiefly because of the superiority of British manufactures as against those from France, Italy, Germany and Czechoslovakia, which were exerting a rapidly growing commercial influence. From Vienna we made a journey of something like eighteen hundred miles, beginning with an exciting run over a mountain pass deep with snow.

We inspected the steel works at Styria and harbour developments on the Adriatic coast. We went to Zagreb, Belgrade and to Sarajevo, the capital city of Bosnia, which was connected with the outer world only through a mountain pass on which lay a narrow gauge railway. It was all a wonderful experience and brought me new and abiding friends, for it was on this trip that I first met the Prpic family, very charming and cultured Yugoslavians. They entertained our delegation at their beautiful home near Zagreb. M. Prpic was a director of a banking establishment and also held large interests in timber, a vastly important concern in that country. Later on, I often stayed with him and he, for his part, made occasional and most welcome visits to London.

When we left England for the continent, the end of Ramsey MacDonald's Government was in sight, and very shortly after my return events moved to a rapid conclusion. The Liberal party (to whom Austen Chamberlain had referred as 'the hewers of wood and drawers of water for the Socialist Government') became uneasy, fearing that some Liberal votes might, in future, be given to Labour members. The Conservative Party were eager to be back in office to prevent further disasters, and the House met after the summer recess in a difficult and belligerent mood. In October, matters came to a head when legal proceedings had been instituted against the acting editor of a Communist newspaper, but were withdrawn on Government instruction. Sir Robert Home moved the Vote of Censure, and on the Government's being defeated, Ramsay MacDonald asked for an immediate dissolution. Barely twenty-four hours after the dissolution was announced, election writs were received. It was a very rushed affair. The socialists were eager to get a wedge into

Unionist Birmingham, and we of the 'Birmingham Club' adopted for our slogan the watchword of Verdun: - 'They shall not pass.'

I found myself with an opponent who rejoiced in the name of Mr. G. Blizzard, a name which lent itself to lighter propaganda from both Parties. When the result of the election appeared, Mr. Blizzard was beaten by roughly seventeen thousand votes, but our Parliamentary brotherhood had been slightly disturbed by Mr. Robert Dennison capturing Kings Norton on behalf of the Labour Party. Although I disagreed with his politics, I was much attached to Dennison, and greatly respected his high personal character. It was at this election that the Liberal Party suffered the crushing defeat from which they have never recovered.

In Mr. Baldwin's new Government, Austen Chamberlain was appointed Foreign Secretary, and his brother Neville was appointed Minister of Health. Some years later, Harold Macmillan was chatting to me about the formation of that Baldwin Government, and the problem as to the personalities who should compose it. Prior to 1925, his father-in-law (the Duke of Devonshire) was Secretary of State for the Dominions and Colonies, yet he was not consulted or even written to on the formation of the new Government. The Duke naturally expected some word, although he did not seek to have a new position in the Government, but he thought that he might at least have received the courtesy of a communication from Mr. Baldwin. A little later, when Baldwin wanted to make a public pronouncement of great importance, and was attending a big mass meeting at Chesterfield, he asked the Duke if he would be so kind as to receive him at his house, and bring representative people from all over that part of the Midland area. The Duke very generously consented, and the result was that there was a very distinguished and comprehensive assembly. During the dinner in the great hall, a peculiar incident occurred which shocked those who witnessed it. Mr. Baldwin, before the dinner had concluded, produced a briar pipe and, to the horror and disgust of both Duke and Duchess, proceeded to light it without asking permission of either of them!

It was at this time (just about a year before the General Strike) that my old friend Professor Hewins compiled a memorandum on imports, exports and general commerce, showing the exceedingly grave position that industry was facing. The quarterly meeting of the Iron and Steel trades on the Birmingham Exchange was a most saddening incident in the industrial life of our nation, for we learned then that this industry as a whole was living from hand to mouth, this industry that should have made up part of a great wealth of the nation. Stocks were practically exhausted, yet orders were few and far between. The shadow of unemployment, starvation and misery was already spreading over the Black Country. Furnaces were being closed down, every day highly skilled craftsmen were being thrown out of employment, and a demoralising gloom was overcoming both employers and employees. In these circumstances, the Trade Unions were gradually becoming a great political force.

The Act of 1913, which permitted Trade Unions to raise compulsory levies for the purpose of taking political action, had established a situation that was becoming increasingly dominant in the working of our political institutions. While evil forebodings expanded throughout Britain there was, at any rate, one bright ray of hope and glory in Birmingham on the occasion of the signing of the Locarno Treaties between Germany, France and Great Britain, in which Austen Chamberlain played such an important role. During the negotiations he made a most striking advance for British prestige in diplomacy, and it was for his brilliant judgement, tact and action that he was made a Knight of the Garter. The following February, Sir Austen was given the Honorary Freedom of Birmingham. Almost forty years previously, his father had been given the same honour on his return from a mission for peace (he was indeed the first man to receive it) and Sir Austen now commented: - "When the day comes that I am to be judged, ... I will plead to be judged by two acts of my long public life, and each of them was an effort for peace. I will ask to be judged for the part I took in the Irish Treaty, and the part I took in the Treaty of Locarno."

Only a few years before I had been present at the ceremony, and afterwards at the banquet, at which Lord Balfour was made an Honorary Freeman of the city of Birmingham. Austen Chamberlain, being unavoidably absent had written: - "To have served under him was itself a political education." Words that could have been applied to the writer of them. Yet again I went abroad for a few weeks to study and report upon economic and trade conditions. Our contingent was headed by Sir Philip Dawson. Philip Richardson was another of the party, which consisted of eight Members of Parliament and two economic experts. We left England towards the end of May, returning about the third week in June and, as always, the trip was both stimulating, informative and satisfactory. Among other things, we saw over the huge Siemens works, where about ninety per cent of all work is piecework. Dr. Carl von Siemens, the head of the business, received us in a magnificent boardroom and made himself most agreeable.

Then we went on to Warsaw, where we dined with the Prime Minister of Poland (M. Grabski) and attended a large, and somewhat bewildering, reception. Bewildering, I say, because none of us could speak Polish and had to depend upon the services of an interpreter who spoke French. I recall our visit to a Polish timber works, whose offices were situated in the late Czar's shooting box, and the ceilings were still covered with paintings of hunting scenes. We learned that many of the men employed here had been members of a private military force that waged war against the Bolsheviks. We saw the largest, or what was claimed to be the largest, cotton goods factory of its kind in Europe and also visited the oil industrial centre of Boryslav. During our tour of the very ancient city of Krakow, the Polish Count who was acting as our guide spoke of its castle as, 'The insolence of architecture', because of its strange admixture of styles. A fitting title, I agreed.

It was particularly interesting to see those oil wells in Boryslav and watch the workmen actually drilling for oil, for I had recently had a hand in preparing a memorandum for the General Purposes Committee of the B.C.U. upon the subject of British oil supply. At that time, the United States consumed seventy-three per cent of the world's output. The memorandum noted: - *"Great Britain has owed her prosperity in the past largely to the fact that she had been Queen of the coal world, but the United States has gradually become King of the oil world."* It was vitally important for us at this juncture to take the right course in the discussions with Iraq and Turkey, whereby we were offered oil concessions in Iraq, then belonging to the Turkish Petroleum company. The Turkish Government was anxious to get Mosul under their control which, by virtue of its great resources, would have given them a powerful commercial and financial position.

There are two other matters I might mention before we leave the year of grace 1925. The first being one of which I am rather ashamed, and the second one of which I am very proud. Knowing what a lot of good Fascism was doing in Italy to raise the standard of living and create employment, I became interested enough in their way of life, as I saw it, to agree to preside at a meeting of British Fascists in Birmingham. Their objects, I fancied, were freedom of speech, private enterprise, and freedom of religion. But the meeting was such a stormy one, with so much heckling (chiefly from a Communist element) and such wild scenes that it had to be cleared by the police, and I vowed I would not put myself again into that position.

The second fact to which I have referred was my election as President of the Aston Villa Football Club. I was already President of thirty-eight football clubs, and Vice-President of fourteen others, but this honour was one that I greatly appreciated, and I am happy to say that it is one which I have retained through all these difficult years. I have always been very fond of watching football, and have seized any spare time that I could to follow the teams' progress. Another sport with which I had some connection in Birmingham, was greyhound racing. When the first electric hare was introduced to that city, I was asked to start it in motion by pressing a silver knob, which was then presented to me in the form of a paperweight.

Young Pat Hannon

Pat Hannon and Mary Hannon (née Wynne)

Pat Hannon and his family

At the House of Commons
with Miss Florence Horsbrugh (Con,Dundee)

September 25th, 1939

HANNON

The People's Candidate for Bristol East.

Social
Reform.

Land
Reform.

Poor Law
Reform.

Tariff
Reform.

National
Defence.

Industrial
Insurance.

UNITY & EMPIRE.

Printed and published by Lawson & Son, 43 West Street, Bristol.

The "Gombeen Man"

Political campaign

The Statesman by Bassano Ltd., 20 January 1926
(©the National Portrait Gallery)

The Statesman by Howard Coster,1930's
(©the National Portrait Gallery)

Sir Patrick

The House on Magna Carta Island
photograph by Bassano Ltd., 8 June 1936
(©the National Portrait Gallery)

Sir Patrick and Lady Hannon, 8 June 1936
(©the National Portrait Gallery)

Sir Patrick with his daughter Violet and Mary Hannon

Windsor 1957

Sir Patrick with Violet and Mary Hannon and his eldest grandson, Patrick Godfrey Hannon

CHAPTER 9

One of the most important events with which I was directly concerned in 1926 was a Conference with prominent German industrialists on the one hand, and on the other a group of British industrialists (of which I was Honorary Secretary) representing every section of productive enterprise. We met under the Presidency of Sir Robert Home at Major Ashley's beautiful home Broadlands, near Southampton. The Ashleys were very good friends of mine. Mollie Ashley was a wonderful hostess, and found herself in her element in giving hospitality to so many friends and strangers. Major Ashley later became Lord Mount Temple, and Broadlands has now become a fitting home for Lord Mountbatten. I took part in the conference with one object only, the revitalising of certain of our basic industries and the enlargement of the field of employment. We discussed at length the depressing situation of the steel industry and tried to make arrangements to allocate steel. Among the German delegates was my old acquaintance, Dr Kuno.

We spent nearly a week in this great country house, for the problem of arriving at an understanding between corresponding groups of industrialists in two countries is, naturally, abounding in difficulties. The detached and individualistic character of our industries contrasted sharply with the highly organised grouping of kindred industries in Germany. This hampered discussion. The Germans, for instance, were able to speak with one voice for the whole of the iron and steel manufacturers in Germany, but our representatives could only speak for a somewhat loose organisation whose individual members might quite possibly be unwilling to conform to obligations imposed upon them by international agreement.

The next year, I organised a delegation for a return visit to Germany, where we were entertained near Cologne by Herr Duisberg and his wife. The Conference was carried on as before, with perfect good humour, and many interesting decisions were made. During the previous autumn, at a dinner in the Midland Conservative Club (at which I presided) Winston Churchill was the guest speaker. The Communist menace was much in our thoughts those days, my own election speeches frequently had warned

Birmingham of Russian lack of faith in the commercial world. I recall Mr. Churchill saying that: - "... our island community stood obviously as a massive obstacle in the path of the Bolshevik revolutionaries, whose aim was to lay low the cause of order and freedom ... to shatter it into fragments ... to grind it into powder."

During 1924, the Russians had a trick of opening up trade negotiations for business with British firms, then duplicating all the replies and distributing them as evidence of the eagerness of Britain to trade with them. After the General Strike in May 1926, while the miners still refused to return to Work, it became known to us that money was being sent from the Russian Council of Trade Unions to aid the strikers, and some Members of Parliament demanded that diplomatic relations with Russia should be severed. But it seemed to me that a better element in Russia was gradually gaining control, and much could be done now in the way of trade with that country. Mr. Joynson-Hicks took a prominent part in the debate, making statements which were bound to aggravate the Soviet Union. On June 11th I received a letter from George Armstrong referring to this, from which I quote an extract: -

"Honestly, when I read tonight's debate, almost a feeling of despair came over me. Just when those who, like myself, know the Russians intimately and have carefully watched and assisted in the gradual metamorphosis which has come over their Rulers during the past three years, are on the point of bringing them to a reasonable and practical course of policy. Russia is once again made the shuttlecock of politics and a target for the 'stunt' press. Such a policy, if persisted in, can only lead to one result, the defeat and disappearance of those Russians who are striving hard to lift their country out of the Morass, and the victory and restoration to power of the vile crew who, until this moment, have been trembling for their own heads. Also, and not least, the loss of a splendid market, and relief for a large percentage of our unemployed."

Upon receiving this letter I immediately wrote to Joynson-Hicks, or Jix as we called him, pointing out that a very important proposal had been put to the Soviet Government by one of our biggest industrialists for the recognition of pre-war debts, the establishment of private rights, the safety of private property and the conduct of business relations on the conventional lines that obtain between civilised countries, which proposal had been accepted by the Soviet Government. I then wrote to George Armstrong as follows: -

"Those of us who are really concerned for the maintenance of constantly improving relations with Russia, have had an exceedingly unenviable task during the past few weeks in negotiation with Ministers to prevent the denunciation of the Trade Agreement. So far, everything has gone very well, but I do most earnestly appeal to you, by the exercise of such influence as you possess with the Representatives of Russia in this country, to induce them to advise Moscow that continuous propagandist effort can only result in the near future in very unfortunate consequences ... It was largely due to the vigorous' efforts which you have been making which prevented, for the time being, disturbance of the status quo."

The following day I received a note from Armstrong, complaining that one of the popular newspapers, coupled with 'Churchill's vulgar outburst' was making the task very difficult for those Conservatives in the House who aim at improving the relations between our country and Russia. Indeed, it is sad to think of the number of times that awkward situations have been aggravated by thoughtless interference.

As the post-revolutionary Russia emerged clearly from the inevitable fogginess and dust of upheaval, we in Great Britain learned more about her Government and peoples, and many opinions were changed. Accordingly, extremists on both Sides took a saner view of events. I remember sending a note to Neville Chamberlain concerning one of the most extreme of all Labour leaders, and one of the most ardent supporters of Soviet propaganda in the country. I thought it might interest him to learn to what extent this fellow had modified his opinions.

That year I had an unexpected and amusing trip to Spain. It came about this way. My friend, Freddie Guest, had been invited by Lowenstein (the great financier) to bring a party of Members of Parliament to inspect the great schemes he was developing in Spain. Guest said to me: - "Paddy, would you like to come to Spain? All expenses paid." So, as I had no other commitments at the time, I naturally said I would be delighted. "If you like you can take your secretary with you," he added. So my secretary and I joined the delegation among whom, I remember, were

Hamar Greenwood and Christmas Williams. We went first to Biarritz, and during a meal there Mr. Lowenstein drew a caricature of everyone sitting round the table (an amusing and clever sketch!). From Biarritz we went to Pau, where a complete hotel had been taken for us, and we had every luxury that can be imagined. It was a lovely old town and I regretted having to leave it so soon, for we started off early in the morning to cross the Pyrenees by way of a nine thousand feet high pass. That journey in the wonderful mountain air made us really hungry, and I have never forgotten the excellent luncheon that we were given on our arrival in Spain, where the local trout was a speciality.

Afterwards we were shown a large new hydro-electric installation, and further on another electric station where American engineers were working on a big project. Tarragona, Barcelona, Montserrat, then home via Carcassonne, Toulouse and Lourdes. My secretary had returned before me, and I travelled home with Lowenstein, who was an entertaining companion. He had a hand in so many financial projects, from heavy engineering to artificial silk. Poor fellow, I don't know what went wrong, but sometime later, he came to London for consultation with the Board of Engineering and on the flight home, via Belgium, he went out of the plane.

The famous Constitutional Club has always been my great interest, ever since I first became a member. Early in 1927 I was delighted, and greatly honoured, to be elected Chairman of the Political Committee on the resignation of Sir Edward Nicholl. This entailed, among other duties, the choosing of Speakers for the political talks which were an interesting feature in the life of the Club.

Somehow, in spite of this extra call upon my time, I was able to leave England for a few weeks to see a part of the world, far across the ocean, which was new to me. I was chosen, that September, to represent Britain at the thirteenth Inter-Parliamentary conference in Rio de Janeiro. We were all guests of the Brazilian government, and a very motley party we were. The representatives from forty-four nations were present. This in itself made the visit of much value and interest. The subjects under discussion included international cartels, industrial agreements, distribution of raw material, the stabilisation of currency and a whole host of other economic topics.

1928 was a year of gloom for me, for my dear wife Mary died early in February, after years of suffering from asthma. I moved from our pleasant home in Ashley Gardens to spend the next three years at the Constitutional Club and worked even harder than ever. The number of obligations imposed upon a Member of Parliament is much greater than the public realise for, apart from his actual work in Parliament, he must attend many political and social functions in his constituency. For myself, I found that the demands upon my time were so heavy that I considered myself lucky if I was able to spend one week-end a month with my family, and during each week I made an average of at least three journeys to Birmingham. On frequent occasions, I have had to travel to my constituency early in the morning (and hurry back as soon as I was free to do so) in order to record my vote that evening in the Division Lobby of the House of Commons.

The end of the Conservative Government's time in office came during April 1929, and we were plunged once more into the hurly-burly of a General Election. There was much dissatisfaction among the wage-earners at this time, for they felt very strongly that they were not placed on a level of competitive equality with their fellow workers in similar industries and occupations in other countries. Much of the election propaganda on both sides centred on the particular Party's answer to the problem of unemployment, Labour especially boasting of their power to find a solution.

Another matter at that time which came into prominence during the election speeches was the much debated question of a Channel Tunnel which, allegedly, would have helped to ease the growing unemployment. In pre-war years I had been a strong supporter of the scheme, but I felt that now England was an island no longer (for air-routes had connected her with the whole world) talk of a tunnel under the Channel seemed, to me, futile. I said that immediate steps should be taken to cease work on the operation.

On this occasion I had three opponents contesting my seat. Bushnell (a Labour Candidate), a Liberal and a Left-Wing Labour Party member (who obtained less than seven hundred votes). The polling was greatly increased all over the country owing to the Government's extension of the female franchise, and in the Moseley Division I headed the poll with something under thirty-four thousand votes. But many of my friends in the Conservative Party were rejected, the Liberal vote dropped still further, and Labour just scraped home. The great Edmund Burke, in his historic speech at Bristol in 1780, said: - "I have read the books of life for a long time, and I have read other books a little. Nothing has happened to me but has happened to men much better than me, and in times and in nations full of good as the age and country that we live in ... and it is in general more unpleasant to be rejected after a long trial than not to be chosen at all."

This historic declaration embodies the philosophic attitude which should be pursued both by individuals and Parties after a defeat at the polls, but there was much moaning and wailing among the fallen after the 1929 election. During the whole period of Baldwin's late administration I had voted steadily and constantly in support of his policy, but we approached the General Election with divided counsels, with conflicting voices and with an unwholesome tendency to employ the methods of expediency, instead of those of courage and resolution. And the result: the Election left our Party in a mood of despondency and almost incoherence. We silently accepted the advent of a Socialist regime with a measure of tolerance unparalleled in the party antagonisms of politics. For reasons which I never could fathom and which were never even explained, Baldwin's vigorous campaign (which was anticipated by an imposing speech at the Albert Hall in October) was not pursued.

And now the first signs of the general depression were making themselves evident, for the United States of America was unable to continue the series of financial loans to European countries which, until this period, had produced a false impression of Europe's economic situation. The unemployment figures, already so large in Great Britain, rose rapidly, despite the efforts of the new Labour Government, and all over the continent the tale was the same. Nothing, it seemed, could be done to stem the rising tide of unemployment everywhere, and to control a situation which appeared to be getting rapidly out of hand.

Imperial Preference was, I felt completely assured, the only answer which met our own case, and at the Annual

General Meeting of the National Union of Manufacturers (of which at a later date I became President) I moved a resolution urging the Government not to discontinue duties on certain goods. I said then that the body politic of this nation had suffered for three generations a disease which arose in the middle of the 19th century, when a wave of feeling spread over the country that our markets should be open to the whole of mankind. Every nation but ourselves made it a first principle of economic policy that their home market should be the possession of their own people. It was not yet too late to apply that policy with full force, for half-hearted attempts made little difference. I gave my wholehearted support to the splendid campaign for Imperial Preference, which my good friend Lord Beaverbrook was pursuing throughout the country. In its boldness, comprehensiveness and magnitude, the project was almost staggering, but, in my judgement, it was calculated to have abounding consequences in the survival of the British Empire. It was the greatest idealistic proposition submitted to the British peoples since Joseph Chamberlain's great speech on Fiscal Reform in 1903. Beaverbrook's appeal to the country through the Empire Crusade for a great, far-reaching Imperial policy was an example of blazing the political trail in national life that has seldom been equalled. Many people were interested and caught up in the first enthusiasm. When the call went out for foundation members of the Empire Crusade, queues of married women, young and old, rich and poor, waited with their enrolment forms outside the offices in Trafalgar Square. I sent a telegram asking to be enrolled as one of the first members. The energy and initiative of Lord Beaverbrook were attributes sadly lacking in the Cabinet. Indeed, the leadership of the Conservative Party itself was not so vigorous, inspiring or aggressive as it should have been. Up and down the country Unionists had doubts, difficulties and embarrassments in their conviction of policy.

The United Empire Society was founded early in 1930, and I welcomed the United Empire Party as being a healthy and stimulating influence in political life. Should it be able to work side by side with the Conservatives without conflict, I felt certain that it would have a powerful effect in bringing home to the people of Great Britain the supreme importance of Empire Free Trade. The announcement of its formation roused great enthusiasm and was widely discussed in political circles. There were more than two hundred thousand adherents, who pledged their allegiance to the launching of the United Empire Party. It was an extraordinary fact that we were the only community under the sun that allowed our own markets and our own doors, both industrially and agriculturally, to be made the scene of exploitation and a source of profit to every foreigner who chose.

Many strange things were said at Geneva by our representatives of those days, and many inexplicable decisions were made and actions taken. At the Naval Conference in 1927, for instance, it was laid down that Britain should have seventy cruisers for the protection of her trade routes and the maintenance of her international communications. But, instead of using this right as a bargaining power, the Government actually reduced the number of cruisers to fifty, thus placing us in a subordinate position for bargaining throughout the whole Conference. Three years later, the Board of Trade proposed at Geneva to have a tariff truce, which would mean suspending for two years all modifications of existing tariffs in European countries. Naturally the reaction of several countries was to raise their tariffs immediately in anticipation.

So, we were to be tied hand and foot for the next two years in an arrangement whereby every cheaply produced article in Europe could be poured into this country and sold at prices against which we could not possibly compete. Every one of the European countries that I had visited was determined to develop its own internal industrial activity by every means in its power, with the protection of a tariff wall, and, at the same time, continually looking to the open market in England as a place where they could dump their surplus commodities. The situation then was to be made even worse by this absurd project of Mr. Graham, the President of the Board of Trade.

In the House of Commons debate upon this, many protests were made, and I declared that to offer a free market for exploitation by other nations was a crime against the working classes. During this controversy (Protection versus Free Trade) that raged throughout the country, I remember very well speaking in the National Liberal Club (regarded as the centre and home of 'Cobdenism') and being agreeably surprised at the respectful hearing which I was accorded. My old friend, Jim O Grady, wrote to me from Hobart, a letter dated May 26th 1930, which I now give in full: -

"My dear Pat,

It was good of you to write me, date February 10th. Your warm compliment as to my work is appreciated, and will be an incentive to attempt even greater service in Imperial work. I watch with keen interest how affairs at home are going on, particularly industrial matters. The feature that I think is at times lost sight of is that the economic depression is world-wide, and that on the whole we are weathering the depression more easily than other Nations. Mankind cannot destroy thousands of millions (£'s) of wealth, as we did during wars 1914-1918, and expect to recuperate rapidly. Personally, I think (and Jimmy Thomas makes the point with force) we have reached bedrock. Indeed, the tendency in matters industrial seems upward already. I note the effect of Snowden's speeches, rather than his budget, was keeping the industrial barometer wobbling, but the fact of the McKenna duties being retained, at least in the main, must result in steadying the position. Apart from affairs at home, does not the fate of industrial history prove that bad and good trade comes in cycles of years, emphasising the old Biblical story of seven fat and seven lean years. But in the present cycle of lean years there is the artificial interference of two great revolutions, Russia, and China, resulting in those markets containing a hundred and fifty million consumers being closed to us in a special manner. I cannot see the probability of any new markets opening up for some while yet. This, it seems to me, gives emphasis to the need of shaping the Empire into an economic unit, self-contained, and supplying the world with the overplus of our products. This is the idea which I think underlines the proposals of Beaverbrook. I notice in this latter matter that Beaverbrook has cut adrift from Rothermere. I don't see how he could do otherwise when Rothermere tacked on to the original proposal two political propositions. I am watching for the effect of the Commonwealth's Governments tariffs in the matter of the 'Old Country's' export trade with Australia. I am afraid it will be somewhat disastrous. Australia has for at least six years been living above her income and been borrowing from outside lavishly. Something drastic of course, had to be done, but the question is should it be done by imposing drastic tariff measures. I will not comment further on this matter simply because Scullin and his Cabinet are really an able team, and I have no doubts that if they find they have gone too far, particularly in the matter of tariffs, they will courageously admit mistakes and rectify them.

Give all my old friends in the House my warm greetings, and tell them my daughter (she is a gem, Pat, and has risen to the occasion and circumstances splendidly) and myself are in good health, and are getting through work to the apparent satisfaction of the folks in Tasmania.

Best of wishes and good luck."

It may be remembered that I had recommended O'Grady to His Majesty King George V for the position of Governor of Tasmania. O'Grady filled the position so admirably that His Majesty wished to bestow honour upon him, but the Labour Party would not put forward his name for a knighthood. When O'Grady returned for a few months to England, the King met him, and said: - "These fellows would not put your name forward? Kneel down." And thus he became Sir James O'Grady. Early in the 'thirties' he left Tasmania to take the position of Governor to the Falkland Islands.

But to return for a moment to Lord Beaverbrook and his great campaign. The Central Chamber of Agriculture (of which I was Chairman) arranged an important meeting at the Caxton Hall, which I invited Lord Beaverbrook to address on the subject of the agricultural policy of the Crusaders. At the last minute, however, I received an apology from him explaining that he had that day received 'a momentous announcement' from Mr. Baldwin, and in this circumstance he could not give effect to the speech which he had prepared. Sir Horace Plunkett, who had now retired and was living in Weybridge, came to the meeting, and I asked him to speak. Next day I received this letter from Sir Horace: -

"It was a kind thought to give me a chance to say a few words to such an influential body of farmers. But as you know, I am the worst of speakers even when prepared. You turned the non-appearance of Beaverbrook to advantage with brilliant ingenuity, but I have no such gift. If I had known what Baldwin had said, I might possibly have been able to support your important statement, that it had transformed the whole situation, which indeed was pretty dark for the unfortunate farmers. I look forward to tomorrow's 'Times' which will have a verbatim report. I don't see why Beaverbrook could not have come to the meeting and have told us that he now hoped to be able to demonstrate that his movement is wholly non-party. I gather that Baldwin must have given him a splendid opportunity to make

that much clear. He could have trusted you to back him in this attitude. Indeed, what you said would have been just what was wanted to introduce him. Of course you were quite right not to say that he ought to have come, but you must have felt that it was a pity to miss such a chance to place his views clearly before as representative a body of farmers as he is likely to meet again. I don't expect ever to speak in public again. I had hoped to write once more on the agricultural situation, but the burden of years and the overstrain of a long struggle for the small cultivators, whose neglect is in my view the gravest mistake of British policy, have worn me out. I was glad to see you in your best form."

Poor Plunkett. He died in March 1932, just two years later, and thus a very pleasant link with my work in Ireland in the old days was broken. Beaverbrook and Baldwin ... Baldwin a baffling and indeterminate personality who had no particular affection for any of his supporters, treating them with an indifference due in part to his self-esteem and his exaggerated concept of his own importance. Beaverbrook afforded the Conservative Party every facility to acquiesce in the achievement of his objective, but there was doubt and hesitancy and timidity on the part of the leaders. At last, a meeting took place and Baldwin's 'momentous announcement' was made (which had disrupted my plans for the arrangement of Speakers at the Farmers' Conference). By arrangement, Beaverbrook undertook to support Baldwin's Imperial policy through the medium of his Press, but thereafter, Beaverbrook was ignored by Baldwin and was not even consulted on matters affecting them both. Then, on June 24th, Baldwin addressed a Conservative Party meeting at the Caxton Hall and, in a vigorous speech, attacked both Lord Beaverbrook and Lord Rothermere. "We are told that the gloves are off,' he said. "If they are, we shall see who has got the dirty hands."

Rothermere had been making persistent and unrelenting attacks upon Baldwin and the Tory administration. After consultation with Beaverbrook, I decided to write to him appealing for his support for unity, not disruption within the Conservative Party, with the object of accepting an Empire policy based upon Empire Free Trade. At the same time, I made a speech in which I appealed for Party Unity and for the support of the Press in order to maintain the vitality of the Tory Party. Rothermere then wrote to me from the Riviera, as follows: -

"My dear Mr. Hannon,

I have received a report of your speech here. I cannot make it too abundantly clear that under no circumstances whatsoever will I support Mr Baldwin … and let me beg of you for Mr. Baldwin to read the name of any other person who may be leading this party … unless I know exactly what his policy is going to be, unless I have complete guarantees that such policy will be carried out if his Party achieves office, and unless I am acquainted with the names of at least eight or ten of his most prominent colleagues in his next Ministry. Unless I am completely satisfied on this point, no appeals will be listened to from any quarter. I much prefer a Labour-Liberal Government to a Ministry of the indolence and ignorance of the semi-Socialist Government we had from 1924 to 1929. I do not like food taxes. There is nothing private about this letter, and I have no objection to its publication in any form.

Yours faithfully,

Rothermere."

This letter I rather stupidly showed to Davidson (Baldwin's Private Secretary) whereupon Baldwin sent for me and I gave him the letter, which he kept. I was sitting with Beaverbrook and Paddy Goulding at the Party Conference and, to our amazement, Baldwin produced Rothermere's letter and read it aloud, the substance of which seemed to have hit him pretty hard. It was, in plain fact, much more than a mere expression of opinion, it was virtually an aggressive demand for a Cabinet reconstruction, and Baldwin was justified in declaring that: - *"A more preposterous and insolent demand was never made on the leader of any political party. I repudiate it with contempt, and I will fight that attempt at domination to the end."*

Sir Gervaise Rentoul then addressed the meeting, also denouncing the Rothermere and Beaverbrook Presses, and expressing confidence in his leader, and moved a resolution to that effect. Colonel Gretton opposed this, saying that Baldwin's policy of 'no food taxes without a referendum' should be altered, and that a free hand be given to leaders of the Party to deal with food tax questions at forthcoming Imperial conferences. The wording of this proposal had already been approved at a private gathering of Conservatives a few days previously. With such organised opposition, Baldwin's position was an extremely delicate one. Indeed, the situation was almost without precedent. A leader had called a party meeting, and now it seemed as though he might fail to secure a majority. Sir Henry Page Croft declared that the country was looking for a lead, and unless the Conservative Party gave this lead the country would turn in another direction.

There were attacks and counter-attacks. Churchill's expression, I recall, was one of restrained fury and, indeed, tempers were rising all over the hall. Then Sir Robert Home saved the day by a quiet but strong appeal for unity, which smoothed down some of the aggression and brought good sense and Party loyalty back to the gathering. Rothermere later issued a statement to the Press in reply to Baldwin's speech, in which he said: -

"I maintain most firmly that a political leader today, and certainly a Conservative leader, should publicly state in the course of an election which of his colleagues are going to occupy the key positions in his Ministry. The electorate have the right to know. This safeguard is particularly necessary in the case of Mr. Baldwin, who has made more blunders with regard to all important appointments than any British Prime Minister in history."

A few months after all that hullabaloo, Sir Henry Page Croft and I got into hot water for supporting Sir Herbert Liddiard as Free Trade candidate at a bye-election for South Paddington. He had lost the support of the Conservative Party, and our critics declared that we were being disloyal to our Party in working for his election. This I strongly repudiated, for I had given (for twenty-five years) my whole efforts towards the furtherance of Imperial Trade, and I would oppose any policy which purposed to favour foreign competition at the home expense. A man who has not the courage to say frankly what are his convictions in the direction of improving the interests of his country is a political coward, and I am confident that I could never have been accused of political cowardice.

On August 22nd 193I, I went to St James' Church, Spanish Place, to be married to Miss Amy Gordon Barrett, whom I had known for very many years (ever since I had become Secretary of the Navy League). She had been one of my most active supporters in the Navy League during the whole of my time as Secretary, and was a member of the Executive Committee of the Ladies Council of the Navy League since 1910, and Honorary Treasurer of the

Kensington Branch. Chief among her other activities at that time was poultry keeping (she was an expert on the management of poultry and a member of the National Poultry Council) add also took an active interest in animals, since for many years she was a member of the Grand Council of Our Dumb Friends League. The ceremony was performed by the Very Reverend Cyril Ryan, Provincial of the Carmelite Order and Prior of the Carmelite Church, Dublin, who had in the dim and distant days of my boyhood been my tutor, and ever since then my friend. Commander Charles Evans was the Best Man, and a guard of honour of boys from the training ship 'Stork' (which my bride had helped to found) saw us launched into married life. Among the numerous handsome wedding presents that we received was a piece of plate from the Executive and Parliamentary Committee of the Empire Industries Association, who gave us a special dinner at which the presentation was made.

Before Parliament opened in the New Year I received, like all my Conservative colleagues, a circular letter from Baldwin which, in stringent terms, stressed the importance of the critical period ahead (of which we were all aware). None of us, however, could have clearly foreseen the appalling state of the economic crises so soon to be revealed, nor could we have forecast the astonishing steps which were to be taken in dealing with the situation.

Baldwin's letter ran thus: -

"The business to be taken in the House of Commons when we reassemble on January 20th will be of particular importance, and it is vitally necessary that every member of the Party should be available for constant attendance during this critical period. I wish, therefore, to impress upon you the urgent necessity for refusing to accept engagements in your constituency, or elsewhere, on days when Parliament is sitting, and it should be noted that the Prime Minister has already announced his intention to take Government business on Wednesdays. It is not possible for an opposition party to anticipate the exact course of business, or to forecast the precise time at which important divisions will be taken; and it is only by a general recognition of the necessity for a much better response to the Whip that the Party can hope to take advantage of opportunities, such as have been narrowly missed during the past few weeks, and which will certainly occur again in the future. It is, perhaps, unnecessary for me to add that no excuse, except illness, is adequate for failure to respond to a Three-line Whip."

On February 11th our Party called the attention of the House to the immediate need for economies in the national finance, and Snowden agreed that drastic measures would have to be imposed. That a Committee should be formed to make recommendations for effecting such reductions in the national expenditure was the Liberal amendment, and in the third week of March this Committee came into being under the Chairmanship of Sir George May (later Lord May of Weybridge). Among those on the Committee was my old friend Ashley Cooper.

The competitive power of Great Britain, faced with free imports in this country and reduced cost of production abroad, had fallen low. The balance of trade against us became more and more overwhelming, and the unemployment figures increased daily. On the 16th June Sir Horace Plunkett wrote me a letter in which he said: - *"I am anxiously awaiting the news of the Liberal-Socialist negotiations. I cannot believe that Lloyd George will force his allies to go to the country. Nor should I like to see you people forced to take over the appalling muddle we are in at the present time. I pity all Parties."*

And on the same day I attended a pleasant luncheon at 10, Upper Brook Street, the residence of Stanley Baldwin, who had asked one or two members of the Party to meet and discuss matters. But the extreme gravity of the situation was not yet clearly evident. On 31st July the bomb exploded, and the Chancellor of the Exchequer (Philip Snowden) informed the House that he had now received the report of the May Committee, and that its contents would come as a shock. The shock was realised when it was disclosed that a deficit of £120,000,000 would have to be met in order to balance the 1932 Budget, and that the recommendations included substantial reductions in the unemployment benefit and drastic cuts in the pay of the Civil, Military and Police services. This deficit, however, was foreshadowed to be even much greater, by the special Committee appointed to deal with the report.

The various members of the Cabinet who were scattered on holiday were recalled, and crisis followed crisis. While I was enjoying a very brief honeymoon in Wales (having decided not to travel out of Great Britain in this time of national emergency) the situation came to a head, and King George V invited Ramsey MacDonald to form a National

Government. This Government was expected to be only temporarily in power, for as soon as Bills were passed to avert the economic crisis, Parliament would dissolve and the country would have a General Election. I was filled with admiration for the spirit of self-sacrifice which had activated Ramsey MacDonald into agreeing to this course, and taking upon himself the thankless task of leading the Government which would impose such drastic restrictions. For a leader of the Socialist Party it was especially bitter; MacDonald had been in Germany when I was there in 1922 and 1923, that terrible time when the Mark was smashed to smithereens, and when the whole exchange of that country had fled from any sort of standard of stability. He had seen the appalling destitution that fell upon the Germans as a result. It was to avoid a similar ghastly situation here, that he took his courage into both hands and faced the people. But we were forced off the gold standard on September 21st, and this action greatly weakened confidence in the Government. A series of Party meetings followed, where the immediate policy concerning electioneering was debated. On 23rd September, Page Croft, Leo Amery and myself had an interview with Stanley Baldwin, who appeared to be confident, self-possessed and assured. He agreed that agriculture should be protected, and said that we should go to the country as a National Government, with a manifesto written by the leaders of the three Parties. "The Prime Minister," he said, "was entirely in favour of a full tariff policy, and the Liberals must be made to accept it." Snowden, he thought, would not stand again, but would give his support to a National Government. The Liberals, however, refused to compromise with their great tradition of Free Trade and a deadlock was reached.

On 29th September a meeting of the Conservatives took place, at which it was decided to send strong representations to Baldwin pressing for a General Election. With the split in the Labour Party, whereby Ramsey MacDonald felt that he had been let down by his followers, and the general dithering of the Liberals, we believed that our Party should have a big majority throughout the country if we 'struck while the iron was hot'. The majority in the House were for a National Party, but a fair number preferred a Tory appeal made through Baldwin, while a very few were entirely against an election being held. At last, a solution to the deadlock was reached and, although the individual Parties could stand by their Free Trade or Tariff policies, no mention of Protection was to be made in the joint appeal, and the country went to the polls on October 27th.

I believed in a National Government as being the only instrument by which the prestige, honour and financial stability of the country could be restored, and I declared this throughout the Moseley Division. Many new municipal housing estates had been built in my area and, consequently, the electorate had greatly increased. The Socialists were putting up opposition all over the country, and I found myself against Frank Lloyd who, in the 1929 election, had increased the Labour vote in Kidderminster by 5500. The result, however, was a majority for me of 39642 votes, the largest majority in the country.

Throughout that year important steps were taken to try to expand our commercial relations with countries far overseas. I had a delightfully interesting morning 'on the air' one day in March, when I sent a message of encouragement from the Birmingham Chamber of Commerce all the way to Australia (quite a novelty in those days) which was responded to by the President of the Sydney Chamber of Commerce. Sir Arthur Shirley Benn, the President of the Federation of Chambers of Commerce of the British Empire, exchanged greetings with Mr. Maitland Paxton in Melbourne. The latter spoke for ten minutes, and I could hear the applause of the people in Melbourne punctuating the speech. The experience of talking across half the world for the first time was one that is not soon forgotten. We were disappointed that the Press did not make more of this event, for it was really of great importance in the industrial world.

At that time also, the Prince of Wales was having a great campaign in South America on behalf of British commerce, and the British Empire trade exhibition was held in Buenos Aires. I was honoured in having my name added to the Grand Council for this occasion. Some nine years later I became President of the British and Latin American Chamber of Commerce. On May 21st, a wonderful banquet was given in honour of the Prince's campaign, and a photograph appeared in the newspapers the next day of His Highness, Ramsey MacDonald and myself at the banquet.

Indeed, members of the Royal Family take (and have always taken) an abiding interest in everything that is directly or indirectly relevant to the welfare and prosperity of our country. I recall so clearly the Duke of Kent's visit to Birmingham as guest of honour at the annual dinner of the Birmingham Jewellers and Silversmiths Association, at which I had to respond to the toast of 'Our Visitors'. This industry is such an important source of wealth to the city, and I have always done what I could to foster their trade. I am glad to say that I was always invited to attend their banquets and even in these, for me, gentle years, when so many activities must be slowed up, I look forward to their annual invitation.

CHAPTER 10

The outstanding event, to my mind, for the year 1932, was the introduction of a new fiscal policy for the Nation. I refer, of course, to the Ottawa Conference, whose resolutions formed a platform of Imperial progress, propaganda and constructive statesmanship. With the signing of the agreement the outlook for happiness, comfort and peace seemed brighter to my eyes than ever before. It was a time of great rejoicing. The new epoch in our national and Imperial life, however, was opened some months before the conference took place at the end of January, the new tariff policy (formed by a committee at whose head sat the Chancellor of the Exchequer, Mr. Neville Chamberlain) was published. Few events more momentous than this, for the future welfare of the people, had taken place for a great many years. Neville Chamberlain, in unfolding the policy, knew he was announcing proximity to the goal towards which his father had endeavoured to guide the country. The policy provided for a ten per cent duty on foreign goods (certain non-essential foreign goods bearing an additional duty) and, where a foreign country showed discrimination against British goods the duty could be raised to one hundred percent. The tariff would not, of course, apply to Colonial produce. In effect, this comparatively low basis of duty could be expanded indefinitely.

It must be realised that in those days this was quite a revolutionary proceeding. For eighty-six years free trade had dominated the financial and industrial life of our nation. It had been adhered to with almost religious fervour, by vast numbers of our population. It had been the subject of intense controversy for more than a generation, culminating in a series of bitter political contests. But in the grinding circumstances of the 'twenties', in the presence of the faltering and fading competitive power of Great Britain in world markets, its doom was inevitable. And so it was that on Thursday January 31st 1932, in the House of Commons, we participated in the first and most picturesque of the series of obsequies which led towards its final interment. Sir Herbert Samuel naturally attacked Chamberlain's speech with great vigour and received hearty support from the Free Traders who were present.

A day or two previously, Page Croft had written to me: -
"Dear Paddy,

I am of opinion that we should insist as a condition of our continued support to the Cabinet that these declared opponents of tariffs should, in any event, not take part in Cabinet decisions or Cabinet meetings with reference to tariffs or Imperial Preference, otherwise the whole thing becomes a mockery."

And what difficulties that Cabinet went through! It was only for the sake of maintaining this newly born National Government that, after great hazards, the members were prevailed upon to accept a majority vote instead of the unprecedented, unanimous decision. But with the Ottawa Conference, Samuel and his Free Trade supporters handed in their resignation. Canada was the real crux, as I saw it, to a full Imperial economic understanding that would enlarge the field for the sale of British products, and give preference to Imperial raw materials. The outcome of the conference depended largely upon the quality, effort, statesmanship and strength of character of the British delegation, and in Neville Chamberlain these attributes were to be found.

On June 9th, I had a long and interesting conversation with Captain Harold Macmillan (as he then was) who proposed to me that we should make arrangements to give a dinner to the delegation before they left for Ottawa. After some discussion on the propriety of inviting certain people to this dinner, we decided to ask a whole series of men connected with banking and industry, including Reginald McKenna, Mr. Goodenough, Sir Barry McGowan and several others prominently associated with the industrial enterprise of this country. The particular point we wished to impress was that the delegation should feel assured of the confidence which we had in them.

On the morning of July 13th, the party left Victoria station en-route for Canada, and we waited for news of their deliberations with eagerness and impatience. The only weakness of the Conference was their attitude towards agriculture. Indeed, Beaverbrook, thoroughly disappointed that things had not gone much further, openly declared that: - "No progress of the least consequence had been made," and that, "the livestock industry of Great Britain had been ignored." But in my view, the important feature of the conference was that now industry in this country would have ample opportunity in the market and, also, for the first time the relationship between the Dominions and Great Britain was placed on a business basis, and the Empire was to have a policy of give and take, whereby the voice of the British manufacturer would be heard in the Colonies. An interesting point I noted at the time was that the 2/- per quarter tax on foreign wheat was the very duty suggested by Joseph Chamberlain twenty-nine years before.

Upon Neville Chamberlain's return, I sent him a note of congratulation, and received the following in reply, written from Aberdeenshire, where he was resting from his labours: -

"Dear Paddy,

Many thanks for your kind message, which I much appreciate. We had a strenuous time in Ottawa, but it was worth it.

Yours ever,

N. Chamberlain."

On December 5th, the 'Birmingham Club' gave a dinner to Chamberlain in the House of Commons, where it fell to my lot (in the unavoidable absence of Sir Austen and Leo Amery) to present our guest of honour with a beautiful silver salver, inscribed with the names of the Members of Parliament for Birmingham and, also, those of five ex-members. There was, in addition, an inscription in Latin which could be translated as: - *"What the father undertook, the son after thirty years accomplished."* with which Neville Chamberlain was particularly touched.

I should like here to quote a few words from his speech. He said: - *"Reading, as I have been doing during the last few days, of my father's early days, so wonderfully described by Mr. Garvin, I feel very humble ... Nevertheless, I am indeed proud and thankful that I should have been able to take some part in bringing to a successful conclusion, the work to which he gave so much, and concerning which he never lost the conviction that a successful conclusion would come. It is curious to think that up to the date of his death, he had no conception that I should ever enter Parliament, or take any more active part in politics than I had done up to that time. He had never asked me to do so."*

Sir Austen Chamberlain's absence on this occasion through illness was a cruel blow of fate which Neville felt greatly, as did all of us who wanted to celebrate together. During my part in the Presentation, I read aloud the letter that I had received from Austen that morning: -

"My dear Paddy,

It is a cruel disappointment to me that I cannot be with you tonight, when the little ceremony which is to be performed has an interest for me second only to that which it has for Neville. Please make it clear to Neville that I had nothing to do with the inception of the presentation, though I gladly joined when you and others proposed it to me. I think what we have all felt is that not only might Ottawa have failed without Neville, but that had it not been for Neville's action alike at the time of last year's crisis, and in the earlier crisis in the Unionist Party, Ottawa might never have taken place. Give him my love. How proud his father would have been of him!

Yours sincerely,

Austen Chamberlain.

P.S. I am up today for the first time, but I dare not come out at night yet, nor at all on a day like this."

What a happy dinner that was; and what a memorable occasion. Through Neville's ability we had protected the home market, we had reduced the import of competitive manufactured goods by some £75,000,000, and all the resolutions passed at Ottawa carried us a little further along the road to that point when the Empire would be playing its full part, to the mutual advantage of the whole. After the dinner, Neville Chamberlain wrote to me: - *"The salver has arrived safely, and the more I look at it the more I admire its shape and lines. It is a beautiful thing in itself, and with its inscription and the signatures. It will become a family heirloom of which my descendants will be very proud. You told me that you and Leo Amery were the initiators; I might have guessed this without being told for you are always thinking of things that others find appropriate, but have not thought of doing themselves. I am very grateful to all who have joined in this gift, and am writing to them individually, but I want to express my special thanks to you for your particular share, and for the most generous terms in which you made the presentation. It was a great occasion for me, and I shall always remember it with pride and pleasure."*

I have already said a word about the sad fact of the delegates at Ottawa overlooking our agricultural Industry, which at that time was in a precarious state. There had been a slump in farm prices the previous year and since then the downward trend had continued, while acreage had decreased, leaving no room for misconception of the intensity of the depression. When, at the end of September,

Major Walter Elliot became the Minister of Agriculture, I wrote a letter to him, publishing it in the 'Daily Express', in which I said: -

"You are taking up your exacting duty at a moment of supreme emergency in our agricultural life. … Arable farming is confronted by a more staggering outlook than at any time in our economic history. It is aggravated by the position in which we find ourselves in regard to our great livestock industry. With the approach of winter, this great branch of wealth production is rapidly being enveloped by creeping paralysis. The value of agricultural land during recent months at public sales has been at a lower level than at any time within living memory. A very bleak future indeed must be faced in many a rural household. In your own country of Scotland, the outlook from the point of view of marketing produce is almost one of despair. … The early solution of the meat problem must prove the turning point in British agriculture. … I am aware that the Central Chamber, of which I have the honour to be Vice-President, and over which I presided last year, is engaged upon the preparation of comprehensive agricultural proposals which will in due course be submitted to you, but in the meantime I am so deeply concerned with the whole outlook, not only in agriculture but in our entire national life, that I have taken the liberty of writing to you on the morning of your entry into the Cabinet."

Elliot wrote in reply: -

"There will be plenty to do and I shall, no doubt, have to draw heavily on the good nature of my friends before the task is over."

My facts were not taken from reports or verbal accounts, for I had just made a tour of Scotland and the North of England, and in every agricultural district I had been met with an attitude of despair. John Beard (the President of the Central and Associated Chambers of Agriculture) fully understanding the farmers plight, said that if he were dictator of Great Britain, he would compel one hundred thousand men to be transferred on to the land for the coming winter. In his position, however, the next best thing he could do was to hold a meeting at the C. and A. Chambers of Agriculture, where we passed a resolution asking the Government to take emergency action to relieve the acute depression, and invited the Prime Minister and Walter Elliot to receive a deputation to consider measures to meet the crisis. I spoke supporting the resolution and, on November 9th, was accorded the honour, along with John

Beard, of introducing the deputation to the Minister of Agriculture. Leo Amery, I recall, was among those on the deputation. We had a preliminary meeting at the Chartered Surveyors Institution (in Great George Street) and then went on to the Ministry, where Walter Elliot was sympathetic, but guarded, in his replies.

Before Elliot became Minister of Agriculture, he had been Financial Secretary to the Treasury, and had had the onus of steering the Finance Bill through, the committee stage while the Chancellor of the Exchequer was at Lausanne. Neville Chamberlain, in a somewhat disappointing speech on the third Reading of the Bill, paid him a very high compliment for the way in which he had carried out his task. After the House adjourned, Walter Elliot and I had a long conversation in the Smoke Room on the difficulties he had met with, and the means he had had to adopt, in solving then.

It was about this time that we lost one who was regarded (not merely in his own country, but throughout Europe) as the clearest exponent of economic thought of his generation, Magnus Alexander, whose death aroused universal regret. I had the privilege of entertaining him to dinner, to meet a number of leading industrialists and economists, on the occasion of one of his visits to this country, and his discourse on that occasion made a lasting impression upon us all. The contribution he made to the appreciation of the subtle and embarrassing financial problems of those times was of inestimable value.

While the Disarmament Conference was taking place at Geneva, Hitler was openly showing his claws in Germany. Well-meaning people had urged me to press for the policy of disarmament, quite unaware that our Navy had been cut to the bone and our Army was a mere skeleton. We had done more to disarm than any other country, and until other nations did likewise, I strongly maintained that we should not go any further. It was our hope (and what a vain one it turned out to be) that the nations of the world would be satisfied with such defensive forces as would ensure their own internal security. I have the copy of a letter I sent to the Foreign Secretary, Sir John Simon, drawing his attention to a comment which appeared in an edition of the 'Kölnische Zeitung' on the 20th September, which was obviously designed to place Sir John Henderson in ostensible antagonism, preparatory to using this situation for propaganda purposes. The comment, translated, ran thus: -

"The English Note has made an excellent impression in Polish Government circles, which is only to be expected since Poland is completely under the thumb of France. Germany, however, has a staunch ally at Geneva, in the person of Mr. Henderson, who is entirely against Simon, and shows a masterly appreciation of England's obligations in the matter of disarmament. Henderson interprets Part V of the Treaty of Versailles in the way we would expect, and is quite open in his opinion that Germany has every right to her claim for equality of status."

Sir John's reply to my enclosure came within a few days: -

"My dear Pat,

I am afraid that the alarms and excursions of the past few days have prevented me from writing before to thank you for your kind letter of September 27th, in which you drew my attention to an article in the 'Kolnische Zeitung' about my supposed relations with Henderson. It was very good of you to bring this to my notice. Geneva is an unequalled breeding ground for this sort of stuff.

Yours sincerely,

John Simon

I was greatly incensed during June to hear that an ex-Zeppelin Commander, Kapitanleutnant Breithaupt, was to relate from the B.B.C. his experiences over England as a raider. I never dreamt that, within thirteen years of the close of conflict, I should witness this insolent disregard of British national feeling, and I felt it to be an insult, particularly to those who had suffered bereavement through the Zeppelin raids. I had been invited (along with a party of Parliamentary Members) to visit Broadcasting House, but, on hearing this extraordinary broadcast, I immediately cancelled my acceptance of the invitation. In the reply which I received from the B.B.C. it was stated, as explanation, that: - *"... the talk was one of a 'Hazard' series, in which endeavour is being made to give first-hand accounts of unique, thrilling, experiences in the adventure sense."* An explanation, which, in my eyes, failed to redeem the broadcast. Among other speakers in the series had been Admiral Evans, who had contributed a talk on Scott of the Antarctic (with whom he had shared perilous adventure), and it is surely obvious that those wonderful feats of courage and endurance in exploration are hardly on the same plane as the cruel and appalling mission of a bombing aircraft. I would have liked to have aired this matter in the House, but under the rules of Parliamentary procedure (in view of the extraordinary powers conferred upon the B.B.C. by the House of Commons) it was impossible to put a question on the Paper relating to its programme or internal administration.

In August, my wife and I spent a very pleasant holiday in Scotland, in the company of Sir Cornelius and Lady Chambers, and, on December 10th, we went on a tour to the West Indies where, with the co-operation of the Colonial Office, I was to examine the economic conditions. The beginning of any voyage always has its particular thrill in the cursory examination of numerous boats of all sizes, and from all parts of the world, gathered in the dock.

I recall dining with Mr. Harrison (of the Harrison Line) only a short while before our trip, and he had given me a long dissertation on the situation in the shipping world. He had pointed out to me that, unless we were prepared to develop the more generous use of coal in relation to shipping, both the coal industry and the shipping industry would be placed in a very difficult position. He held the theory that neither pulverised coal, nor oil, were in any sense suitable for tramp shipping, though of course admitting that in the Navy, oil would be, and must be, the predominant element in the provision of motor power. And soon, I suppose, nuclear power will predominate on all our ships!

"If we were only wise enough," Harrison had lamented, "to use the coal of Great Britain, in relation to the great mass of English shipping for bunkering purposes, the whole policy of the country would be substantially improved."

To return, however, to our delightful West Indian trip. The 'Viceroy of India', in which we journeyed, was the first ship propelled by turbo-electric machinery to visit Port-of-Spain, and this fact created much interest in the Islands. The weather was so bad shortly after we set off, that the ship was unable to call at the Azores without losing too much time and disrupting our schedule in the West Indies. So, with her two hundred and seventy or so passengers, the ship carried on across the ocean and soon the West Indian climate embraced us. We arrived at Bermuda in glorious sunshine! This island was at that time (and very probably still remains) the most thoroughly congested self-governing unit in the

British Empire, and probably the only community in the world which maintains abounding prosperity on its invisible exports.

I remember so well our arrival in the early morning at Kingston, Jamaica, where we were received by the A.D.C. to the Governor and members of the Jamaica Imperial Association. They took us for a drive through the most picturesque parts of the island, and I can assure my readers that, if one could select any motor run through scenes of the most wonderful natural beauty and tropical cultivation, one could find nothing more striking than that drive from Kingston. We went through mountain gorges, past banana plantations and into coconut groves and found beauty abounding. Indeed, I might say that every island seemed to derive the fullest blessings from nature. On the next day, the Institute of Jamaica gave a garden party in our honour, and we were received by the Chairman, Mr. Herbert de Lisser (a very friendly and charming personality). The Jamaican Imperial Association gave us luncheon one day, and Field Marshal Lord Allenby (who was staying on the island) was the guest of honour and spoke recalling the contingents of West Indians who had served under him in Palestine. I found the whole series of islands, from Bermuda to Trinidad, most interesting from the point of view of the development of the British Empire. Indeed, it is no exaggeration to say that the foundations of our Imperial prestige were laid in these Islands.

To one who had, like myself, been Secretary to the Navy League for a part of my life, it was a cause of pure excitement to lunch with Sir Reginald St Johnston (the Governor of Antigua) and see his beautiful home that had once been the residence of Nelson and Rodney; to look at the famous harbour where Nelson had based his fleet, and ponder on the tiny ships of 1801, '02, and '03 in which they planned their great schemes to wipe their antagonists off the seas. Wherever you touch land in those islands, you find features reminiscent of the early struggles for the supremacy of the sea, and with the establishment of British Naval supremacy began the rise of the Empire. Incidentally, the Governor of Jamaica (Sir Ransford Slater) was an old boy of King Edward's School, Birmingham, and thoroughly relished the opportunity to chat about Birmingham and recall his schooldays in New Street.

Of the other islands, I remember best a most interesting morning I spent in Grenada, at a Government ginnery, where the coloured man in charge gave me an absorbing demonstration of the ginning of cotton. I also recall the new lime plantations in Dominica, whose predecessors had been uprooted in a single night by the terrible hurricane of 1926, and the beautiful and go-ahead island of Trinidad. We were met in this latter island by the leading businessmen, who showed us over the big firms of Geddes, Grants and Hubbards (dealing with shipping throughout the islands, and transport going to South America). Their organisation was as perfect as human effort could make it, and I praised them to the press reporters for the magnificent spirit that is evident in their work,

The Tropical College of Agriculture in Trinidad was doing work of untold value for humanity. Dr Evans (who was in charge of the College) was one of those splendid types of Englishmen, prepared to sacrifice every personal consideration to the job entrusted to him. Our usual programme was to come ashore in the morning, lunch with the Governor of the island and have some sort of conference in the afternoon with the local businessmen.

In each case, we discussed the island's future with the Governor, and with many different officials. I was most interested to find in Jamaica that the ideas with which I first became identified in public life (agricultural co-operation) were being given practical application. They had, in fact, taken a most direct, positive and constructive course, by inviting the participants in each particular industry to organise for the promotion of that industry's expansion and efficiency. The most striking feature from the economic point of view in Jamaica was the large number of small cultivators who, in most cases, showed a considerable degree of independence, enterprise, and anxiety to acquire technical knowledge.

Consequently, technical and rural education was making substantial progress. It was good to see that nearly every official with whom I came in contact showed great keenness and enthusiasm in agricultural research and experimental work, which augured well for the future of the islands. But there were economic difficulties also to be faced.

214

These were mainly dealt with by the West India Committee, which had been furthering the interests of the islands for two hundred years. I had first become acquainted with its Secretary, Sir Algernon Aspinall (who was the author of many books on the subject) when I was Honorary Secretary of the movement to erect a monument to Drake. At that time, I learned that the West India Committee was an organisation both expository and diplomatic, for the administration in Whitehall (so fortunate in having an officer like Sir Algernon) was playing its part better and more wisely than any other similar organisation of its kind connected with the British Empire. I wanted to get him to speak to the House upon the subject of the West Indies, and I thought it desirable that a small group of Members might be formed who would keep in constant contact with the W.I.C. so that some of the economic difficulties might be directly faced and smoothed out.

Of course, we had (in Sir Philip Cunliffe-Lister) a Secretary of State at the Colonial Office, who took a most active interest in the welfare of all the Colonial peoples. Many of us in Parliament believed that the development of the Colonial Empire (in regard to reciprocal trade) lent itself to almost unlimited expansion, and I was anxious to spare no effort to forward this conception.

On Christmas Day, which we celebrated many miles away from Great Britain, the 'Sunday Express' paid me an amusing compliment, which I would like to quote. It is taken from an article by William Barkley: - *"It has been my custom every week to give you a bad-tempered biography of a Member. Where, oh where, in this season of goodwill and amity, can I find a fitting subject for this new mood? Big, comfortable, florid, silver-haired Patrick Joseph Henry Hannon, eleven years a Member (for Moseley), is the best-liked man in the House. The secret of being the best-liked man in a body of egoists is unselfishness; being confident and strong, by no means self-effacing, yet free from paranoia. [. . .] Putting his feet down firmly as he walks, he is also flat-footed in his decisions, unswerving in his path. Capable of bad judgement, but never of bad conduct. Courage to a high degree. Cares nothing of criticism. Given a whole House of Hannons, Britain would be supreme in Europe and dominating in America."*

And on this happy, if somewhat absurd note, I shall pass into that period of brighter years which resulted from the

Ottawa Conference, when prosperity among all classes was on the up-grade for six years, till the outbreak of war brought its 'blood, tears and sweat' to the British people. There is, of course, the sad reflection that during this interval the mind of the nation was directed towards the establishment of the pathways of peace, at the expense of preparedness for the fury of the conflict which, to those of us in touch with the situation, was inevitable to a nation as unprepared as we were. Incensed at the reduction of our Naval strength advocated in 1933, I wrote to the 'Morning Post': - *"There is nothing more disturbing in our political life in these embarrassing and, indeed, menacing times, than the frequently sloppy and sometimes calculated indifference of certain politicians, to the outstanding gravity of the problems of Imperial defence. ... The cry of the pacifist to limit our naval building programme, is perilously near an appeal to the British people to commit national suicide ... It is difficult to be patient with the fumblers and faddists of so-called pacifism in their attacks upon the Navy."* On March 6th, I also drew the attention of the House to the intensified activity then apparent in the Skoda ammunition works, but no reply was given. The League of Nations was an admirable institution, unique in human history to that date. Every point of its six-point disarmament programme was academically admirable, yet every point was hopeless from the practical view of securing universal peace. Owing to differences arising out of economic nationalism, military pride, and old prejudice and bitterness, we could not expect (or even hope for) any great accomplishments, and the future proved us only too correct. In that year, we were still settling up the age-old question of war debts, for it was not until June 13th that Chamberlain announced that £2,000,000.000 was to be paid to the U.S.A. in settlement. I clearly recall Sir Austen Chamberlain's words, spoken at a Unionist meeting in Birmingham at the beginning of April: -

"I am not a reader of the Press, I do not draw my knowledge or inspiration from it. I base what I have to say on the utterance of men in Germany, and these utterances reveal a spirit which we hoped had departed from this world. Germany met her fate because, in overweening pride and egocentric vanity, she was not willing to let live while she lived, but tried to dominate and impose her will on the rest of Europe. And now we see the same spirit, kindling again, in her internal affairs."

216

I did everything that lay in my power to fight the appalling persecution of the Jews, but there was so pitiably little that could be done. On April 3rd, Sir Philip Dawson and I sent a letter to Hindenburg, appealing to him to get the Government to end these attacks, and to restore the rights of German citizenship to the Jews. We said in addition: - "It would be a sad day for the German name throughout the world, if it became identified with the cruelty and persecution of a helpless minority of its own people. We feel so deeply the danger of a serious blow to the good understanding of our two nations, that we regard the action we now take as an imperative national duty."

On April 26th a most unfortunate meeting was held in one of the Committee rooms of the House of Commons, under the Chairmanship of Mr. Doran. He had invited a German, Dr. Thost, to explain the true situation in Germany, and I attended the meeting in company with a handful of Members (including Major Proctor and Sir Basil Peto). The Herr Doktor declared that the Jews had acquired a dominant position in Germany, which was unfair to the pure German national, and that when they left the country it was with the best of goodwill from the Nazi officials, who would say politely: - "All right, I am very pleased you are leaving. Here is your passport."

As to the so-called atrocities, continued Dr Thost scornfully, those incidents had been much exaggerated and were very infrequent. He mentioned one case, which had been published recently, and said: - "It was just like an ordinary 'Oxford rag'; the Jew was not hurt at all." When he had finished his somewhat uninspiring defence of the Nazi regime, a motion that the Members of Parliament deplored Germany's attitude towards the Jews was proposed by Major Proctor, and there was immediate uproar. The Chairman made a tirade against the admittance of aliens into Great Britain, and the meeting ended in disorder. It was all a useless and undignified procedure.

This reminds me of another meeting in a committee room of the House that was held that year, causing considerable annoyance and which also dealt with the Jews, but in relation to the Arab problem in Palestine. I had been obliged to leave the meeting before it ended as I had to take the Chair in another committee room, which prevented me from associating myself with the just and fitting protest made by Lord Winterton on the proceedings. Lord Winterton's letter to me explains the incident: - *"I was very grateful for your support at the Arab meeting yesterday, and I would be still more grateful if you would watch out for any possible reply in the 'Daily Telegraph', and which I hope will appear in tomorrow's issue, relating to the proceedings. I take the greatest possible exception to the speeches which were made, which got, unfortunately, worse after you left. At a later stage I suggest that it may be necessary for you and I privately to see the Speaker, and urge upon him the undesirability of allowing committee rooms of the House of Commons to be used for the purpose of holding 'Public Meetings'. I have always understood that the use of the rooms in question, for unofficial Meetings, was limited to those composed of Members of Parliament, though of course a reasonable latitude is always allowed in regard to the participation at such meetings of members of the public, and speakers from outside, but the gathering yesterday was nothing else than a packed propagandist meeting, calculated to do great injury to the cause of the Arabs. I would not venture to trouble you with this letter, if you were not always such a good friend."*

I replied: - *"I am very much honoured by your confidence and friendship, and you will see from the 'Telegraph' this morning that I lost no time in expressing my views on the matter which gave both of us so much concern on Thursday afternoon. I will be delighted to co-operate with you on the matter of the grave abuse of the committee rooms. A good deal of this sort of thing arose when the agitation was in full swing on the Entertainments Tax. We also had a dose of it on the action taken by the Government in relation to the Tote, and there are other instances equally glaring and equally objectionable."*

In my letter to the 'Daily Telegraph' I declared that I was in complete accord with Lord Wintetton's expressed opinion. I went on to say that Members of the House of Commons are always anxious to obtain first-hand information on questions of great public interest, and generous courtesy is invariably extended to Speakers from outside the House who are best fitted to discuss those subjects; but that this was an entirely different matter from using Committee rooms for propagandist purposes, and abusing the opportunity of an exchange of views with Members by making attacks upon Governmental policy and the conduct of those who represented H.M. Government in mandated territories.

1933 was the year of Sir Samuel Hoare's famous White paper on India (resulting in a long controversy) which the late Leo Amery described as producing much of the finest debating I have heard in Parliament. For my own part, I withdrew my membership from the India Defence League and the India Empire Society, believing that it was unwise to interfere with the efforts of the Joint Select Committee (on which Winston Churchill, incidentally, had refused to sit). I felt that it was wrong that Members of Parliament should vigorously put forward their opinions before the Report had become public.

My own unhappy country was also in the news those days, owing to an impasse in the relations between the Free State and Great Britain, and trade relations were almost at a standstill. I quote my letter to 'The Times', published on May 30th: - *"The trade situation between Great Britain and the Irish Free State, as revealed in 'The Times', presents a distressing commentary on the apparently hopeless misunderstanding between these two co-equal partners in the British Commonwealth of Nations. The figures you quoted show that Irish imports from Great Britain fell by 38% in the first four months of the present year, as compared with the corresponding period of 1932. The percentage fall in the Irish exports to Great Britain in the same comparative period is 37%. Now it may be quite true to say that the full effect of current trade conditions must result in a reduction both of the import and of the export trade as between the two countries, but quite clearly the percentages given are in a very large measure due to the unfortunate commercial relations which obtain, consequent upon the decision of the I.F.S. to refuse payment of the Land annuities [...] It is needless to emphasise the grave injury which must necessarily be inflicted upon the Irish people, more particularly the agricultural community, whose market has been, and must always continue to be, Great Britain; on the other hand the inconvenience and loss of trade to a great variety of industries in England and Scotland are, and indeed in many instances within my personal knowledge, of far-reaching consequence in the field of the employment of our workpeople. How long is this unhappy state of affairs to continue? Is the present impasse an example of the bankruptcy of statesmanship and the futility of constructive diplomacy? A fall of seven pounds a head per annum in the commercial vitality of the population of the Irish Free State cannot be contemplated by any Irishman without disturbing apprehension. National pride and national self-respect*

219

are beautiful concepts in the life of nations, but their rigid observance sometimes inflicts severe wounds on the prosperity of people and the peaceful progress of mankind, where a moderate and less highly susceptible self-consciousness would have produced happy relations all round. Mr. de Valera will shortly return from Rome, where he will have witnessed one of the greatest examples of ardent patriotism employed as an instrument of national progress which the world has ever seen; and he will have observed that the economic power which has been created in Italy has, during its development, always had careful regard for measures which led to expansion of trade with the rest of the world. He will also have noted, no doubt, that the tendency of even a powerful nation to become self-centred has its limitations. Can one who still ardently loves Ireland and who is intimately concerned for the success of British industry and agriculture, make a plea for the subordination of the smaller considerations to greater, and urge that negotiations in a kindly spirit of mutual goodwill between Mr. Thomas and Mr. de Valera might be initiated at the earliest possible moment with great advantage to Great Britain, to Ireland and to the Empire and, one may venture to hope, in some degree to the success of the World Economic Conference."

The difficulty of my position can be appreciated in the reconciling of that loyalty which I felt towards the country of my birth, with the loyalty towards the British Empire and the policy that I had advocated for so many years. In my speeches therefore, I defended Mr. J.H. Thomas who, although adamant against conceding any part of the Land Annuity's debt, had done everything that he could to produce a settlement. Yet it was most disheartening to hear that Mr. Lemass had offered to remove the Irish tariff duties (providing that Great Britain undertook to remove her tariffs in a reasonably short time), and that this fair offer on Ireland's part had met with a cool reception. There was no desire on the part of the British Government to inflict any penalty upon the Irish people, but they very naturally wished to recoup the British treasury. There were merits for the case from both points of view, but it was unarguable, and I could only pray with heart and soul that even at the eleventh hour (when negotiations seemed to be permanently in abeyance) wisdom might prevail so that measures could be taken for a further exchange of views such as could lead to a peaceful adjustment. I asked in the

House on December 5th if the door was still open for further negotiations if the Free State desired, and was told by poor Thomas that 'the door has never been closed.' A long period was to pass by, during which the livestock industry of Ireland was to be brought to such a condition by the slaughter of her calves that recovery has only been possible in recent years. As the late Count John McCormack wrote to me in July 1932: - *"She is destined to be the 'Niobe' of the nations, alas!"* And this was very true.

My mention of Rome in the previous letter reminds me of a most interesting trip I made, early in 1933, as one of a party of Members of Parliament attending the International Commercial Conference in Rome. We were received in audience by the Holy Father, one of the most wonderful incidents of my life. The charm of the Pope, his gentle treatment towards us, and the touching words which he addressed to us, are never to be forgotten memories of my visit. I was the only Roman Catholic in the party. We also officially visited the King and Signor Mussolini, who had addressed the Conference at the opening ceremony. I had the good fortune to be able to call privately at the Duce's house with a letter of introduction from a friend.

Once seen, Mussolini's face remains in one's recollection forever; and he impressed one immediately as a man with tremendous personality, power, and unswerving will. I was able, with perfect truth, to praise the transformation apparent in Italy under the Fascist regime, and to tell Mussolini of the interest which I took in that virile movement. Everywhere was order, regularity and cleanliness, and the arable districts would have been a valuable example to the British farmer for the efficiency that was everywhere evident. Another point that impressed me was the fact that no Italian would dream of buying a foreign article in preference to one produced in Italy, and I wished that our people at home had the same loyalty in the economic life of Great Britain.

Through the generous kindness of Brother Clancy, I secured a ticket to the Tribune at St Peter's on Easter morning, and saw the whole of that wonderful ceremony at close quarters. I was present in the Piazza of St Peter's when the Pope gave his blessing to the people. I visited several beautiful churches including Our Lady of Victories, where I saw the famous Bernini statue of St Teresa. On Easter

Monday, we went for a motor tour through most romantic and interesting districts, visiting, among other towns, Viterbo and Alvito. It is strange to think that, within a decade, the people of that pleasant land were to wage bitter war against our army on the deserts of North Africa.

I had connection also with some of the Baltic countries that year! For instance, the National Union of Students sent a group of Lithuanian students to England, where they would see for themselves the way in which British politics and industry shaped the country. I arranged that five of them should meet me to be entertained at the House, and from these I later received most enthusiastic letters of thanks for all they had seen and learned. After their return home, the Lithuanian Minister wrote to me: - *"I know that you will agree with me that the plastic mind of youth is a favourable medium through which to operate in seeking to cultivate and stimulate international contacts of this nature. Such contacts should be, more than ever, encouraged at a time like the present, when the almost universal economic malaise, inevitably perhaps, tends to breed a too narrow spirit of nationalism, hostile to intercourse of this character. Thus, the cultural, economic and political entente between the Baltic States and Great Britain can but benefit from the recent visit."*

In November, the matter of the Riga loan cropped up again. It was a sad business, for the Latvian Government had not yet (after a number of years) been able to repay the British bondholders who had invested their capital in the loan. During my visit to Latvia as far back as 1922, a conference took place with the Minister of Finance on the subject of the Riga loan and we understood that they would settle the matter as quickly as possible. When I returned to England I stressed its importance upon the Latvian Minister, M. Bisseneek, and also arranged a conference with the directors of Lazard Brothers; but, even then, no action was taken. The Latvian Prime Minister promised Sir Philip Dawson and myself, during our visit in 1924, that the matter would be expedited. Yet here I was in 1933, once again directing attention to the Riga loan in connection with that patient and confiding individual, the British bondholder, whose reliance in foreign investments was being so sorely tried.

With trade now on the up grade, that great engineering firm, the Birmingham Small Arms Company (of which I was Deputy Chairman) showed a profit for the first time since the start of the depression. The B.S.A. Company was one of the very few concerns that had come through the post war years without a reconstruction of capital, and with very few lapses from the dividend list. I remember opening a B.S.A. Exhibition that year, which included (among the interesting variety of motors, machines and small arms) an old bone-shaker such as had not been seen on the roads of Great Britain for a great number of years. There was a certain amount of feeling at that time against that department of the B.S.A. which was concerned in the manufacture of weapons, and I repeatedly stated the fact that nobody, neither director, officer nor manual labourer of the company, desired to make arms with a view to waging war. Some British firm had to make them and, as this was the inescapable position, it was as well for Birmingham that our firm was given the contract to make a proportion of these arms, rather than another firm elsewhere in the country.

The jewellery trade of Birmingham had received a severe blow in May, when Mr. Runciman made an agreement with Germany reducing the import duties on jewellery, clocks and so on. So many people are connected with this trade that there was much dismay throughout the city, and Sir Austen Chamberlain led a revolt against the Government which I, of course, supported (along with the 'Birmingham Club' and other Members). There was quite a to-do, and Runciman had to appeal for a vote of confidence. However, Chamberlain's motion was defeated; chiefly because this Anglo-German agreement opened the market in Germany for extra coal from our pits. At this time the Post Offices were stamping the words 'Buy British' upon our mail, and I discovered the absurd fact that, stamped upon these particular machines they used, were the words. 'Made in U.S.A.', or something to that effect!

It appeared from the reply Sir Knapley Wood gave me in the House, that no British machines were available at the time of installation, but he assured the House that replacements would be British. While we were buying goods from abroad because we were unable to make them ourselves, and even though so many of our workers were unemployed, Great Britain received many thousands of immigrants (greatly in excess of our emigration numbers) which naturally intensified the unemployment problem.

Even our ships were manned by foreigners, thus throwing our own sailors on the dole. A big demonstration that attracted a good deal of notice was given on behalf of twelve thousand officers of the Merchant Service. The tug 'Britannia' carried a huge petition from London Bridge to Westminster, where I received it and handed it over to Lieut. Colonel. Moore Brabazon. On the petition, it was stated that owing to the foreign influx into the Merchant Navy, about three thousand officers and forty thousand seamen were out of work. A large number of the public also signed the petition.

Apropos of unemployment, I have, over a number of years, urged that the payment of unemployment insurance benefit should be associated with some kind of work. The almost indiscriminate doling out of money for relief, while leaving the recipient completely idle, is bound to have a demoralising effect. Working hours (so inextricably bound up with unemployment) were much debated at that time and, under the Presidency of Churchill, I was the Parliamentary Chairman of the Early Closing Association. I was disgusted at the extension of Sunday trading which I saw as a serious menace, not only to the moral outlook of the people, but also to their physical well-being and comfort, and I am still saddened to perceive the numbers of people who have turned the Sabbath into a virtual marketing day. I am not one of those people who would like to see the return of the hard puritanical Sunday, on the contrary, I want to see all the amenities and opportunities of life available to all, as long as no section of the public is deprived of their right in the service of the others. But I have no compunction in describing the unnecessary trading on Sundays as a sign of decadence. I believe that it would have been far better for the people of Britain, had the asset of Sunday been preserved on the same high level as it was when I was a child.

In order to commemorate Chamberlain's work at the Imperial Conference at Ottawa, the Midland Conservative Association presented him with his portrait (painted by Oswald Birley) and also presented Mrs. Chamberlain with some jewellery. In his speech of thanks, he mentioned his father, Joseph Chamberlain, saying that it was characteristic of his tenacity of character that, up to the very end, he never wavered in his faith in the ultimate acceptance of his ideas, and he spoke too of his wife, Anne Chamberlain (that delightful and charming personality) telling us how ardently she pursued her husband's interests, and how, sharing all his plans and secrets, she never divulged them to anyone. "No politician," he declared, "could owe more to his helpmate than I do." She certainly inspired him in his career, and they were a devoted couple. He wrote to me afterwards: -

"My dear Paddy,

Although I had an opportunity of expressing my thanks to the subscribers' to the Portrait Presentation Fund on Saturday, I should like to tell you personally how deeply touched by wife and I have been by the wonderful gifts which you joined in making to us. Amidst all the anxieties and responsibilities of public work, such a recognition coming from our fellow workers in our own City is a reward as gratifying as it was unexpected. The picture and the jewellery will be treasured by us as long as we live, and when we have passed on, our children too will value them, equally for themselves and for the association they will carry with them.

With grateful thanks, believe me,

Yours sincerely,

N. Chamberlain

P.S. I should like to add how much we appreciated the opportunity which you and Mrs. Hannon gave us of meeting some friends afterwards. It was more than kind of you and rounded off a perfect day."

Incidentally, I sent a copy of the first and second volumes of J.L. Garvin's biography of Joseph Chamberlain to His Grace Thomas Williams, Archbishop of Birmingham, who replied: - *"Garvin's 'Chamberlain' is as interesting as any novel I've ever read, and I am most grateful to you for sending it to me. I've read the second volume first, because I remember the events of that period, but I am now going on to Volume 1."*

In the late autumn of 1933, I got into hot water with the Labour Party from the effects of a speech I made at the Conservative conference in Birmingham, which was held soon after a particularly rowdy Labour Party Conference in Sussex. I proposed a motion that Conservative leaders should concentrate on questions relating to Empire consolidation and development, and the motion was seconded by Rear-Admiral Taylor and carried after some little discussion. In my speech I had declared: - "Since the war we have had too much internationalism and too much

Geneva. We should concentrate more on the Empire. There is not a faddist nor a fumbler who does not take Geneva close to his heart, and there is not a fumbler nor a faddist in the Socialist or Liberal parties who is not always decrying the Empire. Look at that Socialist Conference the other day. Look at that rag, tag, and bobtail collection at Hastings. Imagine what sort of government this country would enjoy, what sort of social life this country would pursue under the administration of gentlemen who were fighting like Kilkenny cats the other day."

After that speech I received a flood of correspondence, some of it of an encouraging character, but some downright abusive. The phrase 'rag, tag, and bobtail' appeared to have touched a large number of Labour supporters on the raw. At the next opportunity I reiterated my statement about Geneva, adding that the British Empire, co-ordinated and stabilised in the determination of its own policy, should make its own moat safe before using its power (diplomatic or otherwise) to foster and improve the conditions of other people.

My old friends Sir 'Corney' and Lady Chambers celebrated their Golden Wedding during November of that year, and my wife was elected to present a silver-gilt rose bowl, given by the Moseley Division of the Executive Committee of the Birmingham Unionist Association. It was a charming occasion, and one which we look back on with so much pleasure in our own old age together. Sir. 'Corney' paid a delightful tribute to the Division and to myself, when he said that during the whole time he had worked with us, there had existed a fellowship and friendship among all concerned such as he had never experienced in any other political division. By an amusing coincidence, only a week or two previously, I had appeared for a saddler and his wife in a marriage trial contest on the lines of the famous Dunmow Flitch. Some fun was made during the 'trial' by opposing counsel asking if, since he was a saddler, had he kept his wife on a bridle. But although I did my best for my clients, they were beaten by a couple who had been happily married for years.

On August 19th, the Constitutional Club celebrated its fiftieth anniversary, having been founded by the Marquess of Abergavenny in 1833. One of its minor attributes to fame at that time lay in the fact that it was the only Club in London where a 'baron of beef' might be roasted whole! As far as I know this is still the case.

Apropos of such hospitality on the grand old scale, I am reminded of an amusing article in the 'Daily Express' in which it was declared that I would have made a great innkeeper: - *"He is big and florid, with great warmth of heart and a rolling Irish accent. He is the kindliest of sentimentalists. Yet he has a shrewd brain. He has the Irish gift of making you feel as soon as you meet him that you are his oldest friend. His friendships thus reach their climax at once. Oddly enough there is rarely an anti-climax. This gift makes him invaluable at a house-party, or in any mixed gathering. It must also have been useful when he first started out to win the hearts of his Birmingham constituents. Socialists as well as Tories agree that Patrick Hannon is the best liked man in the House of Commons."*

The 'Birmingham News' commented upon this article: -

"I suppose all are qualifications which have stood him in good stead if he had decided to keep a pub instead of keeping the largest majority in the country."

Of all the many things that have been said of me, some good and some bad, one which gives me particular pleasure, said by a colleague in the House, is: - *"Young Members look up to him like a father for guidance on procedure and etiquette."*

I have always made a point of helping new Members to feel at home in the House of Commons, and to find their feet as quickly as possible. I recall asking some of the younger men to dinner, one time, and inviting Baldwin to join us, but the Prime Minister (as he then was) was unable to accept. He was not in any sense a genial man, and often offended fellow Conservatives by his abrupt manner or by his coolness, but he wrote to me on that occasion saying: - *"As you know, I always enjoy meeting some of the younger members of the Party, and I would very much have liked to have accepted your invitation."*

Ashridge (the Bonar Law College held its annual course for Peers, M.P.s and Parliamentary candidates during May and, whenever I attended, I found a number of keen young Conservatives, as well as a sprinkling of older men. Major-General Sir Reginald Hoskins was Principal at that time (he resigned in 1938, and died during the war). I used to motor over to Ashridge about tea-time, always at weekends, and after dinner we would get together and have a formal discussion at which I sometimes took the Chair. On certain occasions I was engaged to lecture there, and it was warming to see the interest and enthusiasm among all those who came.

CHAPTER 11

The gathering clouds of war which, black and oppressive, were to overshadow all our activities in the last half of the 1930's, were, in the beginning of 1934, already mounting fast from the horizon. Stories of terrorism were brought from Germany and Austria by persecuted refugees who sought sanctuary in Great Britain, and the terrible massacre in June, followed a month later by the murder of Dollfuss (the Austrian Prime Minister) sent the war-clouds scudding across the sky on a wind of fear.

In reference to the abortive revolution in Austria to overthrow Dollfuss, Leo Amery said at a Conservative meeting on the 2nd March: - "If an aggressive Germany, contemptuous of the public opinion of Europe, determined to reverse the verdict of war and tear up the peace treaties, was allowed to swallow up Austria, in violation both the letter and the spirit of international law, then it would not be long before, encouraged by her success, she would swallow or coerce into subjection and dependent alliances the rest of Central and South-East Europe. That meant that Europe would once more be divided into two armed camps, and that we should be face to face, once again, with the very danger which Locarno sought to eliminate." I quote these words of Amery's to illustrate one school of thought to which many members of the National Government subscribed.

At the same time, the National Disarmament Committee had a large percentage of support from influential and leading personages. I remember cancelling an appointment to speak at a League of Nations public demonstration because of some preposterous document issued and conceived, as I thought, by the League but which, in reality, came from the Disarmament people. At the end of July, I attended a solemn Requiem Mass for Dr Dollfuss in Westminster Cathedral, and many of us came away with the feeling that this would not be, by any means, the only memorial service from such a tragic cause that we would be bound by melancholy duty to attend.

On January 22nd, I received a letter from Austen Chamberlain, in answer to my suggestion to him that something constructive might be done to deal with the large number of German refugees. He said: - *"I joined in the appeal made at the Albert Hall some time ago on behalf of the refugees from Germany. Their case is indeed a sad one and must attract English sympathy. Owing to the amount of unemployment still existing in this country, we cannot receive them in any numbers here, but we can do something to relieve their suffering by subscribing to the funds raised on their behalf."* Indeed, until our own affairs were more completely settled, it was impossible to help those unfortunate homeless wanderers to any great extent. There was, at that time, a strong feeling that members of the Cabinet were becoming too complacent, and there was a certain animus against Sir John Simon, Minister for Foreign Affairs. This was increased to such an extent that the Press actually printed the news that Sir John was moving to the Home Office, but, as the object of their benevolent reporting was unaware that he had contemplated such a move, the matter faded out. I was most indignant, however, to find that a speech I had made in Birmingham (when supporting a plea for the inclusion of Sir Austen Chamberlain and Leo Amen in the Cabinet) had been somewhat mangled, to give the strong impression that I had made some sort of attack on the Foreign Office.

I had not done so, but had merely pointed out (with very strong conviction) that the Government would have been strengthened if these two Statesmen had been included in its personnel. To correct this false impression I wrote both to Sir John Simon and to Anthony Eden, assuring them that much of what had appeared in the newspapers was completely at variance with my actual words. Had Sir Austen, in particular, been in his old post of Foreign Secretary during those years, I am satisfied that he would have rendered services of incalculable value.

I was at this time, in conjunction with my wife, about to present the busts of Peel and Palmerston to the House. I had noticed that neither of these great statesmen was represented by statuary in the House of Commons. Therefore, I waited for an opportunity to acquire something really suitable, and was fortunate to buy the two marble busts executed by Mathew Noble. (Peel in 1851, and Palmerston in 1860). Noble was renowned for more than one hundred busts, which is quite surprising work for an extremely delicate man. Peter Howard of the 'Sunday

Express', commenting on our presentation, said: - *"They are fine works of art. The curl on the front of Palmerston's head is strangely like the curl on the forehead of the jovial donor."*

On June 8th, I addressed the following letter to Lord Beaverbrook: -

"It has occurred, to me, that the time has arrived when a bust of Bonar Law should be placed in its appropriate situation in the Palace of Westminster. My wife and I are presenting two busts of Peel and Palmerston which are going to be placed at the foot of the great stairway, and which we decided to give because I want my name to be associated with the story of the House in the golden days to come. I saw Freddie Sykes and Isabel at the India Office reception today, and they are both very keen that something should be done to commemorate Bonar in this way in the House of Commons. You have been his greatest personal friend, and before I move further, I would like to have your advice and suggestion as to what is the appropriate course to take. I am quite confident that all the Members who sat in the House with Bonar, will be delighted to subscribe to provide the bust. I propose to ask Austen and Neville to a small private meeting, or luncheon, or dinner at the House to discuss the proposal, and I would like very much if you would be present. Of course I shall ask Paddy Wargrave to take a hand in the affair."

Beaverbrook replied by return: -

"My dear Paddy.

Very many thanks for your letter of June 8th. I hope very much that you will erect a bust of Bonar in the House. Needless to say, I will gladly subscribe. But I should not go to any luncheon which you may hold for the purpose of promoting it. Wargrave was Bonar's greatest friend, barring myself. He should go.

Yours ever, Max."

In October, the almost legendary figure (friend of Tim Healy and one of Parnell's most pugnacious followers) Jasper Tully, re-visited his old haunts in Westminster, and I was there to welcome him to the House. And what an extraordinary character he was. In the stormy and energetic campaign against Irish landlordism, waged in the early eighties of the last century, Tully was an uncompromising advocate of the three Fs for the farmer: fixity of tenure, fair rent, and free sale. So fearless was he in his bitter antagonism against the Government, which he believed to be responsible for the misery of the Irish tenant farmer, that he frequently exposed himself to the charge of slander and libel in the vehemence of his words. His contributions to debate in the House of Commons maintained the obstruction tactics of the Irish Nationalists, who thoroughly embarrassed the Government of the day by their irrepressible loquacity. As I wrote of him in 'The Times' on his death in 1938: - *"The columns of Hansard during the 'obstruction' period are eloquent testimony in volume of output to Tully's faculty of saying nothing, and saying it within the rules of order over hours of Parliamentary time."*

There was nothing he liked better than a good row in the House, which of course was appropriate to his red hair and moustache, and he was a favourite subject for the cartoonists. At one time he had been in Kilmainham jail with Parnell, and he would have followed his leader to the ends of the earth. Yet withal, his was a gentle and kindly personality, and he bore no malice even against those whom he most often reviled. On his arrival at the House of Commons I gave him tea on the terrace, and we chatted of old times and old friends both in Parliament and in my old homeland, for he came from Boyle where he successfully managed the local newspaper. Then we went inside and listened to speeches from Churchill, Baldwin and Sir John Simon. That day, one of the evening newspapers came out with the headlines of: - "Tully-Ho."

Tully naturally wanted to know if any progress towards reconciliation had been made between the Free State and Great Britain. I told him of the replies which I received in answer to the questions I put at intervals in the House, that 'no-one would welcome a settlement more than the British Government', and 'we have never closed the door to any settlement', and 'De Valera said they would never pay, so what earthly use is there in taking the initiative'. Thus, the situation had dragged on over weary years, and it was not until the end of January 1935, that an informal understanding was reached between the two Governments, and the end of the 'economic war' came in sight.

I had an interesting letter from Macassey that summer in connection with my speech at the Annual Dinner of the Drapers Company. He said: - *"It may afford you a background for a little free play of your imaginative fancy, to know that the Drapers Company was, of course, one of the twelve Livery Companies of the City of London which co-operated with the Irish*

Society in the colonisation of the counties of Tyrone and Londonderry, at the time of the Ulster 'plantation'. The Draper Company's 'proportion' included the area about Draperstown and Moneymore. Last year, when I was Master of the Company, and was entertaining the Lord Mayor and Sheriffs, I protested against the way the Corporation of London had planted their citizens in the 'Proportion's' of the twelve Companies and having done that, had never gone back to Ulster to see how they fared. The result was that the Lord Mayor and Sheriffs went over last July to Ulster in 'state', accompanied by the Master and Clerk of each of the twelve Livery Companies. After making a tour of Ulster they assisted in the opening of the new bridge between 'Ulster' (more correctly Northern Ireland) and the Irish Free State in Derry and got a reception from every section, class and creed of the population, which was the most impressive and spontaneous of anything I have ever seen."

If only the gulf between North and South could have been as effectively bridged (in the figurative sense) at that time, the effects of the war might not have widened the gulf of Partition and brought the country of my birth to a state of virtual isolation. While the livestock problem was desperate in Ireland, the position was somewhat precarious throughout England, and I had numerous interviews with the Minister of Agriculture (to whom I had constant access). Unfortunately, he was terribly hampered by some of his colleagues in the Cabinet, particularly those Free Trade adherents, although he was not afraid to stand up against them.

During June, I had a reassuring letter from Baldwin, to whom I had written in appreciation of his speech concerning the 'agricultural problem. He replied: - *"Thank you very much for your letter. I much appreciate what you say regarding my speech. I can assure you that we are all deeply sensible of both the importance and the urgency of the livestock problem, and it is no empty phrase when I say that it is engaging our most earnest and unremitting attention. I have every hope that it will be possible to make a statement on the subject well before the House rises for the summer recess. As you will no doubt have seen from the official notice in yesterday's press, negotiations with the Dominions are in active progress. I am sorry I cannot say more at present, but we are, believe me, sparing no efforts."*

The number of unemployed persons in Great Britain was still a most serious problem, and the hunger marches were a source of great controversy in the House and elsewhere. The Prime Minister refused to grant any facilities for the marchers, and certain of the Liberal and Labour members objected in strong terms. I remember Baldwin's declaring (at a big Unionist rally) that the present restlessness was caused by the subordination of the human by the mechanical, and in the large sense he was undoubtedly correct, but it was so necessary to come to grips with the difficult problems arising out of this subordination. The Archbishop of York urged the Chancellor of the Exchequer to restore the cuts in the allowance for the unemployed, if this were at all possible. Whereupon John Morris and I wrote immediately to 'The Times' in support: - *"The unemployed 'cuts' were taken in the throb of circumstance; they must at the earliest moment be restored. The burden of income-tax demands relief, and should be treated on an equal footing with other demands for relief ... but unemployment must be the first concern of us all."*

It was with great satisfaction that we heard on the announcement of Chamberlain's Budget in April that there was to be a reduction of income-tax and the restoration of unemployment benefit cuts. It was the most satisfactory Budget since the close of the war. But many of us were worried by the flood of imports of foreign goods, and in particular steel, and the Parliamentary Committee of the Empire Industries Association (of which I was a member) started a movement for higher tariffs. The late Herbert Williams, M.P., was determined to find a way of securing a full-dress debate in the House on these matters, for statistics showed that in many instances the tariffs were not nearly high enough. Leo Amery and Page Croft were also prime movers in the affair.

As an example of commodities dumped in Great Britain, I might mention cycle tubes, which were sold at sixpence each, and pocket-knives for ten pence a dozen wholesale. Yet, as Neville Chamberlain said, at the British Industries Fair in February: - *"Although trade has shrunk to a shadow of what it was, nevertheless we in this country are maintaining and increasing our proportion of it."*

For nine years, from 1921 to 1930, I was Chairman of the National Council of Inland Waterways, and I have always taken the greatest interest in the furtherance of our canal system. Both in the House, and out of it, I have spoken for our inland waterways over and over again, yet mine was too often a lone voice, for they are a sadly neglected means of transport. The original Birmingham canal dated back to 1768 and now (in amalgamation with four different canal companies) the system comprises an intricate network of artificial waterways passing through the city, and in and about the industrial districts to the north and west. The total length equals approximately one hundred and fifty-five miles. Some hundreds of industries, blast furnaces, chemical works, flour mills, glass works, timber mills, iron foundries, potteries and a host of others are situated alongside the canal, some of which use the public wharves to tranship their goods to the railways, others the private basins and branches connected with the system.

In 1927 a Parliamentary group, over which I presided, drew up a scheme for the reconstruction of canals with a view to forming a network across the country, on which would be used diesel-engined boats. Periodically, suggestions have been made that the canals should be adapted for larger boats, but the Royal Commission of 1906-1909 decided that the scheme would be prohibitive on account of the enormous expenditure that would inevitably be incurred. However, the whole length of the canal from Birmingham to London was (at this time) under improvement, whatever money was available being used to reconstruct old locks, build new ones and widen the canals wherever possible. By 1934, fifty-two old locks in our canal system had been reconstructed, and I was present at the opening (by His Royal Highness the Duke of Kent) of the new locks at Hatton. Less than a week before this opening, his brother (the Prince of Wales) had laid the foundation stone of a new hospital site at Edgebaston. He said, and indeed this might be said of all the Royal family: - "I always take the greatest possible interest in what I believe I am right in describjng as the second biggest city in England."

These two occasions are a good example of the engagements which it was my duty and, usually, my great pleasure to keep. I was a sort of 'jack of all trades' in Birmingham. I tried to attend as many exhibitions, bazaars and fetes as I could, so long as they contributed to the welfare of the community. Sometimes, when the speakers were well-known personalities, they were most entertaining. I remember Lady Tree speaking at a motor-car exhibition; and telling how Sir Herbert Tree, Ellen Terry and herself were once stuck in a car at the bottom of a hill all night long until they were rescued in the morning by a carriage and two horses. Those were the good old days, when the advent of the horse-less carriage was a wonder and excitement to all.

An event which I attended with the deepest interest took place at the beginning of July 1934. This was the opening of the Chamberlain Museum at Highbury. To its collection of letters, I contributed some which related to Chamberlain's entry into Birmingham municipal life. The opening was performed by Sir Austen. In his speech he said: - "We were a very united circle, and my father's influence and presence permeated the whole of it. I never remember his preaching to us except by example. The few maxims he tried to instil into his children were of the simplest, that truth was sacred, that whatever you do was worth doing with all your might [...] His name will live; he made his mark not merely on the policies of his own time, but on the development of our Empire and our country. Whatever his occupation and wherever he might be, his thoughts returned to his people in Birmingham, and his heart, his dearest feelings centred in this room." Sir Austen also told us of their great interest in the design and detail of the house, and also in the laying-out of the garden and the erection of the greenhouses.

Another very pleasant event which stands out in my memory of that year was a Conservative Party cruise in the liner ' Adriatic', which lasted for nineteen days, during which we visited Portugal, North Africa, Malta, Sicily, and other Mediterranean spots. There were seven hundred passengers (all Conservatives) among whom were some Members of Parliament. Many of the passengers belonged to the newly re-organised Unionist Club, which had been founded forty-seven years before, and of which I was now the Honorary Secretary. The Club consisted of 109 members of the House of Lords, 159 members of the Commons, and close on two hundred Conservative supporters who were not in Parliament. Lord Daryngton was Honorary President, and Sir Austen Chamberlain one of the Vice Presidents. I resigned the Secretaryship in 1938. The official flag of our party flew from the mast as the boat sailed, and throughout the voyage we were fortunate in having wonderful weather. Sir John Smedley Crooke and I drafted a message to the 'Birmingham Daily Mail', in which we stated how much we were enjoying ourselves, and how we recalled with grateful appreciation the valuable services of the 'Mail' and the 'Post' in promoting the maintenance of the National Government policy. On my return, I wrote to the 'Morning Post': -

"It was my good fortune to visit Malta at the beginning of the present month, and ample facilities were offered me to examine for myself the attitude of mind which now obtains on the new outlook presented to its people. I left the Island strongly convinced of the loyalty of the vast majority of the Maltese population to His Majesty the King, and to the maintenance of its place in the British Empire, of which it regards itself proudly as a vital constituent part. There has been a wholesome and stimulating change in local political feeling. The bitterness of past controversy has happily subsided. Such differences as are still manifest will, I am persuaded, be adjusted by the exercise of common sense and a generous desire for mutual accommodation. The present Governor and Commander-in-Chief, Sir David Campbell, has given abounding evidence of his administrative efficiency, and conciliatory purpose, in the very difficult duties which he has been called upon to discharge. Sir David deserves the warm appreciation of everyone interested in the welfare of Malta for the achievement which stands to his credit in dealing with the thorny and tantalising situation which faced him in his acceptance of this office. The attack upon the Secretary of State for the Colonies at that time wholly unwarrantable. It was the unqualified view of all schools of thought in Malta, that Sir Philip Cunliffe-Lister has shown a very high level of statesmanship in dealing with the basic troubles of the island. I had the privilege of a long exchange of views with the Hon. Mabel Strickland. She can be, and I am confident, will be a moderating influence of inestimable value in the future of Malta. The present excellent administration under Sir David Campbell, with the co-operation of a public-spirited leader like Miss Strickland, will in due time bring peace and content to the Colony. Gallant little island. The heroism and determination of her people in their great trial during the war will live long in the world's memory. During our cruise the Jewish New Year began, and a service was held on board the 'Adriatic' which I attended. It was claimed that this was the first time that a Jewish New Year service had ever been held on board a liner on a Mediterranean cruise."

1935 brought another General Election upon the country, and my own personal fight was against a young Leeds barrister, Councillor Silverman (a Labour candidate). Moseley had grown to such an extent that it was now the biggest of the Birmingham Divisions, and I kept my seat with a majority of 26,342 votes. But, before the election we had a change in Prime Ministers, for it will be remembered that Ramsey MacDonald resigned, his place being taken by Baldwin. MacDonald had been ailing in health for several years, and his powers of concentration and vigour had gradually waned. Yet at times it seemed as if he would regain his prowess, times when the 'old Ramsey' returned to us in the House. But it was not to be. After one of these temporary rejuvenations, I wrote to him a letter dated February 14th, 1935: -

"My dear Prime Minister,

May I offer you my respectful congratulations on your clear, moving and forceful speech in the house this afternoon. You have risen, if I may venture to say so, to your old form; a leader of directive and inspiring power in the National Government Administration. For some time past, many of us who admired your many fine qualities of statesmanship, and who are profoundly grateful for the sacrifices you made to save the Nation and Empire from disaster, were somewhat disturbed and distressed that you had not asserted more vigorously your personal magnetism in the stimulation of Parliamentary debate, and the heartening of your supporters in the House of Commons.

This afternoon you were splendid, clear, concise, logical: a leader in fact as well as in name. Scores of Tories who have been in doubt are in happier mood. Do, please, follow this by coming amongst us a little more: meet us, mix with us, talk to us, give us something of your human and friendly side. The Members of this House who support the National Government are friendly to you on personal merits alone. Let us know you better."

In reply, MacDonald wrote: - *"I cannot tell you how much I appreciate, not only the words, but the spirit of your letter of yesterday. What I am afraid some of you have not quite appreciated is that the enormous burden of detail, which a Prime Minister must now carry, is creating a revolution in his work and his relations to the House of Commons. I hope it will pass, but, if it has come to stay, you will have to look upon a Prime Minister in a way very different from what has been the case hitherto. This is really not a reply to what you have said. It is only lifting a little corner of the curtain. Again and again I have instructed those who make my engagements to try and find ways for leaving me at liberty to mix more with my friends in the House, and I hope your letter will help them to do what I should like. Again, thank you with all my heart for what you have written."*

But the burden was too much for him, and Baldwin took his place. Prior to the election in November, I suggested that I should support MacDonald in his Divisional campaign. He wrote: -

"My dear Paddy, … I hear from Rose that you have been good enough to say that you would be prepared to come to Seaham and speak for me during my campaign. This is, indeed, most kind of you and I should be extremely obliged if you would. If you would let me know upon which day we can expect you, we will make the necessary arrangements for meetings. Your assistance will be of great help to me and I deeply appreciate your offer. I was sorry to learn that Mrs. Hannon was not very well; please give her my kindest regards and say I hope she will soon be perfectly fit again. With all good wishes to you in your fight, believe me to be yours very sincerely,

J. Ramsey MacDonald."

In all I addressed three meetings at Seaham, which was in a part of the country not well known to me. On my return, MacDonald wrote: - *"I hope you did not take away with you too bad an impression of the condition in which you found my constituency. We still have a great deal to do before we can count ourselves victorious, but we are leaving no stone unturned to retain the seat."* He was heartened by the fact that the three Parties forming the National Government all came to his support in his election campaign. The Conservative Party, and their supporters throughout the country, were wholly in favour of the continuity of the National Government, for their abounding success in the field of economic revival and social reconstruction was impressive. The protection of the home market had produced results so far-reaching, and of such advantage in the period of time, as none of us could have anticipated during the depths of the depression. Public opinion, too, dictated the unlikelihood of any one Party being restored to supremacy, but we had to keep in mind the possible danger that, because our traditional Party loyalty was being mobilised to maintain a National

Government, we might eventually find ourselves becoming an essential part of a National Party, bound to support such a Government far into the distant future. It was unthinkable that the aims and ideals and policy of such great leaders as Beaconsfield, Bonar Law, and Joseph Chamberlain could be destroyed and put aside for the sake of upholding a National Government, therefore, while we wholeheartedly lent our support, we kept in mind, and indeed in some anxiety of mind, this disastrous possibility.

The support for the National Government was not, of course, unanimous, and I remember one stormy meeting at which I tried to speak and was continuously interrupted. This was on the occasion of a meeting of the South Paddington Conservative and Empire Association, which had been called to review the progress of the Government during March 1935. Among other things, I arranged that the Birmingham Small Arms Company should provide MacDonald with a car for his use during the General Election, as had also been the case with Baldwin. MacDonald was deeply grateful and, although overwhelmed with work, he wrote to me saying: - *"A most beautiful car arrived from you this morning, for my personal use, and I cannot thank you enough for having sent it, nor can I say how grateful I am to you for having troubled to come up here personally to support me."*

Earlier in the year, I was involved in an unhappy split in the Conservative Party, when the Wavertree Division was contested at a by-election by Platt (a Conservative Nationalist Candidate whom I supported) and Randolph Churchill (who was standing as an Independent Conservative). There were also Liberal and Labour candidates, and many of us were fearful that a split vote would result in the loss of the Conservative seat. The Junior Conservative Association were indignant with Churchill's claim to represent Conservative youth, and wished him to stand down. In every way, it was hard to understand his point of view. He professed to be attached to the old Tory principles, yet set out with more or less irregular forces to strike at the foundations of his Party. He appeared fairly confident of success, and made the usual self-confident electioneering speeches, warning Platt that he should stand down before it became too late. And, he added, that although such a gesture might make him appear ridiculous in some quarters, he would become much more ridiculous when he found himself at the bottom of the poll.

We could not get Randolph to realise the stupid situation he had created in the Wavertree Division, and in despair I wrote the following letter to his father, dated January 23rd: -

"My dear Churchill, May I venture to appeal to you on the basis of the generous and kindly consideration which you have extended to me for many years, and urge with much respect that you would take such steps as may commend themselves to you, to prevent the possible loss of the Wavertree Division to the National Government. Until the unhappy developments on the question of Constitutional Reform in India, you showed me many marks of friendship and goodwill. I recall with grateful feelings your kindness to me when I was in charge of Agricultural Organisation in Cape Colony, when you were Under Secretary of State for the Colonies, and we have been colleagues in the House of Commons for fifteen years. During my Secretaryship of the Navy League, when you were First Lord, it was my privilege to plead your policy for the 'Command of the Sea' at thousands of meetings over the length and breadth of the land. Thus, my apologies ... poor thing in itself, but certainly sincere. No statesman has borne more striking and touching testimony to the record of the National Government in saving the Nation and Empire from the sloppy ineptitude of a Socialist Administration than yourself. Your son has a charming and attractive personality. I had the privilege of entertaining him at the House of Commons when he came down from Oxford. He made a speech which delighted everybody, and which indicated the outlook of a great career in public life.

But his intervention in the Liverpool by-election must fill your, and his, friends in the House of Commons with mixed and disturbed feelings. I observe that you have stated that you are in no way responsible for his action in becoming a Candidate at Wavertree. But surely you still possess the priceless quality of amiable parental advice. I have been in consultation with Liverpool friends and colleagues in industry, and they tell me that a split Tory vote may allow the seat to pass into the hands of the Socialists. Can you contemplate such a result with indifference? If a plebiscite of our people could be taken in the selection of a knight in political armour to pulverise socialism, the choice would undoubtedly fall upon you. Can you, therefore, survey from afar, with self-imposed detachment, the loss of a seat to the protagonist of a creed or cult in political life upon which you have roused for years the biting scorn of your unchallenged invective.

The world is small after all; time is the supreme healer; the ups and downs of political affairs are part of your own place in history; your boy is young; he has a great future; the name he bears is an asset in our island story; why should he at a moment so critical in our national affairs strike a blow - a deadly blow - at the fortunes of our Party and, incidentally, at the heart of the nation itself. Think!

Yours ever,

P. J. Hannon."

And on 30th January I addressed the following to ' The Times': - *"Sir, I am confident that the great majority of loyal members of the Conservative and Unionist Party must regard with grave anxiety the political contest now in progress in the Wavertree Division. Nothing could be more unfortunate than the effort to drag the great problem of Indian Constitutional Reform into the whirlpool of a by-election, on the eve of the debates of the Government on the 'India Bill' in the House of Commons. I was at Liverpool yesterday. I addressed a large meeting there last night and was present at another. I had talks with several Liverpool colleagues and friends who have been workers and observers during the whole of the election campaign. From what I have seen and from what I have heard, the local electorate takes a quite perfunctory and casual interest in the Indian question, and would take none at all if it were not forced upon its notice from outside. The intervention of the Indian Defence League cannot be justified on the grounds of wisdom or common-sense, or public duty of those responsible for the direction of the policy of the League, but they would hardly rejoice if the part they play adds to the number and prestige of the Socialist Party. For such a misfortune the members of the League must take the responsibility and it will be poor consolation to them that misdirected zeal may place a further dangerous implement in the hands of the Indian agitator. The abounding concern of the people of Liverpool, is the continued improvement of the industrial condition of the country, with the expansion of our overseas trade, which so intimately affects the prosperity of its port. The economic revival of the last three years is warmly acknowledged by Liverpool businessmen and there is a general testimony that there could be no more competent exponent of local needs and possibilities than the official Conservative Candidate, Mr. James Platt.*

I am, Sir, your obedient servant,

P. J. Hannon."

The upshot of all this was the refusal of Randolph Churchill to withdraw, and the seat was won by his opponent. While we were able to survey with some satisfaction the economic triumphs of the past three years, it was heart-breaking to us to reflect upon the pitiful and ramshackle structure upon which international friendship and world peace rested. There arose, at this time, a number of semi-hysterical campaigns for the duration of peace, supported by people who almost laid claim to a monopoly in the prosecution of an abiding peace, which all peoples of the British Empire desired to create. Most of the methods were foolish and ill-balanced and, if anything, heightened the confidence of the Nazi leaders in their war plans.

The so-called Peace Ballot launched by Robert Cecil in June 1934, and exploited in Birmingham by a mixture of sloppy sentiment and malignant political dishonesty, was an example of the obstructive tactics that added to the difficulties of international relations.

The result of the Ballot, appearing in June 1935, and widely advertised as indicating the considered view of the people of Birmingham on the problems of peace and war, claimed among other things, that the great majority of voters were in favour of an all-round reduction of armaments. The Ballot was of course wholly worthless, but was the subject of much comment, argument and controversy. I most strongly protested against the mischief-making tendencies of these people, and again and again pointed out that it would constitute a national crime. if we, who were on the fringes of the seething pot of Europe, should neglect to prepare defences for our shore.

I repeatedly urged the people to labour untiringly for peace, but stressed that it must be peace with security, otherwise it would be worthless. A feature which aroused the greatest indignation of these misguided citizens was the manufacture of armaments and the private profit therefrom. As a matter of fact, at the Annual General Meeting in 1935 of the Birmingham Small Arms Company, the shareholders were concerned at the report given to them of the Company's miserable profit. But it was generally supposed that armament manufacturers were necessarily reaping enormous profits 'out of murder'. When the Government announced that the War Office had decided to give up the

Lewis gun, manufactured by the B.S.A. Company, and use the Bren gun manufactured by the Royal Small Arms factory at Enfield, there was consternation among the shareholders.

While these campaigners created excited emotion at home, the League of Nations was desperately trying to bring about a peaceful settlement between Italy and Abyssinia. Negotiations in Geneva waxed and waned. Mussolini's blatant demands for the annexation of Abyssinia were countered by various proposals, all of which he rejected, and the Emperor Haile Selassie repeated his dignified appeals for aid. Sir Samuel Hoare prepared, in collaboration with Neville Chamberlain, a speech which he delivered to the League on September 12th 1935, and in which he stated that: - *"... my country stands ... for steady and collective resistance to all acts of unprovoked aggression."* This firmness so greatly appealed to me, that I wrote at once to him in appreciation, sending my 'heartfelt congratulations on your triumph at Geneva'. I said: - *"The speech which you delivered on Wednesday, and the broadcast which you gave last night, will rank as the greatest contribution to the political history of our time. I am proud to feel that the great responsibility you were called upon to discharge in giving expression to the policy of H.M. Government, and to the deep-seated conviction of the whole people of this nation, has received almost unqualified approval in every civilised community under the sun. It will give intense gratification to the whole British race in the reflection that you have done more than any living statesman to lay the foundation of permanent peace in the world."*

So many people were uplifted and invigorated by this speech of Hoare's. Churchill recalled how, he too, felt stirred as he read the report of it, for it was indeed a wonderful contribution to the relationship of nations with reference to the establishment of permanent peace. Our only course, and indeed the plain duty of every citizen at that time, was to give the League of Nations all possible support. But how difficult it was to encourage loyalty towards it.

When, in the early summer of the following year sanctions were dropped, I was inundated with correspondence. But the League failed, and in its humiliating failure our dreams were shattered. I recall with gentle irony, that at the Jubilee fete of the Birmingham branch of the Navy League that year, there was exhibited the original bell of H.M.S. Birmingham (the ship, that during the Great War, had sunk the first German submarine). Many of the people present believed with high idealism in the infallibility of the League, even more believed that the danger to European peace was not Germany, but Italy. But very few, I suspect, imagined that relics such as this of the Great War would so shortly fade into insignificance beside the relics of the Second World War. In my speech on that occasion, I pointed out that the continuity of the food supplies for the people of Great Britain in times of war depended entirely on the protection of the thousands of miles of sea routes (which was the especial function of the Navy) and that the safeguarding of these routes must always occupy a premier place in our national policy.

Talking of food supplies in this connection reminds me of an unfortunate mishap that occurred at the Naval Review in July. Sir Austen Chamberlain and I were invited to attend an inspection of a certain warship, along with a large number of foreign visitors of some importance. Many of us had had an early meal followed by a long journey, and the sea air heightened our appetites, but something went wrong with the catering. The expected meal could not be served and we returned to London feeling very hungry indeed, and not a little cross, some of the foreign guests appearing positively insulted.

Of the many pleasant events which occurred in that year of grace, I remember of course the Silver Jubilee of their Majesties King George V and Queen Mary. On that day of rejoicing, it was well for the Royal Family that they could not foresee the immediate future [...] the shattering crisis of the abdication. But perhaps the most pleasurable event of that year for me, personally, was the acquiring of Magna Carta Island for my wife and myself. Some years previously we had stayed with the owner, Mr. Hepworth Thompson, and had fallen in love with the beautiful house and grounds, and all its romantic association. On June 18th the house was put up for auction, and the moment that my wife realised that the house was on the market, she arranged to be represented at the auction. When word came through that her bid had been successful, she telephoned me at the House of Commons to say that she had a lovely surprise for me and was coming up to tell me all about it. I first heard, however, from a 'Daily Mail' reporter, who forestalled her. When Magna Carta Island had first been put up for sale, it had been bought by a purchaser acting for speculative builders. There was intense local dismay at the prospect of a growth of bungalows over that lovely spot, but unfortunately (or as it turned out for us, fortunately) the island is subject to flooding, and so the purchaser put the house again on the market and it eventually came to us. It had been very cleverly modernised and the Charter Room, which held the stone-topped table bearing the inscription, had been built some time ago by a member of the Harcourt family, one of whose ancestors was present when King John 'made his mark'.

We determined to give every facility to delegations from schools, colleges, and other institutions and societies to view the historic place, but we would not throw it open to the public. We planned also to entertain as much as possible, and the memory of some of the large parties which we held during the summer is a pleasant recollection. Although the house itself is not old there are, or were at that time, many old trees in the grounds. One in particular, an evergreen oak, was supposed to be from five hundred to seven hundred years old, and it was claimed to be the biggest in Europe. Among other trees remarkable for their age and size were an ilex tree and a magnificent chestnut. There was a delightful sunken garden, surrounded by topiary and clipped yews, which provided great shelter and warmth. Other spots have been claimed as being the place where the great charter was sealed, but I think Magna Carta Island is the most likely. Mathew Pariss (who died at St Albans in 1259) indicated that this was the historic spot, and a group of three walnut trees, descended from those that were believed to have surrounded the actual site, stood to support the story.

Sir Patrick Hannon by Howard Coster
(©the National Portrait Gallery)

CHAPTER 12

The year of 1936 opened brightly for me, for my name was among those who were knighted for political and public services! Of course, the Birmingham newspapers had something to say about me. It may be of some amusement to quote from a couple of reports. From the 'Birmingham Gazette': - *"Our jovial friend, Mr. 'Pat' Hannon, who is reputed to possess the biggest diary list of social engagements of any Member of Parliament, has won his way to public respect by sheer personality. Nature has endowed him with a picturesque and pleasing appearance, in addition to a certain comfortable 'roundaboutness'. As a speaker, he is adaptable and fluent, and naturally is in great demand for all kinds of public and social functions, and he seldom refuses. In the House of Commons, Pat is a greatly loved character. This I have on the word of several of the Midland M.P.s. The fledglings of the House regard him as a paternal guide and mentor, for on points of Parliamentary etiquette he is unchallengeable."* And from the 'North Eastern Daily Gazette': - *"Of all the 615 Members, Pat Hannon most nearly resembles the typical M.P. He is a trifle explosive, and he combines heartiness with dignity. He brims over with good nature. Pat, or Paddy as they call him, is as straight as a die. He typifies the essential honesty of Birmingham politics, for say what the cynics like, Birmingham politics are honest. In America and elsewhere, men go into politics to make money. Here they have to abandon politics to get rich. The House is full of men like Pat Hannon, who are there because they really believe they can serve their country by being there."*

The Knighthood was conferred upon me by His Majesty King Edward VIII (whose father had died just a month previously, and therefore it was a private investiture), and we were asked to wear either morning clothes or lounge suits. It was a very delightful ceremony. I had the privilege of following Colonel Sir Bertram Ford, that distinguished citizen of Birmingham. His Majesty was most gracious to everyone, the function was arranged with great care and exact timing, and we all left the Palace in happy mood. My friends in the house and in various business concerns were most generous in celebrating my knighthood. Among the entertainments which I remember best was a dinner that was given in the house by thirty M.P.s, presided over by Leo Amery. On 24th April, three hundred guests were present at a dinner in my honour, in connection with which I received the following letter from Ramsey MacDonald: - *"I have received a notice today that your friends are giving a dinner in your honour. Needless to say, I should be delighted to attend were it possible. Unfortunately, they have chosen a day which is included in a little block of time I have had to mortgage to meet calls that are being made upon me. Should it happen that between now and Easter the commitments I have made are shifted, I can assure you I will be present to show how I value your services and friendship. I am writing this to yourself straight away, so that you may know why I will, for the time being at any rate, make no response to the convenors of the dinner."*

I replied: - *"My friends are most kind and I am, indeed, a little embarrassed by the compliment which it is proposed to pay me. I may, however, say to you at once that I do not think I have ever been paid a compliment which has given me so much pleasure as that which you embody in your letter. It would give my wife and myself the very greatest joy if the exigencies of public work could make it possible for you to be with us on the occasion of this dinner."*

That year was indeed a year of great events, and none more momentous than that which concerned our Royal family. For it brought to Great Britain and the Empire the passing of a great and wise king, the accession of a prince whose abdication in circumstances of profound pathos brought a surge of loyalty from the British people towards the throne, and then the accession of His Majesty King George VI (who was to prove himself a monarch of outstanding courage, unselfishness and sensibility). In the crisis of the abdication, the whole British family throughout the Empire had behaved with calm and quiet understanding, and Stanley Baldwin displayed extraordinary thoughtfulness and foresight in his most difficult position.

I had been honoured by 'Punch' during the previous summer, through a cartoon and rhyme in their series, 'Our Back Bench Who's Who'.

No one is more spic and span on
Any back bench than Mr. Hannon.
Him one naturally dubs
(He has eleven) the King of Clubs.

I was elected Chairman of the Constitutional Club, an honour that I retained until my resignation in 1955. I was very proud indeed of this honour, which was in no small measure due to Lord Wargrave's great friendship and kindness to me. I certainly do not lay claim to having been the 'King of Clubs', but I admit that I found club life very congenial; and the Constitutional Club has always had my particular regard.

There were (and no doubt still are) in the House of Commons, various groups comprising territorial assemblages of Members who could combine to press local claims. At that time I was Chairman of the Midland Unionist Group, which consisted of members from Warwickshire, Worcester, Staffordshire, Derby, Shropshire, Nottinghamshire, Leicestershire, Gloucester and Lincolnshire. Smedley Crooke was Secretary and the meetings were convened at fortnightly intervals. Much useful work was accomplished in this way. In 1934, I joined a group of Roman Catholic Members of Parliament, which had just been inaugurated for the purpose of keeping together those of us who were of that religion. We were able, thus, to deal collectively with any incident that affected our interests.

In connection with religion, I recall an embarrassing experience one summer when the Anglican vicar of St John's Church, Sparkbrook, invited me to speak from the pulpit to a congregation of men. I was considerably shaken when one man created a scene and left the church in company with three supporters. I had been pleading for friendliness and toleration, and this was apparently too much for him. The vicar apologised, saying that when the meeting of the 'Men's Own Club' took place in the church, the pulpit was open to any man or woman who had a message to give, and as I represented 100,000 people it was proper and fitting that I should speak to them. I have had a certain amount of interruptions and heckling in my time, and have learned to deal fairly successfully with the perpetrators, but I was at a complete loss when this happened to me in the pulpit of St John's Church.

It was at this time that the Church in Spain was suffering great persecution, and some prominent newspapers, including the 'Daily Mail', raised a strong protest. On September 5th, this following letter of mine was published: -

251

"Sir, ... The Daily Mail deserves the profound gratitude of the Christian world in the chivalrous attitude which it has adopted towards the unspeakable atrocities perpetrated by the Spanish Government upon the Church of Christ in Spain. The direct and positive purpose and policy of the existing Administration, in Madrid, are not directed at the suppression of a political revolt against the sinister tendencies of social and economic disruption, but have as their ultimate objective the destruction of Christian ideals and the ruin of Christian influence and inspiration in the national life of the Spanish people ... The directive power of British civilisation in the march of world progress has been broadly based upon the teachings of the 'Master', whose benevolent example and sublime charity are the most precious, as well as the most sacred, treasures of mankind. Surely the Christian people of the British Empire cannot regard without a shudder of horror the devastation of churches and institutions raised by the piety and genius of generations, accompanied by an unparalleled orgy of rapine, torture and murder, without making some forceful and unqualified protest. Whatever critical attitude the people of the British Empire may feel impelled to take up in relation to Germany and Italy in the complexities of international affairs, it must in its soul feel convinced that both these great nations are now acting with strict correctitude in relation to Spain. The nations of Europe which still adhere to the Christian spirit as the dominant factor in world peace and progress should unite in common effort to save the Spanish people from the desolations of anarchy."

As things turned out, the Great Powers adopted the policy of non-intervention proposed by France, who believed that the appalling Civil War must inevitably die down if deprived of aid and arms from outside. But Russia, Germany and Italy broke the agreement, joining in the bestial struggle, and finally France (under communist pressure) sent arms and equipment to the Republican forces. Sir Austen Chamberlain told us on one occasion of a meeting of the Birmingham Unionist Association, that there was a Chinese curse, "May you live in interesting times." There was little doubt that by the year 1936, the curse had fallen upon much of Europe. In March, Germany violated the Treaty of Versailles, which had been conceived in the spirit and framed in the letter of a permanent understanding. German forces crossed the frontier of the Rhineland and occupied all the principal towns, and this aggressive act occurred on the same day that Hitler had proposed a period of twenty-five years peace in Europe. In cold fact, France herself had paid somewhat scant regard to certain of the obligations she undertook in that Treaty. We had forgiven her the debt to us to the tune of £400,000,000. It was not a pleasant thought that while we had been steadily disarming, France had spent the financial resources thus made available on developing a big military organisation. Yet even so, she felt unable to act against Germany alone and asked for our aid, which of course could not be given.

In May, I spoke at a meeting called to stimulate interest in the national defence schemes, but people were lethargic and the result disappointing. Although I am myself an optimist, and believe that optimism is one of the world's greatest assets today, I believe also in being prepared for any event, and I most strongly felt that our best way to avoid a possible war was to be fully prepared to face it. Early in September, in response to an invitation from the Prime Minister, I left for Canada in company with Councillor Dalglish, a former Lord Mayor of Newcastle. On account of a Unionist Council Meeting on October 8th, I had to return to England within a month (which gave me less than three weeks in Canada) but I managed to crowd a lot of lectures and inspections into that short time. The object of my visit was to tour the Province of Saskatchewan, and to address the Immigration and Settlement Convention then being held, so that I might be in a position to advise upon the problems of British emigration to Canada.

The Chairman of this Convention was Garrett Neff K.C., but it had been largely organised by Brigadier Hornby, whom I think of as being the Sir Horace Plunkett of Canada. He was quite a prophet in the distribution of the British race, and had excellent schemes for introducing the settlers into the Canadian way of life. He was rather disturbed that over fifty per cent of the population of Saskatchewan was foreign (representing forty-two different countries) and he planned to people that part of the Dominion with families from the same stock as himself.

In one school that I visited I saw children from no less than seven different nations which, according to Brigadier Hornby, was a fact to be greatly deplored. His plans were for the British people, plans for their happiness, welfare and advancement. One of his suggestions for the contentment of the immigrants was that they should be settled in blocks of families from the same district of Great Britain and Ireland. He arranged that they should first receive five years training (a virtual apprenticeship) on certain farms owned by the emigration organisation in England, for they would be sure to meet many unknown difficulties and differences in Canadian farming.

These settlers had, of course, to be guaranteed by the British Government. Not everyone was in favour of such large-scale immigration of the British people. For instance, when a resolution was passed (at one meeting at which I was present) that the province was now ready to receive five thousand families from Britain, there were several speeches of protest. Some of the speakers told of abominable living conditions of which the delegates were in ignorance. Others declared that Canada was not yet prepared for mass immigration.

Others again advocated the welcoming of Scandinavian or Dutch families which, they said, were more advanced in many respects than the British. There was actually in the city of Saskatchewan, a vigorous anti-immigration Association, which voiced its protests loudly and at some length. But no one could deny the successful results of British settlers already living in the Province and, from my experience, I would say that wherever a British settler finds a home, he brings with him culture, toleration, a spirit of fair play and an observance of the rules of the game to a greater degree than those persons whose customs and tendencies are at variance with British ideals. I do not refer to the Scandinavians or Dutch, with whom we have a lot in common, but to an infiltration of persons of many other nationalities who were setting foot on Canadian soil.

In the town of Humboldt, I was most interested to see settlers from the Midlands of England, in particular three Birmingham families who, with little capital, had established themselves happily in their new homeland. In Melfort I was shown an experimental farm which greatly impressed me in its excellent design and management, and I learned, too, of the wise schemes that were being put into operation to combat the drought of the middle western area.

Our tour was not strictly supervised, so that I was able to

visit such places and farms as I wished. One thing that I especially noticed was that every Canadian housewife had her larder well stocked, with row upon row of home-canned goods, and it struck me that the thrift and housekeeping qualifications of the women rivalled in their vigour the activities of their men-folk on the land. In my mind, I contrasted the life of the immigrant family of the thirties with that of the colonists under the Bam scheme of 1903. Two thousand of those settlers had sailed from Liverpool to Canada where they journeyed over unbroken prairies to forge a home in a tent city, and struggle with the wilderness without the aid of modern machines. Yet at last their reward came; broad acres of oats and wheat stretching out to the horizon, glowing in the sunset of a typical Canadian evening. Their achievement was surely the greater, for they had triumphed over worse difficulties with much less help.

It was an unfortunate fact that Canadian exports to Great Britain greatly exceeded their imports, thus creating a very lopsided situation, and I urged my Canadian audiences to open their door a little wider to us. I was pained from time to time to see the obvious indifference and misunderstanding, in trade circles, on the preferential regard which I had expected to be accorded to British goods. The Anglo Canadian trade agreement had made a distinct advance in our favour, but it was obvious that some modifications were now essential.

Upon my return home I spent a weekend in France, in that very interesting region of the Champagne country, and shortly after that I paid a brief visit to Ireland to speak at the Philosophical Society in Dublin University on Anglo-Irish relations. Kingsley Martin, Frank MacDermot, and Mr. Dulanty were the other speakers, and I thoroughly enjoyed this very pleasant experience at which, as well as renewing acquaintance with old friends, I made some abiding new friendships.

We were now settling happily into our home on Magna Carta Island and I invited an Irishman, the Bishop of Clifton, to bless the house. The celebrated room was converted into a temporary chapel, and Mass was said at the famous table. One of our first parties on the Island was held to celebrate the seven hundred and twenty-first anniversary of the signing of the Charter, and very many guests were present, including the Polish Ambassador and the Austrian Minister.

I think it was in the same month of the following year that Lady Baldwin planted three walnut trees, to commemorate the Coronation.

There were many parties and social functions of every kind that year, for money was once again circulating and European affairs had not dampened the spirits of the people. Apart from luncheons and dinners, dances and afternoon parties, I attended a number of social functions as the official 'opener'. I remember one interesting occasion, when it fell to my lot to open the London offices of the Ideal Benefit Society, of which I was the President. This was one of the most progressive societies of its kind in the country, and the whole aim and character of the society was made of the stuff for which the world seeks vainly today . . . safety and security.

The 'Birmingham News' said of me on February 22nd: -
"Sir Patrick Hannon M.P., has without any possible doubt, created a record among members of the House of Commons for the time he bestows upon his constituency, in paying frequent visits to the Division and attending all manner of social functions. Practically every weekend, and frequently during the week of every year he has been Moseley's Member of Parliament, he has been present at one or another social event, to say nothing of the numerous city engagements he fulfils."

The Press had not exaggerated and, in view of the seriousness of the situation abroad, and the vital character of trade and industry, I decided to 'put the brake on'. It was really becoming impossible for me to comply with the great demands made upon the time of Members in the House (with regular attendance on the various committees on which I sat, with the careful examination of stacks of Government papers which it was my duty to peruse) if I continued to open bazaars, fetes, give away prizes, and all the hundred and one other social affairs that fall to an M.P.'s lot. So, I was reluctantly forced to tell my Constituency that I could not go down to Birmingham in the middle of the week while Parliament was sitting.

It was apparent, however, from the sparse attendance in the House on some occasions, that other Members had not thought of doing the same thing. The result was a letter to each of us from the Prime Minister, dated April 16th, 1936: -
"My dear Sir, ... I am writing to draw your attention to the poor

attendance of Members in the House during the period of the Session which has just terminated and, particularly, to the division on Wednesday, April 1st, when only 139 Conservatives were present to support the Government, out of a total Party strength of 381. I fully realise that 22 Conservatives thought fit to vote against the Government, but even so, 220 Members of the Party did not take part in the division when the Government was defeated. If the Government's prestige and strength is to be maintained, it must be in a position to command a majority at all times. The National Government has only recently received a majority from the country during a critical stage in our nation's history. We are faced with many grave problems, and any signs of waning support in the House of Commons must weaken the Government's authority at home and lessen its influence abroad. I am aware that Members have many calls on their time, and for this reason some find it difficult to give regular attendance at the house. I fully appreciate the support of those who by their constant attendance enable the day to-day Parliamentary business to be successfully carried through. The response which the Party has made to three-line Whips on matters of first class importance has been most gratifying. I hope, however, that all Members will in future pay more attention to two-line Whips, so that the Government may be sure of a majority in any eventuality, and the chance of another defeat as far as possible eliminated.

Yours sincerely,
Stanley Baldwin."

I wrote an immediate reply assuring him that: - *"I do everything in my power to give constant and continuous support to the Government during the whole Parliamentary Session. I attend various political meetings in Birmingham and in other parts of the country, but I always acquaint the Chief Whip with the reasons for my absence and, of course, whenever possible, secure a pair."* It so happened that I was among the 22 Conservatives who, on that occasion, voted against the Government.

That year, 1936, was the Centenary of the birth of Joseph Chamberlain, and the Empire Industries Association formed a Committee (of which I became a member) to decide upon a fitting memorial. The late Leo Amery (who was made President of the Chamberlain Centenary Committee) showed us a vivid picture in his autobiography of the memorable occasion in the Albert Hall in July, when the eight thousand people present stood in dimmed light to pay tribute to the great Protectionist. An enormous portrait, about fifty feet high, picturing Joseph Chamberlain standing on a map of the Empire, was exposed to view at a given moment, creating an indelible impression on our minds. I quote from a letter I wrote to a friend: - *"... I do not think any tribute so great and far-reaching has ever been paid to any statesman in our history. You would have been much impressed by the great crowd of working class people who assembled at Hockley Cemetery, and all around it, when we visited the tomb yesterday and placed our wreath upon it ... Neville's speech in the Town Hall yesterday afternoon was one of the most exquisite in language, and appropriate in form that I have ever heard during my whole public life."*

Undoubtedly, the establishment of protection wrought a more beneficial influence in industrial development than any legislative measure since the Repeal of the Corn Laws. In the first year in which I sat in Parliament, an assault was made with devastating effect upon the crumbling citadel of Free Trade. By the passing of the 'Safeguarding of Industries Act', we laid the foundations of the economic policy which made our industrial life so successful. It was all the more disappointing that the Ottawa Conference should have produced some unfavourable results for our trade at home, but these were small factors against the many great advantages by which we benefited. The following extract is from a letter I wrote to Lord Beaverbrook, who had been disappointed by the lack of response to his Empire educational activities discussed in his Press: - *"After all, the Joseph Chamberlain campaign, opened under the dominating influence and fiery vigour of its author, only produced rare and flourishing fruit in 1932. The promotion of the Joseph Chamberlain policy was sustained by most leading newspapers in addition to your own. It had the full acquiescence, if not active co-operation, of the official Conservative organisation during twenty-nine years. And yet, the Import Duties Act was only passed in March 1932."*

It is from history that we learn how slowly the wheels move that eventually lead us into different ways of life. Apropos of the Empire, the Parliamentary Group of the New Commonwealth Society (of which I was a member) sent a request to Winston Churchill that he should become President of the British section. In his reply, he stated that he felt it his duty to accept, and that he believed that we realised that: - *"I am doing my best to procure effective measures to put our country into a state of safety."* Less than a year later, Sir Austen

Chamberlain died. I looked upon him as my godfather in politics. The place he occupied in the minds of his fellow countrymen was on as high a level as that of any statesman in the Victorian era and afterwards. His character and quality as a statesman and Parliamentarian, and as one of the greatest of English gentlemen, should be an example for all who wish to serve their country and their people. I heard the sad news of his death when I was just leaving the House to go to a Chamberlain Centenary meeting at Wood Green, and it was there that I broke the sad news to my audience. An incongruous feature at the very large funeral were the Coronation stands being erected outside the church of St Margaret's, Westminster. For, while we mourned a great statesman and friend, we were reminded that in little more than two months' time we should be rejoicing at the Coronation of His Majesty King George VI.

We could not tell that immediately after the Coronation, Baldwin would resign and Neville Chamberlain would take his place. It was sad that Sir Austen did not live to see his brother become Prime Minister, for they were very attached to each other and it would have given great joy to Neville to receive his brother's appreciation and congratulations. I was present at Neville Chamberlain's first public appearance in Birmingham as Premier, and was delighted with the splendid ovation he received. He had an audience of some thirty thousand people, to whom I also said a few words. An extract from his speech may be of interest in the light of events that came so shortly to pass. He said: - *"What we hope this Government may yet do in the time that is left to it may be summed up in four sentences: To keep the peace. To make our country so strong that nobody shall treat her with anything but respect. To maintain and to increase the prosperity and activity of trade and employment. To carry on steadily the improvement in the condition of the people."*

Yes, that July day was a day of rejoicing, and I for one, did not believe that before the end of 1939 our country would once again be involved in a Great War. Much has been said against Chamberlain's policy of peace, and many violent arguments have arisen over it. The loyalty of his colleagues in the House, which he valued so greatly, faded in some cases in the shattering events of his brief Premiership. He received strong support, however, from the first action he took in his new position. I have kept a letter written to me by Sir John Simon, apropos of a speech which he made on May 31st 1937, moving the second reading of the Finance Bill in which the Prime Minister proposed to raise money for the National Defence by getting a modest contribution from the future growth of business profits. He wrote: -

"My dear Pat,

... Thank you so much for your kind letter of congratulation. I was not feeling very fit yesterday when I made my speech, (the doctor had ordered me to bed with a touch of bronchitis), but I was determined to show everybody that Neville had got a loyal colleague who would not start by giving him away. I am sure that by joint effort we can get a solution to these troubles we have.

Yours ever, John.

P.S. So many thanks for Gogarty's amusing book. I come out rather well."

I spoke at that time in a lively debate in Hall Green on the subject, 'Which way to Peace?' where good-humoured verbal encounters were the order of the day. Many of my audience were in favour of disarmament, and to those I pointed out the analogy that it was no use suggesting that by doing away with our police force we were going to get rid of crime. The only assurance against war was a strong defensive organisation. That spring, an air-raid precautions committee had been formed in the House of Commons, and I was a keen member of it. Of course, there was a certain amount of trouble from one set of people about our sending of troops to the North-West frontier of India, and from another set who demanded that we should intervene with force in Spain. One of these sets of wrong-thinkers happened to be the Birmingham Trade Council, who sent me a copy of their resolution protesting against the inactivity of the British Government in the face of the Basque massacres. I was very angry, and had published this letter to their Secretary: - *"In my long experience in the receipt of hopeless and helpless resolutions from the Birmingham Trade Council, I cannot recall anything so completely detached from common sense and common political honesty as that upon which you have now done me the honour to invite my comment ... I ask you, in the name of common sense, whether you cannot induce your council to give a little more reflection, a little more maturity of thought, a little more sanity of outlook to your fatuous resolutions. If it had not been for the rigid observance of the non-intervention agreement by the British Government, God only knows what would have happened to Spain."*

Among other letters concerning that country, is one I received from Madame de Navarro (who had been Mary Anderson, the well-known Shakespearean actress). She began by commenting on the 'unforgivable blunder', made by Attlee on his visit to Spain. For it is impossible for a Member of Parliament, and particularly one in the position then held by Mr. Attlee, to visit a country in times of trouble without appearing to carry with him the conviction that he represents his Party, or even the voice of his country, and Mr. Attlee should have realised this. Madame de Navarro said: - *"He is paid £2000 a year as leader of the Opposition, and his apology in the House of Commons, in which he tried to detach himself from his capacity as a Party leader, and represent himself in Spain as an ordinary member of the House of Commons, carried no conviction to anybody, and intensified the ridiculous position in which he found himself. I make no secret of my sympathy with the Spanish National movement led by Franco. The horrors which stand to the credit of the so-called Republican Government are an ever-lasting blot upon Communism and those responsible for the trickery and corruption which marked the triumph of the Madrid faction to securing the control of the Spanish Government two years ago. The situation in Spain is deplorable beyond words. The only happy reflection is that through the wise statesmanship of the British Government, we have prevented the struggle in that country involving us in a European war."*

Our defence programme, however, was bound to have unfortunate repercussions upon export trade and, as President of the National Union of Manufacturers, I wrote to Neville Chamberlain (then Chancellor of the Exchequer) urging him to consider the peculiar relation of the defence programme to the export trade and to the national finances. After a delay of some weeks, he replied in a letter dated April 23rd 1937: -

"My dear Hannon,

... The problems to which you refer are problems of the first

importance, and I am in general agreement with the views expressed in your letter, that the issues involved cannot be left to be determined by individual firms, without co-operation between the Government and the representatives of the industries concerned.

*The specific proposal made in your letter is that there should be an
enquiry, by representatives of the Government and Industries, into
the general issues raised by the impact of the Government Defence
Programme upon commercial work. After consultation with those
concerned, the conclusion has been reached that these matters could
not be dealt with effectively by a general enquiry of the kind
suggested. Experience has shown that the industrial problems
resulting from the Defence Programme are of so varied a nature and
are so constantly changing that the only practicable method is to
deal with them individually. I wish to emphasise, however, that the
Government fully shares your anxiety that the Defence Programme
should be carried through as economically as possible, and with the
least possible interference with ordinary trade. This object is
facilitated by the close contact that the Minister for the Co-
ordination of Defence is, in fact, maintaining with the
representatives of the industries most closely concerned with the
Defence programme. It is not without interest in this connection
that, in his discussions with the Machine Tool Trades Association,
the Minister definitely agreed that the Association's plans for co-
operating in the programme should be framed on the basis that
approximately 25-30% of their output should continue to be devoted
to the export trade and that, to meet any resultant difficulties,
recourse should be had as necessary to purchase abroad by the
Defence Departments. While, however, I do not see my way to
accept your suggestion for general enquiry on the lines proposed, I
wish to emphasise that, if the National Union at any time have in
mind any particular case of difficulty and would be good enough to
furnish the necessary details, the Minister for the Coordination of
Defence will be glad to have the matter carefully investigated.*

Yours sincerely,
Neville Chamberlain."

At that time, I was urging the promotion of trade with
Egypt which, under our tutelage, had prospered to the
extent of greatly enlarging her trade with foreign countries.
A straw will show how the wind blows and, even then, it
was the tendency in Egypt to treat Germany and Austria on
the same terms as England. They had, however, recently
placed an order with a British firm for railway rolling stock,
and I hoped that this might encourage the promotion and
expansion of further commerce between the two countries, I
saw King Farouk for the first time that year. He was but
seventeen years old and, accompanied by his mother, he

paid a visit to the B.S.A. works. As Deputy Chairman of the firm, I had the honour of meeting him. The feature that interested him most in the great factory, was the testing of arms at the rifle range, and we allowed him to try out one of the rifles. He proved himself to be a good shot, scoring a bull's-eye.

This extract is taken from an article I published on July 30th: -

"When Napoleon called us a nation of shopkeepers, over a century ago he did not mean it as a compliment, but we have always taken it as such. What he failed to realise was that commerce is the life-blood of any great nation. You can live by commerce; you can feed hundreds of millions of people. But glory, Napoleon's ideal, is not such satisfying fare.

Strange that a man, who knew so well that an army marches on its stomach, should fail to grasp the fact that the same test applies to the civilian nation from which the army must be raised. We have not always realised ourselves the true significance of our Imperial heritage. There were times when Little Englanders very nearly gained the power to do away with the British Empire altogether, but, fortunately, we had our Disraeli, and after him that immortal champion Joseph Chamberlain."

Alas! Our Imperial heritage has sadly shrunk these days, as the idealistic and impractical countries demand their independence, one after the other. Apropos of the Empire Exhibition that was held the next year, and whose plans were then being discussed, I urged that a series of Empire Exhibitions might be staged in various centres throughout the country, stretching far into the future. The public of this country needed, and still need, educating upon the subject of what they can buy and sell within the Empire. If the war had not intervened, I maintain that much could have been done on these lines.

Towards the end of November, I was one of a deputation to the Prime Minister on the subject of Empire Migration and Development, and we discussed matters with him for about an hour. A lengthy Conference had been held at the Guildhall in October, and a Committee had been formed to report on plans, and this was the outcome of it. Until that year, the Dominion Governments had not been inclined to co-operate, but from then on the surge of people from Great Britain to Canada, Australia, New Zealand and South Africa was interrupted only by the war.

CHAPTER 13

What can one say of the year 1938? It incorporates that period when we were brought to the brink of war, and guided away from it by that great peacemaker, Neville Chamberlain, with the hope that war would not come again 'in our time'. Looking back across the tragic years of conflict, and the grim period that followed, 1938 seems far removed from this present decade. The disillusionment which hit those of us who believed that peace would prevail was made all the greater by the suspense of the Austrian and Czechoslovakian tragedies, culminating in the relief of our fears. I received the following letter from Chamberlain, dated June 3rd, 1938: -

"My dear Paddy,

... it was indeed kind and thoughtful of you to discover and send me the volume of my brother's books in German. I am delighted to have it in my library, and I must say I am very gratified to think that it has found such a ready market in Germany where, I should have supposed, Austen would have been regarded with some suspicion and even dislike.

I believe that the German people are sincerely disposed to friendliness with us. It is, therefore, very regrettable that the German Ministry of Propaganda, and the Government controlled Press, should keep up this barrage of abuse and misrepresentation. One would say that it was deliberately done to make bad feeling, but I am inclined to think it is rather to be ascribed to the vexation and disappointment which the Government feels in realising that they have lately suffered some loss of prestige.

Yours ever,

N. Chamberlain."

The startling news of the resignation of Herr von Schusnigg (the Austrian Chancellor) due to Nazi pressure, followed immediately by the German military occupation of that country, was told to me just as I was about to address a meeting of the Moseley Unionist Association. I informed my audience of the facts, but, naturally, did not comment upon such a matter of grave consequence. Yet these events were not, apparently, of such portent to the majority of the British people (at least so far as the youth of the country were concerned). For barely a month later, I spoke at a recruiting meeting to an audience of grievously small number. It was in May of that year that the Aston Villa Football team travelled to Germany and met with some unpleasantness. I went to Berlin to support their players, and attended a banquet in honour of the team at which many prominent Germans were present, and I spent an interesting afternoon talking to Goebbels. This was the Villa's second visit to the continent in twelve years, and their trip lasted more than a fortnight. They visited Hamburg, Dusseldorf, Cologne, Berlin and various other cities, and returned home by the Hook of Holland. The incidents which occurred in Berlin were greatly exaggerated in England, they arose chiefly because the spectators were unaccustomed to certain decisions concerning the offside rule, and they felt that their team would have won the match if the referee had behaved fairly, which of course was rubbish for the referee was perfectly impartial. Neville Henderson wrote to me about it on my return to England: -

"... The visit of your team to Berlin was a great pleasure to me. I noticed with distress the comments in the British papers about the match. Much as I love democracy, the antics of a democratic Press are a constant source of worry to me. It is unfair enough in politics, but when it even gives distorted versions of sport, it is no wonder that, abroad, foreigners believe that we are losing our sense of fair play and sportsmanship."

In July I was once more on the continent, this time as the guest of the Czechoslovakian Government (in connection with the Sokol Festival) and while there I had the happiness of meeting President Males. The Sokol Movement represented the growth of spiritual and moral forces over the previous seventy years or so. The main consideration of the Czech patriots was a high standard of moral purity with discipline, solidarity and vigorous health in their nation as a whole. I watched, enthralled, the phenomenal display of mass physical drill and gymnastics at the Masaryk Stadium, in which nearly forty thousand men took part, as well as many thousands of women and children. If only the Nazi organisation of youth could have achieved, and then remained at, this splendid level!

I also went to Danzig that year, so in fact I visited the chief scenes of the tragic drama that was soon to be enacted on the European stage. Among the many diplomats and statesmen whom I met on the continent that year was Dr

Burkhardt, the League of Nations High Commissioner. He described Neville Chamberlain to me as the most respected man in Europe. After Chamberlain's dramatic meetings with Hitler in September, Amery wrote me the following: -

"I applauded Neville's courage in flying over to Germany, and I have been in favour of the definite cession of, at any rate, a corner of Czechoslovakia. But that is very different from a general mutilation of the country by ceding every district in which there may be a local German minority, irrespective of how many of that majority really wish to be under Hitler. Moreover, it is one thing doing that as a negotiated policy, and another doing it in desperate haste, and on almost any terms, as a capitulation to Hitler's threat of war. If Neville can say to Hitler that he has got to give time for discussion, and that any act of aggression on his part, meanwhile, puts an end to all talks and sees us and France lined up against him, then we should have made a real contribution to peace. As it is, it does look like a sheer surrender to violence. That may save our own peace for the time being, and may be justified, even at the cost of humiliation, if it gives us more time to prepare, but it certainly would not be a contribution to the permanent peace of the world."

Frankly, I regarded the Munich meeting as the opening of a great peace period and had full confidence in our Prime Minister. Earlier in the year I had, together with Amery, Page Croft and Lloyd, sent a letter to the 'Times' protesting against the large importation of German motor cars and pointing out that the factories from which these cars came could, with only a little modification, be applied to the manufacture of munitions. At the municipal elections in October, the Socialists based their appeal (as I wrote in a letter to the 'Birmingham Post') on: -

"... ill-formed and bitterly prejudiced antagonism to the international peace and goodwill policy of the Prime Minister."

This was naturally and immediately denied, and the Socialists accused me of trying to make capital of the Munich agreement.

At the beginning of November, a memorandum was circulated among Members of the House of Commons by Brigadier-General Spears on some 'deficiencies revealed by the recent emergency'. He gave a list 'of some of the major scandals which were in evidence in the recent mobilisation of the anti-aircraft defences of London.' These included statements that 'no permanent gun positions were yet ready, and if the guns were put on wet grass their accuracy would very soon be destroyed' and that 'there was no earthwork protection, nor camouflage in necessarily open spaces, nor even temporary hutments for officers and men.' He claimed that the distribution of material was so chaotic that, often, the instruments and guns did not coincide and, in many cases, there were no cleaning materials.

"London," he declared, "was defended by 1914 Peerless A.A. guns and Lewis guns which constitute a major menace to the population of London, while providing virtually no protection … It appears literally criminal that guns should be installed for the purpose of making a show which could not possibly embarrass hostile aircraft, and which could be certain to cause numerous deaths among the civilian population ... The whole organisation of A.A. defence is grossly incompetent ... The constant complaint of unit commanders is that there is nobody at the War Office to whom they can go, and from whom they can get decisions."

I was horrified when I read this communication, not because I was necessarily surprised at the statements, nor because I doubted their accuracy, but because such vitally secret information should have been broadcast among Members. I immediately drew the attention of Leslie Hore-Belisha and David Margetson (the Chief Whip) to this memorandum by sending them copies of it. I also wrote to the Prime Minister, and I sent the following letter to Spears himself: -

"...I am shocked to think that an officer of your rank should make himself responsible for the circulation of this document. It would be impossible to suggest anything more calculated to injure the National Government, of which you are a supporter, and tend to lower the prestige of the Defence Departments, than the circulation of the allegations which you make to Members of the House of Commons. It would appear to me that information drawn up by a number of officers belonging to Territorial Anti-Aircraft Units should be brought before their respective commanding officers, and a memorandum communicating secret intelligence for distribution to Members of the House of Commons one must regard as direct and positive violation of discipline. Apart from the great objection which must always obtain from compiling information in this way for the use of a Member of the House of Commons, it would be the obvious

duty of such Member to communicate it to the Secretary of State concerned, or the First Lord, instead of putting the alleged defects into the hands of Members, with the inevitable result that they will be used against the National Government, with the further possibility of communication to a potential enemy of this country. I am so disturbed by what you have done, that I regard it as my duty to submit a report of your action to the Prime Minister."

He replied by return: -

"Dear Hannon,

Your letter of the 14th shows clearly a complete difference of point of view between us. Party questions are all important according to you, according to me the safety of the country transcends all other considerations. The Territorial Officers who gave me this information had previously informed the War Office of the facts, but felt that the points they, as patriots deeply anxious concerning the safety of the capital, had raised, were not receiving the attention they merited. I am sorry you should think that information given confidentially to Members supporting the National Government might eventually reach a potential enemy. I do not share this view, and think that Members of Parliament are quite as discreet as Territorial Officers. None of the information contained in the Memorandum was of a secret nature, and it was known to all Territorials in charge of the defence of London, who naturally observed these deficiencies. I might add that not a single service member, and many have discussed the memorandum with me, has raised the least objection to it, or to the method of its communication.

Yours sincerely

E.L. Spears."

If he had thoughtfully considered 'the safety of the country', he would surely never have put such lamentable facts in writing except to the proper authority. However, the weak and paltry excuses contained in his letter tell their own tale. To Chamberlain I wrote:-

"I feel it my duty to call your attention to a gravely objectionable and ill-advised memorandum which has been circulated to Members of the House of Commons by Brigadier-General Spears. In my judgement it is difficult to conceive anything more calculated to undermine confidence in the administration of the Defence Department and expose the National Government to charges of incompetence, if not indeed of criminal neglect of their primary duty to the safety of the State, than this catalogue of instances of *unpreparedness extending over six quarter pages. This so-called list of 'major scandals' is marked 'private and confidential', but anyone familiar with the whispering gallery of the House of Commons must know that the allegations may rapidly become the gossip of every club in London, and will probably have startling headlines in the sensational Press . . . The statements of Brigadier-General Spears are not the hearsay of Press reporters. They are given an air of authority and technical correctitude. I am not concerned at the moment with the validity or accuracy of the allegations, but I am profoundly disturbed by their distribution by means of a circular statement . . . The charges embodied in General Spears' memorandum should, in my view, be placed before the responsible Ministers, and not scattered abroad with the possibility of coming ultimately into the hands of a potential enemy."*

The Prime Minister replied: -

"I, too, regret the action which he has taken, and for the reasons which you give. But I should like you to know that the matter is being dealt with, so far as it can be now."

Hore-Belisha also replied the same day: -

"My dear Paddy,

... I am most obliged by your sending me copies of your letters to the Prime Minister and Spears, and also of the action you have taken. It is characteristic of you to have upheld so promptly and decisively the tradition and code which bind us.

Always,

Leslie."

It was, perhaps, rather significant that, although I was among a party of some eighty Members who were invited to Northolt R.A.F. Station to inspect recent types of fighters and bombers, I did not receive, nor as far as I am aware did my colleagues in the House, any invitation to inspect the guns for the defence of London.

Our relations with Italy at that time were being weighed in the balance, and many prognostications were being made as to whom Italy would give her support in times of international crisis. On January 8th, 'The Times' published a letter from me on the subject of British friendship with Italy, in which I said: -

"The comments in Italian newspapers, as quoted in the 'Times' of the past few days, on the British policy of broadcasting news in foreign languages will have increased the anxiety already entertained in this country by all who desire the early restorative of

full and frank Anglo-Italian friendship. The recent unhappy growth in Italy of an atmosphere of mistrust and misunderstanding of British policy in relation to world affairs, must find the great majority of the people of this country with a feeling of profound regret ... Italian history presents abiding evidence of the contribution made by Great Britain to the achievement of Italian nationhood, Italian unity and Italian economic progress and power ... One of the most interesting monuments which Signor Mussolini has raised in Rome is the huge cross in the Colosseum, which stands on the spot where St Telemachus was martyred when he tried to prevent men murdering one another to satisfy the bloodlust of a decadent Emperor. On the cross are engraved the words: ' ... the spirit of the cross lies the hopes of all the world.' ... Perhaps one may venture, with all moderation and respect, to submit to the Italian people the substance and implications of the inscription."

At this time an Anglo-Italian Parliamentary Committee was formed, of which I was a member, the purpose being to try to bring back the old friendship between our two countries. My erstwhile companion in travel, Sir Philip Dawson (who knew Italy so well) was appointed Chairman, but to our great regret and loss he died in September of that year. As I said of him in the 'Times': - *"He was the embodiment of good humour, kindliness and tolerance, and possessed in generous measure the faculty of making friends."* He had a wonderful gift for languages, and was as fluent as the natives themselves in many different tongues. It was partly through his friendship that I met so many interesting foreigners, particularly connected with Italy, whom I was glad to entertain when they visited London, although in my own right as a member of the Church of Rome, I naturally had many contacts there.

Does anyone now remember the big Atheist Congress held in London in September 1938? It was a dreadful business that such a thing could have originated, and come to fruition, in a Christian country. We held a meeting in the House to discuss what action could be taken about it, but, as this is a free country where men may express their individual opinions, we could only use our positions to speak against the anti-God crusaders, and to support all Christian movements. Dr Frank Buchman was very much to the fore in those days, and the Oxford Group movement had swept the country, adding many well-known personalities to its ranks. Some of us in the House gave him a dinner, at which I spoke of the need of riveting home the important work that must be done in Great Britain. Many Roman Catholics were interesting themselves in the Movement, and during the following year I sent a message of encouragement to the sponsors of the national meeting of moral re-armament, held in Washington. I received the following telegram, signed by five Senators and four Congressmen: -

"We wish to express appreciation for your support of this great undertaking so necessary for men, nations and peace of mankind. Your message presented on Senate floor and recorded with your names affixed congressional record."

On September 22nd, a procession of Roman Catholics marched from Southwark Cathedral to Westminster Cathedral, in some reparation for the congress of Atheists which had been held the previous weekend. With other Members of Parliament I marched in the first rank, immediately behind the crucifix, leading a vast number of Christians indignant at the affront and blasphemy of the anti-God enthusiasts. One of the most unusual dinners that I have attended was held in the Birmingham town hall that December. It was organised to aid distress in China, and the guests were provided with chopsticks, which provoked amusement. At the end of the dinner, I auctioned the pair used by the Chinese Ambassador, which fetched £2. The Chino-Japanese war had aroused sympathy for China (the victim of aggression) and I had been doing what I could to help China, and to show friendship towards those of her people who were in England. Henry McGowan wrote the following letter, dated July 27th, after one of my entertainments: -

"My dear Paddy,

... A little note of gratitude for a delightful and instructive evening. Your Chinese guests must have seen where our sympathies lie in their struggle against Japanese aggression. I am sure the Professor was right when he said that China was fighting for Democracy. I am having a talk tomorrow with the Under Secretary for Foreign Affairs on this important matter.

Yours ever,

Harry."

One thing that I saw very clearly through the years of my life as a Parliamentarian, was the necessity of keeping politics in close touch with industrial life everywhere. Although our internal Empire trade was steadily developing, we were suffering in general from a slight industrial depression, due partly to considerable over-buying. We might have got more benefit from the various international trade agreements in which we were involved. The United States was then the most closely protected nation in the world, which raised almost insuperable problems in regard to her commercial connection with Great Britain. It was significant that engineering firms all over the world had made good profits, some for almost the first time. The B.S.A. Company, for instance, had increased its profit for the year 1935 over four hundred times. Motor cars, too, were taking the roads in ever-increasing numbers.

His Majesty King George VI visited the Daimler factory in Radford (of which I was a Director) during the early spring, and we watched with delight his drive in an 1899 Daimler built for his grandfather, Edward VII. The ancient car drove round from one entrance of the factory to another, and His Majesty expressed his admiration of the fact and, I think, thoroughly enjoyed it.

During September I attended the International Exhibition in Paris, where I visited the displays given by forty countries. The Great Britain Pavilion (I was glad to find) occupied one of the four best positions in the Exhibition, being practically under the Eiffel Tower, and in the direct approach from the main entrance gate. One point that I noticed with great pleasure was the delightful display of work from the Gold and Silversmiths of Birmingham and London, whose wares received great admiration.

The one folly of our economic policy was the fantastic situation created by paying out something like £2,000,000,000 in unemployment benefits, for which the country received nothing in exchange. Not only is this form of relief distinctly bad for the morale of out of work men, but there was no other country in the world at that time that did not couple schemes of relief with active work, making roads, building, dykes, draining land and so on. So much could have been done, where nothing was done at all.

In spite of wars and rumour of wars, and in spite of trade slumps, we managed to have some very pleasant and happy and festive occasions in our lovely home on Magna

Carta Island. July is the season for the marking of the Swans on the Thames, known as 'swan-upping', and every year we held a garden party for the occasion. The 'Swan-uppers' set out from a point near Southwark Bridge and handle about three hundred birds on their route up river. It takes them a week to do the stretch as far as Henley. The young birds are pinioned by cutting their flight feathers, and those belonging to the Vintners and Dyers Livery Company have their bills nicked. It is a very old custom, stretching back far into history, and is performed by the Swan Masters to the Queen. The Royal swans are allowed to go unmarked. The costume of the swan-uppers is very gay scarlet predominating in their colourful get-up, and each man sports a swan's feather in his cap. At the time of which I am writing, the three Swan Masters were brothers and famous Thames watermen. During the party that we gave, a member of the crew was trussed up and marked to show how the swans were treated, an incident that caused great merriment. Mrs, Chamberlain came usually every year, and always there were many other prominent people among the large number of guests. Our outdoor entertainments on other occasions sometimes centred round the planting of a tree or trees, for what we have received from our ancestors should be handed on down to posterity, and where there are beautiful trees, there should be planted others eventually to replace them.

I think that Mrs. Chamberlain felt this, too. She wrote to me from Downing Street after planting a tree in the grounds during July 1938: - *"Thank you so much for the photographs which I am delighted to have. Should you be keeping one in your collection, I hope it will be the one in which you are holding the hat and not the carnations, as I did not like myself in the latter one! The first, I think, is extremely good in every way and includes the guard of honour. May I add how much I enjoyed the whole ceremony, and how proud I was to plant the trees on behalf of the Prime Minister and myself? I was extremely happy that you should have chosen a tulip tree, seeing that there is a very ancient and beautiful one at Chequers. I like to think that these other trees will stand on Magna Carta Is}and for many hundreds of years. I only hope that some unkind storm will not uproot them and necessitate a replacement. I like to think of the early connection between my 'de Vere' ancestor and the Charter. Yours sincerely, Anne Chamberlain."*

So far as I could ascertain, there is no recorded visit of a Lord Mayor to Magna Carta Island since the sealing of the Charter, so I invited the Lord Mayors of London and Birmingham to plant trees on our grounds one day in July. What a happy memory that is, and one among the last of the entertainments at the Island before the outbreak of war. The weather that day was perfect, the band were seated in the shade of the trees, and we strolled to and fro among our guests or sat chatting to especial friends in that leisurely and delightful fashion so particularly traditional to an English garden party. Our last entertainment there, before the war was declared, was a dance held in early August at the conclusion of the Wraysbury and Old Windsor Regatta. My wife presented the prizes in the late afternoon. Although that was a pleasantly hot day, we had a miniature cloud burst which nearly spoiled amusement. But the ladies came outside again in their pretty frocks, and the grass dried quickly in the hot sun that succeeded this freak storm.

Two other entertainments in those immediate pre-war years stand out in my memory, both of them in connection with the stage. When Julia Neilson attained her fiftieth anniversary on the stage, we gave a banquet in her honour, and I was proud to be in the Chair. I think there were about seven hundred guests and they, and many who were unable to come, subscribed towards the presentation of a George I 'loving cup' and a James II Monteith bowl. Lord Hailsham presented these to Julia Neilson, and Sir John Simon proposed the toast of 'Our Guest'. There was a letter, too, from Queen Mary, who wrote sending her congratulations. Some months later, towards the end of 1938, I was again Chairman at a luncheon given, this time, to Lady George Alexander (widow of the famous actor-manager). She had done ceaseless work for all sorts of charities and hospitals, and a very large number of people came to honour her.

This reminds me of an occasion when I was partly instrumental in the demolition of a theatre! It was the old Surrey Theatre, London, which was situated next door to the Royal Eye Hospital (in which I was greatly interested). The hospital needed a room for expansion, and an appeal was launched (of which I was Chairman) and a large sum of money collected for the demolition and rebuilding. Jack

Hobbs and I directed oxy-acetylene burners on to a huge girder, which soon carne crashing down on to the stage, to the cheers of the nurses who were off duty and had come to view the fun. The theatre had originally been the Royal Circus, and had housed many circus performances and canine acts. Later on, the 'Drama' took over.

The year 1939 (which became such a tragic and terrible date to recall) began for me in a very pleasant way, for my wife and I set off in the middle of January for a two months cruise in the South Atlantic. Tristan da Cunha, the most lonely island in the world, was, once again, in bad plight, and the Island's Society (of which I was a member) launched an appeal, which was well responded to. The result was a shipload of food and necessities of all sorts, also toys subscribed by former passengers of the 'Viceroy of India'. If the weather had been bad, men would have had to land the cargo at the Cape until it could be shipped to the island. But fortunately, all was well, and with good conditions we arrived at Tristan da Cunha. I formally handed over the gifts to the Reverend H. Wilde, who distributed them where they were most needed. Nearly all the passengers landed with me, including Sir Cornelius and Lady Chambers, and they received thanks from the islanders for their gifts of a treadle sewing machine, and a gramophone (which I had bought at Rio with money subscribed to me on the voyage).

Among the passengers was an official photographer, who took many photographs of the island scenery and people, which were afterwards exhibited in London at the Ilford Gallery. It was most interesting to see Tristan da Cunha after all these years, for I had very much wanted to visit it during the plight in 1906, when some of the buildings were actually burnt down to attract attention of passing ships. Although I organised the scheme for its relief, I could not go myself; but now at last I was able to see the place for myself. We arrived back in England early in March, having called in at St Helena, Sierra Leone, Capetown, and other places en route. At Las Palmas, I found I was the first British Member of Parliament to stand on Spanish soil since the new regime took control. Neville Chamberlain was very interested to hear of my project, and hoped that I would have "an interesting and pleasurable journey", which was certainly the case. I suggested that he could send a message to the people of the island, which he did. The message ran: -

"I am happy to have this opportunity of sending to you, by Sir Patrick Hannon, my friend and colleague in the House of Commons, my very best wishes for the year 1939, and my assurance that the interests of the inhabitants of Tristan da Cunha are not forgotten by His Majesty's Government. May you continue to live together peaceably as loyal subjects of His Majesty the King, and to work together for the general benefit of the community to which you belong."

On my return, I received the following letter from him: -

"My dear Paddy,

Thank you for your letter of the 9th March, and for forwarding to me the very appreciative letter from the Chaplain of Tristan da Cunha. I am most interested to hear of your visit to the island, and of your trips generally. It must have been an instructive experience, and I am grateful to you for letting me have your impressions of it. In particular, I appreciate, of course, the kind references which were made to myself.

Yours ever,

Neville Chamberlain

P.S. You must come to my room some time next week and tell me more about it."

Shortly after this, we were very forcibly reminded of another island (the one, in fact, next door to us). Ireland. For some fanatical, misguided members of the race to which I belong decided to wage war against England by putting bombs into letter boxes and other places, regardless of who should be at hand when the explosion occurred. These acts brought great discredit on the Irish nation, and profoundly disturbed me. The fanatical delusion of these soldiers (the Irish Republican Army) that they were playing a gallant part in Ireland's 'fight for freedom' was a tragic example of obtuse patriotism. In those months, whenever a stupid act like those I have mentioned was perpetrated, I felt ashamed of my fellow countrymen. The Hierarchy of the Roman Catholic Church, both in Ireland and Great Britain, were strongly averse to the actions of those advocates of a mad policy, but even they could do little to influence the I.R.A. men.

When two of these men were arrested and condemned to death, I thought it my duty to point out to the Prime Minister the effect that their execution would have upon a certain section of the Irish nation, both at home and abroad. We are adept at creating martyrs out of murderers, and it seemed to me to be a grave mistake that these men should be put into the position of potential martyrs. Although the war had been in progress for five months, and although the Prime Minister was overwhelmed with work, I addressed the following to him: - *"... I am, however, so profoundly concerned for the consequences which will ensue the execution of the two fanatical condemned men who are now awaiting the death sentence at Winson Green, Birmingham, that I hope you will forgive me if I ask you to give this grave affair your sympathetic consideration. The atrocious quality of the crime committed by these misguided creatures must be condemned by every decent Irishman, in every corner of the globe, ... there exist groups Irishmen ... particularly in the United States, who still entertain in the traditional Irish way, the bitterest antagonism to the British Empire. To such people, the making of martyrs will be the pretext for envenomed opposition to this country in the process of the war. You may, perhaps, recall the incident of the execution of three Fenians at Manchester in the 70's of last century, which gave rise to a flood of organised crime in Ireland against the State. A song, 'God save Ireland', written on this incident, became the Irish revolutionary national anthem down to the days of the Sinn Fein rising in 1916. I have been approached by one of our Unionist colleagues, Mr. W.J. Stewart, Unionist Member of Parliament for Belfast South, who entertains the same anxiety in the event of execution taking place as I have endeavoured to outline in this letter. Nobody would dare to approach you with a plea of mercy in view of the circumstances of the crime, but I am satisfied that the substitution of life sentences would have repercussions advantageous to the war effort of the Empire, and to more helpful co-operation with the United States."*

Chamberlain's reply was what I expected of him, for in the midst of his overwhelming cares and pressure of work, he was prepared to consider the matter carefully: - *"I can say at once,"* he wrote, *"that the arguments you put forward have been and are present to my mind. I could, however, be pleased to have a word with you on the matter in the House, if you think this would be helpful."* Readers may remember, however, that these two men (James Richards and Peter Barnes) were executed on February 6th, despite last minute efforts on their behalf by Mr. Delanty and others, whose interest in their fate was very pressing.

Shortly after the war began, I wanted to ask a question in the House concerning the exact statue and function of Sir John Maffey (Lord Rugby) the British Representative in Eire, as the whole position seemed somewhat vague. But, at Sir Anthony Eden's written request, I withdrew the question, realising that a certain embarrassment might arise. Throughout the first half of that fateful year I felt confident that war could be averted. I was sure that the majority of the German people were averse to war, and I thought that the strength of our fleet (which was now greater than ever before) would do much to steady the mad ideas of the Nazi leaders. Dictators understand only methods that pinch their toes, and I strongly advocated the boycott of German goods as an effective reply to the barbarism and the rape of central European countries. At the same time as believing in ultimate peace, however, I pressed for the recruitment of more fighting men, and did everything in my power to impart to the youth of the country the knowledge of our imminent danger, and the part they could play in combating it. During May I wrote to Leslie Hore-Belisha suggesting the establishment of a London Midlanders Territorial unit, but the reply I received was disappointing. The War Office stated that my request could not be granted because it would create a 'redundant unit'.

One aspect of those times that greatly dismayed me was the lack of support accorded to the Prime Minister. In those dark days of menacing danger, it was essential that the country (as voiced by its political representatives) should stand solidly behind their leader. But a new political group arose, whose statement of policy reflected the childish type of mind responsible for its production, idealistic and impracticable. They reviled the weakness of our foreign policy but could suggest no alternative. They declared that there must be no surrender to force and urged a solid front of peace-loving nations pledged to resist aggression. And they had their supporters. From the lobbies of the House of Commons arose rumblings and grumblings of political revolt against Neville Chamberlain, which made his heavy task more difficult still. There was simply no room for division among Liberals, Conservatives and Unionists in the face of danger. The alternative was inevitable weakness.

Those of us who had faith in our leader, exerted

ourselves to stress our support of him on every possible occasion. The 'Thirty Club' (of which I was a member) invited him to be the Guest of Honour at one of the forthcoming dinners. But Chamberlain refused, as he refused so many invitations during that year, explaining: -

"... It is now clear to me, after two years of experience, that the pressure upon a Prime Minister is continuous rather than intermittent, and that, if I am to preserve my usefulness, I must confine my engagements within the strictest limits. For this reason, I have had to refuse dinners and lunches right and left, even for the autumn, and I am afraid that I must ask to do the same in this case. I feel sure that you and the President will understand and excuse me."

CHAPTER 14

The last meeting before the House broke up for the summer recess was memorable for the atmosphere of tension which prevailed. When Chamberlain proposed that we should reassemble on October 3rd, there was some heated opposition. Arthur Greenwood retaliated, by suggesting a date in August, and the subsequent speakers became so heated that Chamberlain ironically commented that, "it seemed obvious that they needed a long holiday." He had already explained that the House had done all it could for the moment, and that an earlier reassembly, unless in the case of emergency, would be somewhat pointless. During the speeches, I once again stressed Birmingham's profound belief in the Prime Minister.

I was in Harrogate, enjoying three weeks holiday with my wife, when Parliament was recalled. From all over the country, and from outside the country too, Members of Parliament hurried back to Westminster, filled with apprehension. I arrived in the House at about half past seven that August morning and was, I believe, the first member from the Midlands to appear. As the House began to fill, I think that we all knew what must lie ahead, and for me it was particularly difficult to reconcile the practical inevitability of war with my belief in peace.

On September 5th, I sent a letter to the various Chairmen of the branches of Moseley Divisional Organisation, saying: -

"... There may also be made a call for sacrifice and service on the part of men and women, young and old alike, such as has never been made before. But when it is clearly understood, as I know you and all our devoted people will understand, that this struggle against tyranny and aggression will probably be the greatest in human history, your desire to serve will respond to the magnitude of the obligation which rests upon you ... The time ahead of us all will test the spiritual strength and moral fibre of British manhood and womanhood."

And how magnificently they withstood this test, under constant anxiety and frequent danger. Meanwhile I had been continuing my friendship with, and interest in, the Italian nation, and was one of the many who cherished the profound hope that Italy would not enter the war against us. As Chairman of the Anglo-Italian Parliamentary Committee

I had, in July, sent an invitation to Count Grandi (the Italian Ambassador) and his wife, to a farewell dinner at the House of Commons to be given by that Committee. Count Grandi was leaving to take up the post of Minister of Justice in Italy. In October he wrote to me: -

"I have hoped so much that circumstances would have allowed me to come back to London to say goodbye to my friends, the members of the Anglo-Italian Parliamentary Committee. This, alas, has not been possible in this moment, but I hope it will be in the near future. I wanted so much to thank you and them all, personally, for the precious help they have always given me during my seven unforgettable years as Ambassador in London. If my mission and my work have not been entirely unsuccessful, that is because my friends helped and trusted me. I will never forget the constant affection by which I have been surrounded, even in some difficult moments, making me always feel hopeful and happy. I beg you to remember me to all my friends on the Anglo-Italian Parliamentary Committee, and to believe me, my dear Hannon,

very sincerely yours,
Dino Grandi."

During the first days of the war, I had an interesting assignment (together with Major Proctor) to interview the Slovakian diplomatic representative, Mr. Harmincz. It was thought possible that he would be of more importance if he concealed the fact that he no longer was prepared to act for the Slovakian Government which, of course, was under German rule. It was hoped that use could be made of the thousands of Slovakians in the U.S.A., that they might be brought to Canada where they could be trained and equipped to fight against Germany.

Although we were naturally very worried about the import trade, which it was essential to maintain, industrial dislocation was not so noticeable as in the 1914-18 war. Yet the allocation of raw material, the various inevitable restrictions, the rigid censorship and officialdom (sometimes carried much too far) played their exasperating parts. I supported a deputation to Leslie Begin (Minister of Supplies) asking that the small engineering firms in the Midlands could have work allocated to them, so that they might play their part in the battle. I also asked in the House to heed applications from firms employing skilled armament workers for exemption from call-up to the Forces.

Both requests were received most sympathetically. During October, the Frances Day Penny Fund was launched at the Dorchester Hotel to provide comforts for the Services, and how well the public responded during the long period to follow. The inimitable Gracie Fields arrived unexpectedly that day, so I was surrounded by talent and beauty! I remember she had been ill, so ill that I had to assist her to stand up. She described herself as: - "... a bit of a cripple, but all right once you get me on my feet." Frances Day is an old friend now, and what a help she was to us all during those black, tense years of war!

Several notable old friends of mine died in the latter half of 1939, Lord Mount Temple (or Wilfred Ashley, as I knew him best) passed away some weeks before the outbreak of war, which was most merciful for him, for one of the greatest objects of his life was the restoration of Anglo-German friendship. In addition to Broadlands, his beautiful home where the Anglo-German Steel Conference had met in 1926, he possessed a picturesque and romantic estate in Sligo, where he had many happy hours fishing. In the death of Mr. R. Hewins (Secretary of the Birmingham Unionist Association) we lost a staunch Conservative, and an indefatigable worker with whom I had been associated since my successful entry into politics.

That first winter of the war (so bitterly chill and relentless, when our people at home in the snow and frosty air learned their preliminary dread of the black-out, and some of our men in the British Expeditionary Force were found frozen at their posts, that cold winter of the 'cold' war) seemed never-ending. Various members of the War Cabinet gave a series of addresses over two months in order to keep the country informed of the progress of the war. The Prime Minister spoke in Birmingham town hall at the final meeting, and of course I was present to hear him. He said that he: - "... felt that the nation was united now as it had never been before in its whole history." And he declared that: - "... he no longer felt as much strain and anxiety, paradoxical though it must seem, as he did in those days before the war, when there was still a possibility that it might be averted."

Hore-Belisha's resignation from the Cabinet in January roused a tremendous lot of feeling. Nobody likes to change horses crossing a stream, much less a roaring torrent, but

Chamberlain believed that it was the right action to take, and I upheld his view whenever necessary. When, however, Chamberlain's own resignation was contemplated in early May, I felt that we must be swept away by the roaring torrent should this come to pass, and in consequence I wrote two letters to him. The first, on May 7th, on behalf of the Birmingham Group in the House, was designed to uphold his fortitude in that dark period. He replied by return, saying that he: - *"... was very touched by the letter"* and that it gave him: - *" the greatest pleasure to receive an assurance of our loyalty and support at this time, although, of course, I have never for a moment doubted it."*

Then, on May 9th, I wrote him the following letter: -

"My dear Prime Minister,

I have been making contacts in the House during the whole of yesterday afternoon, and until the midnight hour last night, on the embarrassing and embittered situation which has arisen in our Party. For reasons which nobody can explain, there is intense antagonism to John Simon and Sam Hoare. I have tried to find out from Attlee, Greenwood and Archie Sinclair the reason of this attitude towards the Chancellor of the Exchequer and the Secretary of State for Air. It is just like the case of Dr Fell, there is no explanation but violent opposition.

For yourself personally there is profound admiration and, indeed, affection among all Parties, and I beseech you for the sake of the future of humanity, not to haul down your flag. Many years ago, when the late Lord Balfour showed me his friendship in taking me for a country walk, he said, "It is easy to haul Up a flag but how difficult it is to haul it down.

So far as I can gather from Attlee, Greenwood, and Sinclair, they are prepared to serve under you if the two statesmen whom I have mentioned will be eliminated. Lloyd George's speech yesterday was an atrocious violation of all the decencies of debate, and the great majority of us who love you so much, were distressed that our deliberations could not have been conducted in private session.

As I left the House this afternoon, the universal feeling was that it would be a disaster of the first magnitude if you were to resign your leadership in the presence of the most appalling situation with which we have ever been confronted. I saw George Courthorpe a few minutes ago, and he will write you a short letter embodying what is the majority feeling of our Party.

My earnest and abiding hope is that whatever decision you may take, you will be guided by God's blessing, and that you yourself will still remain the Head and Leader of the National Government. Please forgive me for writing you in this way, but I feel it is my duty, as one of your devoted friends, to convey to you as an old campaigner, and after twenty years in the House of Commons, my deep-seated feeling of the unspeakable tragedy which would fall upon our people if you were to cease to be our Leader."

His reply came when Churchill had taken over control, and he himself had retired to the Office of Lord President of the Council: -

"My dear Paddy, ... Many thanks for your kind letter. I am sure it would have been quite impossible for me to carry on in any circumstances, however many of my late colleagues I had shed. A National government was required and the Labour Party were adamant against serving under me. Perhaps I may consider myself well treated in that they have now, I understand, consented at least to sit in the same room with me.

Yours ever,

Neville Chamberlain."

He received a tremendous ovation from the Conservative Party on his first entry into the House in his new position, whereas Churchill, we felt, was in the process of being weighed in the balance. Early in 1943, Beverley Baxter published a stirring defence of Chamberlain's immediate pre-war policy and, although I disapproved of the raising of the issue at that moment (and told Beaverbrook so), I prepared an article in support which I sent to Beaverbrook. In comment he wrote: -

"Why do you depreciate Baxter's decision to raise the issue? Surely democracy depends upon public judgement of great events. Baxter's defence has already provoked ninety-three replies. in the space of thirty-six hours."

I replied: -

"... The reason why I felt uneasy about Baxter having raised the Chamberlain issue is because I felt it may have unpleasant reactions on political relationships within the Government, and in the House of Commons face to face with the War Effort. You will recall September 2881, 1938, when Chamberlain made his dramatic speech in the House of Commons, during which he received the message from Mussolini. You will recall the slobber poured over him by Attlee and Sinclair. You will also recall the speeches made on

October 5th, seven days afterwards, in which Attlee and Sinclair denounced Chamberlain by bell, book, and candlelight. I think your sympathy must have gone out to Chamberlain in those days of misery and frustration. I am sure Baxter's article will do much good, if only to prevent the rag, tag, and bobtail of Socialists and Liberals in the House of Commons from screeching against Munich, and forgetting that they voted against conscription and all the Defence Estimates as late as April 1939."

And here I should like to quote at some length from the article I composed: -

"Mr. Chamberlain had an intimate knowledge of the gravity of the European situation. He was well served, with exemplary efficiency, with information of every move in the devilish Hitler game, by our Ambassador in Berlin. His position was one of overwhelming difficulty. On the one hand the gloomy terrors of impending war; on the other hand the deliberate infiltration of poisonous claptrap into the minds of the people of this country against war. When one looks back upon the unholy and unwholesome activities of the League of Nations Union, and the ferocity of Socialist and Liberal leaders against the enlargement of personnel and mechanical equipment in modern armaments for the Defence Services, the embarrassing situation confronting Mr. Chamberlain can, in some measure, be understood."

So far as I can recall in a hurried moment, there were few outstanding figures in the House of Commons who could give unqualified support to a vigorous policy of rearmament. The present Prime Minister, Sir Austen Chamberlain, Mr. Amery, and Mr. Duff Cooper may, in particular, be mentioned.

If I may say so in all modesty, Mr. Chamberlain treated me for many years as an intimate friend. In my rough and tumble way I wrote him on all sorts of subjects. If I were asked, in a hurry, to name one of the greatest gentlemen I have ever known, I would say Neville Chamberlain. But this view of mine does not matter here or there. What does matter, is the case established by Mr. Baxter, that Mr. Chamberlain rendered supreme service to his country, his Empire, and the cause of Civilisation, in the gigantic effort he sustained by indescribable sacrifice of mind and body, to prevent what he knew would be the bloodiest war in human story. It is my profound belief that there will be no more glorious page in British annals than the recital of British achievement in war preparation between Munich and Armageddon. This was Chamberlain's great year, and he had the wisdom and good fortune to bring into partnership the present

Prime Minister, whose grasp of the grinding need for the co-ordination of sea and air power, with a vitality and drive and organisation, which was then, and is still more now, unique.

Only those of us who have been associated with the production of armaments knew of the deplorable situation face to face with preparedness for a European war which weighed so heavily on the mind of Chamberlain in his flights to Berchtesgarten, Gotesberg, and Munich. I happen to be familiar with a good deal of the stirring energy and enthusiastic devotion of management and work people, in shipyard and factory, during the tense weeks and months in what the armchair critics would insolently describe as the Munich or Appeasement period. The triumphant achievement of Churchill, before the outbreak of the 1914-18 War, when he raised British Sea Power to the highest level in our 'Island story', was repeated with what might be called accelerated velocity before the War outburst, and designed the great framework for the phenomenal expansion which followed. This was Mr. Chamberlain's great triumph and, it may be added, Mr. Churchill's great triumph also.

During a Baltic cruise in 1938, I spent a day with Mr. Burckhardt, the League of Nations' High Commissioner at Danzig. I met at that luncheon one of Hitler's private secretaries. I also met the Gauleiter of Danzig and other protagonists of Nazi philosophy. I was staggered by the detailed knowledge that these people possessed of the weakness of British defence organisations. Mr. Burkhardt was a great friend of this country, and within the limits or his influence, strained every nerve in the cause of peace. After a long private conversation with him, I made up my mind that war was inevitable, and I wrote immediately, for what it was worth, a full report to Chamberlain.

I had three or four extremely interesting days in Prague 1935, and left that city just before Lord Runciman arrived. With my colleague, Sir Alexander Roger, we had a full morning, and indeed the greater part of the day, with Dr Benes and the Prime Minister and Foreign Secretary of Czechoslovakia. I left Prague completely convinced that Henlein was playing the Hitler game and that, with the Austrian frontier of Czechoslovakia being wholly undefended, it was only a matter of time until Hitler would seize upon what was then the best governed, and the most financially stable democratic country in Europe. This is not the place to discuss the tragedy, which developed with merciless rapidity, but I feel bound to bear testimony to the complete confidence which the Czech Government placed in Mr. Chamberlain. If he (Mr. Baxter) succeeds, through the influence of the 'Evening Standard', in eliminating from the ignorant, slipshod vocabulary of the times the words 'appeasers' and 'appeasement', he will have rendered outstanding public service."

The inspiration of Chamberlain's advice and the correct political standard he maintained will always be for me, and for many others, a treasured memory. Amery wrote of him, in a letter to me a few weeks before his death: -

"We all hope he will get better, but I think it means the end of his chapter of public service. Whatever differences some of us may have had with him in detail, he has been a great citizen and a devoted servant of his country and of the Empire."

A few days after Churchill became Premier, Sir John Simon became a baron and left the House of Commons for the Lords. His letter to me, replying to my note conveying the esteem in which we held him, embodies a somewhat sad tone: -

"My dear Pat,

… Thank you for your characteristically kind letter. I shall miss the House of Commons, and perhaps it is only human to hope that sometimes they may miss me a little. But I shall not wind up the debate for the Government any more.' For all your kindness to me through these many years I shall always be grateful. Indeed, I do not think that there is anybody in my generation who has so much reason to be grateful to his House of Commons friends, and any regard they had for me, such as you express, is very sincerely reciprocated.

Yours ever,

John Simon."

As the new National Coalition Government came into power the storm broke, and in less than three weeks our gallant Expeditionary Force made its epic retreat via Dunkirk. And soon we were to learn who were our friends and comrades, to stand by us in the fight for our very survival, and who were to turn from us and ally themselves to Nazi Germany. On July 4th, the 'Times' published my letter in which I quoted Garibaldi's words: -

"Cursed be the Italian who would not step forward in her (England's) defence."

For now, to my heartfelt sorrow and to the dismay of us all, Italy was arrayed against us. Then began the Battle of Britain, with that terrible onslaught upon Coventry, followed shortly by the slaughter of hundreds of

Birmingham's citizens. Those raids showed, only too clearly, the great mistake of securing a large part of industrial production in one place. I shall never forget my sight of Coventry after the bombardment. Churches, hospitals and many institutions were in ruins, and of the beautiful Cathedral only the tower was standing.

Lord Beaverbrook wrote to me, strangely enough, at the time when the bad raids on Birmingham were commencing: -

"It is not necessary for me to tell you what we feel about Coventry. And it should not be necessary for me to say that all concerned are working whole heartedly to get the wheels turning again. It has been a sad blow, but it only strengthens our determination. And we shall strive to ensure that Birmingham is protected against such attacks as were made on Coventry."

But this was not possible in such short time, yet the people of both towns (and of, Indeed, all the bombed towns and villages throughout Great Britain) would echo Beaverbrook's words: - "It only strengthens our determination." Another blow, one which greatly distressed and puzzled us, was the inglorious attempt and failure to liberate Dakar. When the news carne through that our fleet was abandoning the attack, I felt gravely concerned for the effect this would have upon our people at home, who were already undergoing so much hardship and danger. Accordingly, I addressed the following letter to Winston Churchill: -

"I regard it my duty to inform you that the disastrous result of the Dakar adventure has had and, unless an early statement from you is forthcoming explanatory of the debacle, will have a disturbing effect upon the morale of the country in these grim and exacting days through which, under your leadership, we are battling our way to victory. Why, in the name of common sense, and in the presence of the attitude of the miserable and demoralised clique who constitute the Vichy Government, the flotilla of ships under the French flag which proceeded to Dakar should have been allowed egress through the Straits of Gibraltar without examination of the quality and character of their personnel is an act of consent on the part of His Majesty's Government which your loyal and devoted supporters in war effort cannot understand.

I have been in contact through my various clubs and organisations with comments on the depressing news of this morning, and the feeling of criticism and resentment is acute. Frankly, this Dakar retreat is regarded as a cardinal blunder; more grave and far-

reaching than the recall of our expeditionary force from Norway, in which, at all events, we saved our national prestige and self-respect.

You have the unqualified confidence of the nation; any appeal you make will have instant -sympathetic response; but it is difficult for your supporters, who face the masses of workers from day to day, to encourage the highest level of duty and sacrifice if there is want of foresight and vision in high places."

Churchill's interesting account of the Dakar incident, related in his volume 'Their Finest Hour', shows how many of us felt, in some degree or other, the emotions which enveloped me at that time, but he decided that no explanation would be given to the public. Churchill's decision to appoint Lord Beaverbrook as Minister of Aircraft Production was a brilliant piece of assignment, for the situation needed a man with Beaverbrook's tremendous energy and drive to organise this vital concern upon which the life of the British people, and possibly of the British Nation, depended. He constantly consulted the B.S.A. works with regard to arms, so that this firm played no small part in the immortal Battle of Britain. Here is a letter, typical of those I received from him: -

"My dear Paddy,

Thanks for your letter. I am delighted to hear you are putting every ounce of energy into production. The gun which interests me is the Browning. Do not let me down over that. I know you will not.

Yours ever,

Max

As Churchill records, the production results of Beaverbrook's Ministry were "magnificent."

While the people of Britain were suffering frequent and terrible bombardment, their morale was being assailed by that master of voice production, William Joyce (or Lord Haw Haw, as he was better known to us all). I had the notoriety of being mentioned by name in one of his broadcasts, and was interested to receive a letter from Stafford Talbot, Director General of the National Council for British Commercial Propaganda Overseas: *"Miss Parker, directly she heard Lord Haw Haw mention your name, made a note of the noble peer's remarks. They were roughly, so Miss Parker tells me, to the following effect: -*

"The British Trade Unions were all out to force the Government to make peace at all costs with Germany, notwithstanding the fact that the leaders of the Trade Unions had expressed their willingness

289

to work in harmony with His Majesty's Government, so that the latter might be assisted to defeat the Nazis ... Sir Patrick Hannon had made various vigorous speeches in the House of Commons, in which he stated that in such times as these no attention should be paid to malcontents among Trade Union members, and in fact that these should be suppressed quite ruthlessly. Sir Patrick Hannon had urged in the strongest language that a line of policy towards the Trade Unions should be adapted by His Majesty's Government which would entirely subordinate the Trade Unions to the control and scheming of Big Industry in Britain, ... Sir Patrick Hannon was, in fact, a thoroughly bad egg, and it was only to be hoped that the unfortunate British working man would eventually succeed in seeing satisfaction for his keen desire for peace, and that in due course the likes of Sir Patrick Hannon would be put where they properly belonged."

The above was the gist of Haw Haw's remarks, and as I listen to them I picture you perhaps also listening to them, and crowing with satisfaction and delight at the realisation of the fact that you could now count upon becoming gloriously immortalised thanks to Haw Haw's personal reference to yourself."

CHAPTER 15

With the onset of winter came the glorious certainty that we had won the first battle of Britain, and Hitler's air force must retire for a space to lick their wounds while their lord and master considered fresh plans. Our soldiers were fighting in the desert, our sailors grappling with mines and submarines, but at home, for large portions of the year (in the Midlands at least) there was only a little hindrance by air raids of the work so vital in our factories. The blitz descended on the ports that year, and many deaths resulted. But, apart from a bad attack once more on Coventry, we worked in comparative peace. Production was the key word in all the manufacturing firms throughout the country, and nearly every man and woman worked with willing vigour and abounding enthusiasm.

I found that an immense amount of good work could be done by the continuous contact between directors and workers, who were thus stimulated to the importance of their task, so I made it my duty from the very outbreak of war to be with them as much as possible, day and night. In a letter to Beaverbrook, dated July 11th 1940, I said: -

"I am constantly in touch with our B.S.A. factories, and am proud of the vigour and devotion of all staffs everywhere, and the splendid spirit that animates the whole of our work people. You will have all the reports of output before you, so I need not quote figures, but I am happy to say that all round ... we are ahead of estimated possible results. We are perhaps a little weak on night shifts here and there, but this phase is only temporary."

I have mentioned above that nearly every man and woman worked well and willingly but, alas, there were subversive elements in some of the factories. One of our works managers, for instance, dismayed me by stating that certain types of workers were taking a mean advantage of the protection given them by the Ministry of Labour, and were interpreting it as a means of 'dribbling' and 'stone-walling', and were preventing the main body of workers from giving the maximum effort. Time-keeping was getting lax, and becoming worse. Absenteeism had greatly increased, and the flimsiest excuses were being given in certain cases. On June 12th, I wrote advising Lord Beaverbrook to work steadily towards unified control. He was now Minister of State, and I gathered that he was not in favour of a Ministry of Munitions on the model created by Lloyd George and directed with such inimitable capacity by Churchill in the 1914-18 War. With respect, however, I urged him to move in that direction: -

"There is a certain amount of overlapping and criss-crossing of ministerial instruction in relation to production efficiency as between the various Defence Departments. Nobody can desire more rapidly or effectively than yourself a programme with the ultimate object of achieving this objective. ... Canada has set us an admirable example in fixing the number of hours for a working week before any premium time for extra working hours can be booked; at the same time, in Canadian industry, it was laid down at the beginning of the war that no premium time could be paid to any worker until a minimum of a certain number of hours had been completed in any one week. If this could be introduced into British industry, it could, I think, provide a helpful correction against absenteeism which is giving many of us so much worry at the moment. ... Steps must be taken to insist on workers dropping, for the time being, what they call their privileges, and throwing themselves heart and soul into the effort which means life or death to the Nation and Empire."

In February of the following year (at a Conference held in Birmingham convened by Lord Dudley) I was interested to find my arguments again pressed forward, for it was agreed unanimously by all those concerned with production that a vast saving in manpower would be effected by short-circuiting Whitehall, and by closer co-operation between the Ministries. On June 29th 1941, Beaverbrook was made Minister of Supply. *"Urgency is everything now,"* he wrote to me shortly afterwards, *"and we must all put forth, over the coming weeks, all the energy we can develop."*

Brendan Bracken had been appointed Minister of Information, and in reply to my note of congratulation he wrote: -

"When the Prime Minister drafted me to this job, he had the hardihood to say that it was worse than running a bomb disposal unit."

The Ministry of Information played a vital part throughout the years that followed. The most startling and, as a consequence, the most selfishly heartening news of the year came in December when, as result of the terrible bombardment of American ships in Pearl Harbour, the United States formally entered the war on our side. In March 1940 a Chinese friend, Mr. Nieu Y. Yao had written: -

"The American people are charming and hospitable, but in them there is no depth. The sympathy for the Allies is obvious, but at the same time there is a very strong fear of being involved in the European conflict ... I do not believe the Americans really understand conditions in England, and there is a lot to be done in that direction. And, I think, it is to the interest of the peace of the world that England and America should understand each other fully ... As regards the Far East, they are very suspicious of Britain. They think Britain may make peace with Japan and abandon the Chinese ... I have told them that Britain will not go so far as that, though she might be compelled to give way to the Japs in certain things. On the whole, the Americans are very good to China, and I think they are clear in their attitude, because when the war in the Far East is over they will enjoy a better position in China than most other powers."

Without the United States, the outcome of the war might have been very different, Now that great nation had become our vigorous and forceful ally, we looked forward with confidence towards the events of 1942. There was, however, a certain element of unrest amongst the Irish-Americans, and it was vitally important that no excuse should be granted to them to raise hostile voices. Therefore, when Churchill proposed to introduce conscription into Northern Ireland, I wrote to him immediately: -

"My dear Prime Minister,

... I am reluctant to add, even for a moment, to the burden of responsibility which you bear in these grim and menacing days, but I feel it is my duty to express to you in unqualified terms my conviction that the introduction of conscription in Northern Ireland would not merely be an embarrassment, but a dangerous experiment at this stage of the war. Nobody entertains a more wholesome contempt for the obstinacy and arrogance of De Valera in relation to the Battle of the Atlantic than I do, and if the question at issue were merely the value which would attach to public opinion in Eire or to the Roman Catholic Nationalist population of Northern Ireland, I would not regard the consequences worth a 'two-penny damn'. But I am profoundly concerned in these grave moments regarding the disturbance of Irish- American sympathy in the United States' which the approval of conscription in Ulster by His

Majesty's Government in the United Kingdom is bound to create. You will have observed recently a message from the most influential organisation of Irish American Catholics to the Eire Government, imploring sympathy with this country in the Battle of the Atlantic, and urging De Valera to consider the free use of the Irish ports to our naval organisation. The Nationalists of Northern Ireland are almost wholly Roman Catholic, and they are led by one of the most forceful and uncompromising leaders of the Roman Catholic hierarchy, Cardinal McRory. You are fully acquainted with the unhappy relationships between Protestants and Roman Catholics in Ulster, which one hoped the passage of time would soothe and soften, but which, unfortunately, so far retain most of the qualities of bitterness and antagonism which have their roots in the darkest shadows of Irish history. Conscription in Ulster will, in my view, intensify this deplorable situation, but worse still, it will afford a pretext for every enemy of this country in the United States to declare that the Roman Catholic minority is being sacrificed at the instance of a Protestant ascendancy.

I wish I could take a more hopeful view of the proposals of the Ulster ministry, but I am thinking of the increased difficulty with which Mr. Roosevelt will have to contend from Irish organisations in the United' States, and the intensified efforts which I fear will be made by Irish American extremists to encourage strikes, sabotage, and slackness of munitions production.

You will no doubt have taken far more competent advice, but as one of your most loyal and ardent supporters, I feel I should give expression to my views."

The two big problems in any war are lack of machines and armaments, and lack of manpower. In order to augment our man-power, farm labourers left the land to learn the intricacies of a disciplined service in uniform that could hardly have been in greater contrast to their former way of life. And the land-girls took over! I have the greatest admiration for those gallant ladies who put in so much hard work on the farms, but, with the best intentions in the world, they could not fully supply the agricultural labour that the farmer so badly needed. It was in January 1941 that I first made direct contact with an organised unit of the Women's Land Army. I was asked to speak (and present good service badges) to the Warwickshire Women's Land Army, whose members, I am sure, fully merited the awards.

Yet despite all their labour that year, I noticed to my dismay that a considerable portion of the oat crops in Warwickshire were still in the stock at the end of September, and in some cases the aftermath was making its way up among the stubble. It was sad that their work should have been wasted for want of extra hands, and sadder still that the country's needs should be endangered. The Government should have been more considerate towards the farmer when he was deprived of the labour so essential to him, and to all of us.

During the debate on the augmenting of industrial manpower, I declared that industry could not depend on the voluntary system of recruitment while we were fighting for our lives. At the beginning of the war, the trade unions showed a magnificent spirit, sacrificing many of their own principles, but after a year and a half of war their initial vigour was fading. We needed a Minister of Labour, who would make the immobilisation of manpower his first duty; fortunately for Britain, we discovered the right man in Ernest Bevin.

It was natural, amidst the grinding strain of winning the war, that we should forget to make provision for future peace, but towards the end of the year I began to feel uneasy about our position in world trade when the war should be ended. If our present policy continued, I thought (and I was not alone in that unhappy conclusion) it was quite possible that we should lose the whole of our trade in the Western Hemisphere. After consultation with fellow members of the National Union of Manufacturers I wrote to the Prime Minister: -

"I think you ought to know that there is a growing feeling of concern amongst manufacturers at the drastic cuts now being made in the established export trade to the Dominions and elsewhere, in deference to the Americans, and the anxiety as to the effect of these cuts on the vitality and recuperative power of the country in the difficult period after the war. They entirely agree that Lease-Lend materials must be regarded as a trust, and the Americans are entitled to be fully satisfied that this trust is not being in any way abused.

They also know that all export trades must, in war, be absolutely dependent on the amount of material and transport which can, from time to time, be made available. It appears to them that the present cuts are going rather further than what, so far as they can see, is required at the moment, owing to either or both of these causes.

You know how vital the established export trade is to the country, and how difficult, if not impossible, it is to recover these when once they have been lost; also, how important it is that the country should be strong enough to be able to play its proper part when war is over."

Churchill replied: -

"I am in full agreement with the National Union of Manufacturers about the vital importance which our export trade will have in the period after the war, and I share their anxiety that no unnecessary obstacles shall be put in the way of its maintenance while the war lasts. But it is not correct to attribute the drastic cuts in our exports to deference to the U.S.A. The reduction of exports is due to our increasing occupation with war-like measures. The Lease-Lend undertaking is a declaration of our understanding that, while the United States is willing to stint its own citizens in order that we may be able to prosecute the war more effectively, it should not be expected to do so in order that we shall escape necessary sacrifices even in our export trade. The differences with which we have to deal are inherent in our own situation. Our problem is to balance the merits of the various demands which are made upon the resources under our control. ... I shall be glad to see that any representations which the National Union may care to make receive the most careful consideration."

This correspondence was published in the Press. Certainly, it was clear that world industry would find itself in a state of economic paralysis when confronted with the problems of peace in a battered and shattered world. Fundamentally, our overseas sales constituted part of the lifeblood of the country. As President of the Institute of Export, I had much correspondence with Sir Andrew Duncan, President of the Board of Trade. He thought that in connection with the establishment of mutual understanding between manufacturers, here and in the States, the initiative ought to come from the firms themselves. I submitted to him that the matter was one of Government responsibility. The Government £should (I felt) not only give a definite lead, but should provide machinery quite detached from the war effort, to concentrate upon our future policy in trade. The Institute of Export gave a dinner in my honour just before Christmas that year, and I think from the applause that greeted my speech in which I gave voice to the above opinion, that most of those present quite agreed with my views.

A part of my pleasanter duties during the war was the

entertainment of foreign statesmen and officials, and I recall one July day in 1941 when members of the Icelandic delegation were our guests at Magna Carta Island. Incidentally, I was one of the few Members of Parliament to have spoken in the ' Althing', their thousand year old Parliament. Early jn August, Winston Churchill visited Reykjavik, where he received a vociferous welcome.

July and August held a personal sadness for me; for Lady Chambers died at the end of June, and her husband, my dear old friend Sir Cornelius, followed her early in August. They had been married for nearly sixty years; and their names (I have no doubt whatsoever) will be remembered with love and admiration in the city of Birmingham for many years to come. Sir Cornelius had come to that city as a young man intending to be articled to the law, but, soon, he became associated with commerce in the shape of a well-known brass-founders, and in less than fifteen years he held a leading position in the trade. He was very keen on tariff reform and, in 1906, he opened a 'dumping shop' to emphasise the wide range of imported articles and the need for Protection. First in Edgbaston, and then in Moseley, he held nearly every office in the Unionist Party, and he was made the President of the Midland Conservative Club in 1930. He was an enthusiast for any cause which he espoused, and with it he had the priceless gift of good humour. His wife was a gracious personality, animated by a lofty sense of public duty and endowed with great human sympathy. For twenty-one years she was president of the Moseley Division of the Women Unionist's Association, and she and her husband spent many happy years working together for the Conservative Party, and for the prosperity of Birmingham.

Early in the New Year, 1942, I opened the Warship Week in Swadlincote. In the nine weeks since this form of raising money for our Royal Navy had begun, already £100,000,000 had been subscribed. During Wraysbury's Warship week I lent the Magna Carta table, and presented a gilded book in which everyone was invited to sign their name for the price of a savings stamp. In the first half of 1941, financial support for the war effort was mainly concentrated upon the Spitfire fund, and I still possess a file of letters acknowledging the generous gifts of the people of Moseley. Our target was

£5000, and although it appeared that we had set the target too far away to reach, we could congratulate the Division on a near achievement and a very splendid effort. So many people worked so hard in their different ways to raise the money. One little boy of nine years old collected over £10 by his initiative in selling jam-jars and magazines to his neighbours, and acorn pipes and cookers to his school friends. Letters of thanks came to me from the Ministry of Aircraft Production: -

"Your constituents have made a most valuable contribution to our air strength. And you have every reason to be proud of their efforts."

An Irish Spitfire Fund was inaugurated too, for which I received most generous subscriptions from some of the citizens of Eire. The bombing of London was at its height at that time, and when I saw the Debating Chamber in the House of Commons, with all its traditions, turned into a mass of rubble, and heard of the savage attack being made upon numerous historic buildings and charitable institutions around Westminster, I rejoiced all the more in the large sums of money that were being sent for our defence. In spite of the grievous strain on nerves and emotions, the morale of our people remained at a high level.

"I think Hitler is making a very great mistake if he hopes to break our spirit and determination, by such devilish work," and "Faith is the greatest thing in life," are extracts from letters typical of those which were written to me during those terrible months. Everywhere one heard praise for Winston Churchill, but dissatisfaction was expressed towards his colleagues (a state of affairs which I deplored, for one cannot win the match by supporting the captain only and abusing his team). On February 17th 1942, the Midland Group of Members of Parliament passed a resolution urging certain reconstruction of the War Cabinet, so as to remove its members from Departmental responsibility and enable their entire energy and thought to be concentrated on the war effort. During February, various changes were made in the Government Ministry (including the transference of Lord Beaverbrook from the Ministry of Supply, to the Ministry of War production). On his appointment I wrote to him: -

"You will have the abounding goodwill and cordial support of

the whole country in the gigantic task you have undertaken, and I need hardly assure you of my ardent good wishes for your triumph in what is, in plain, homely language, the biggest job under the sun.

I have been in contact with the production problem since the beginning of the war, and although, as you said to us at the private meeting in the House, development and expansion are beyond the wildest dreams of a few years ago, there are still disturbing incidents, and plenty of room for increased output.

I am quite convinced that the delegation of wider executive power to local Regional production Boards will improve the smooth running of the machine. There has been complaint of prolonged delay in giving decisions where local difficulties have been referred to the Central Authority. I think it would be wise to take workpeople more into the confidence of the management in cases where diversion of labour or suspension of production on a particular contract become necessary. There are also cases in which particular firms are overloaded with contracts, where diversion could, with advantage, take place.

In all the works of B.S.A., Daimler and James Booth, I think I can say that efficiency and productive effort are at a high level, but, of course, the defect in skilled labour supply is a continuous worry."

When a man with the energy and abounding enthusiasm of Lord Beaverbrook overtaxes his strength, there is but one inevitable conclusion, rest and resignation; so it came about that the Prime Minister most reluctantly accepted Beaverbrook's resignation from Ministerial position, barely two weeks after his appointment. Many of his colleagues did not realise his serious state of health, and could not understand why he had been, apparently, passed over in the reconstruction of the War Cabinet. I wrote to him on March 3rd: -

"You may perhaps like to know that in the House of Commons, and outside, there has been much discussion on the reason why, having regard to your immense achievement at the Ministry of Aircraft Production, and at the Ministry of Supply, and the inestimable services you rendered the Empire in Moscow and Washington, you are not still retained in the service of the State.

It is an amazing development in the politics. of our time that Stafford Cripps should be leader of the House of Commons. There is, moreover, a very strong feeling that the changes which have taken place will raise the influence of the Socialists to position in the body politic, which may ultimately lead to the wreck of the Unionist

Party, Notwithstanding the changes which have taken place, there is still the grinding need of impressing upon the nation, the peril with which the whole Empire and, indeed, civilisation itself, are confronted. Many of us feel that it is a national misfortune that in these grave and dangerous moments you are not still playing your great part in national administration."

I am proud of the telegram Beaverbrook sent to me on July 27th of the same year: -

"Your telegram gives me the greatest pleasure and most complete delight in the exploit of my son Max. ... You have been to me just as good a friend as I ever stumbled on in my long life. ... Max.'

Towards the end of November I spoke on the Lease-Lend system and how it would effect our future trade, to a meeting of the National Union of Manufacturers in London. Among other points made I declared that: - "Notwithstanding the immense contribution to the war effort of the Lease-Lend system, it struck a major blow, at all events for the time being, at a wide range of British enterprise, whose prosperity was identical with our export trade ... One would suggest that the case for greater &freedom for British export trade, on a perfect understanding with the United States, should have been arranged with a little more constructive touch of the British statesmanship in relation to trade with which we were familiar in the golden days of long ago. ... Many of us ask ourselves seriously, what will be the fate of the Ottawa resolutions ... It is no doubt premature to discuss some of these weighty matters until the end of the conflict is in sight, but questions such as these press themselves upon the minds of thoughtful people. ... The burden of taxation, from which little relief can be anticipated, will hang like a mighty millstone round the neck of industry."

This speech was much publicised, and copies of it were sent to my fellow Members in a broadcast discussion on Lease-Lend. We (that is Edward Murrow, Harold Laski, G.M Young and I) met at Broadcasting House, and for two hours discussed all the issues that were to be raised during the half-hour programme. For my part I spoke on the future of the export trade, and how anxious I was that we should cultivate a working agreement with the United States, with the primary consideration that Britain's industrial power should be restored after the war. I pointed out, too, the immense combined power that could be wielded by the United States and Great Britain. I remember Laski commenting that my arguments assumed a pattern of British commerce on the lines of the pre-war period. If only this had been allowed to come to pass!

It was at this time, about December 1942, that the great Beveridge plan was proposed, and much discussed. Although I thoroughly approved of it on paper, I did not see how a financially exhausted nation could possibly support a proposal of such magnitude. In a few weeks he became a national figure, exalted by his fellow countrymen. Yet I still maintained that the social structure which he visualised was the nearest approach to the millennium that stood on record since the publication of Moore's 'Utopia'. Sir William was an idealist, but his plan laid the foundation for our present scheme of social welfare.

Another figure very prominently in our more peaceful news at that period, was Lord Woolton, the Minister of Food. He was responsible for the creation and expansion of one of the most complex, but highly effective, organisations in our economic history. His somewhat thankless task should have earned the warm gratitude of every housewife in the country.

Yet another scheme was presented to the House of Commons within twelve months, for Sir Kingsley Wood, presented, unfortunately, on the day of his death. This was the 'Pay As You Earn' system of taxation, which was proposed to extend only to weekly wage earners. This seemed to me to be a somewhat lopsided legislation, for I wanted the monthly wage earner to be taxed by the same method.

There were at this time a number of members from both Houses who used to meet together to discuss policy for when the war should be ended. We called ourselves the Post War Policy Group, and we consisted of eight peers, twenty-nine Conservatives, (including myself) and one Labour Member. It was pleasant to feel that we were planning for a time when peace should once more be with us. Our aim in post-war reconstruction was threefold: political, economic, and financial. Although the war was to last a further two years, all the world over there were countries who were looking forward with more confidence to the end of the grim struggle. From Jamaica came a letter from Herbert-de Lisser: -

"My dear Hannon,

... I received your last letter of May 18th, but cannot agree with you that you are a bad correspondent. I think, indeed, considering the multiplicity of calls upon your time, prevailing war conditions and the difficulty of letters arriving early anywhere in the world, that you are an extraordinarily good correspondent. I wish I could follow your example. Enclosed I send you a copy of an important letter which we have written to Sir Percy Hurd M.P., whom, of course, you know. Hurd was one of the men who, with the late Lord Burnham, began the formation of the British West Indian Parliamentary Committee in 1923, at a luncheon I remember giving at the Savoy Hotel. We in Jamaica sincerely hope that this Committee will be reorganised; it seems to the Jamaican Imperial Association that it is very necessary in these days, and will especially be necessary in the days to come. Of course, the other British West Indian Colonies agreed with the formation of the British West Indian Parliamentary Committee, and I may say that copies of these letters to you and Hurd will be sent to them immediately.

We need hardly suggest that you should do your best to get the Committee started again. You have always worked for these British West Indies, and, believe me, we are very grateful.

Sincerely yours,

H.G.de Lisser"

Those unfortunate parents and wives whose men had been taken captive were bearing with great fortitude the meagre news they received, but I was constantly being asked if I could say what the true position of the treatment of prisoners of war was. At last, I wrote to Eden, on behalf of the parent of a lad was incarcerated in Stalag VII. Eden replied: -

"You say that your impression is that the position of prisoners of war is very much worse this winter than last. Our information is, I am thankful to say, that, taking them as a whole, conditions have not deteriorated. Much depends on the German officer in charge, and in some districts there have been frequent changes which have prevented improvements from taking place."

When the war was over many autobiographies appeared showing that until 1945, prisoners of war in

Germany, on the whole, received fairly good treatment, so long as they conformed strictly to the regulations and did not try to escape. During the last few months of the war, of course, when the Germans were in desperation, when food was scarce for all, when the advance of the enemy meant evacuation of camps and enforced marching of prisoners, then the story of conditions among our prisoners was very different.

The Church of which I am a member suffered a great loss in the death of Cardinal Hinsley (who passed away in March 1945) and, on behalf of the Roman Catholic Members of Parliament, I sent a message of sympathy. Only six weeks earlier I had attended a luncheon at Claridges, on the invitation of the Cardinal, at which I had met a number of most interesting people who were largely leaders in their particular walks of life.

However, to turn from people and personalities to industry. The coal trade at that time, and for a long period thereafter was, as my old friend Commander Evans expressed it in a letter to me, 'very depressing reading.' He remarked how strange it was, that in all the past history of the coal trade, whenever the wages had been raised the output had fallen off: -

"I reckon that in most colliery districts," he wrote, "they are largely isolated communities; there is but little to buy, especially in war time, and so there is no incentive to work, and they are so self-centred that Patriotism does not appear to weigh with them. Also, I reckon the Parties in Parliament who have had to deal with the mines have messed up the whole thing, as was pretty well the case in the last war. "

And again, with regard to coal: -

"With requirements for ourselves and Europe after the war, I cannot see much prospect of the Export trade of Great Britain assuming any large proportion for some time after the conclusion of the war, and then may come the slump. I need not go back to the mistake the Labour Government made over the Coal Trade, such as making German coal to be used in reparations, whereby the French, Belgians, and Italians took care of their own skins and got a lot of cheap coal for their own requirements at the expense of the British Coal Export."

It was no uncommon thing, to see foreign coal brought to, and unloaded at Newcastle. On September 1st, the 'Daily

Telegraph' published a letter of mine in which I admitted my mistaken views of pre-war Germany. The war on our nerves waged with Hitler's latest type of terror-bomb had, I suppose, put the final bar to any thoughts of friendship I had kept towards the places and people in Germany which I had once known. I quote from my letter: -

"The mass of German people have sustained, for five years, the barbaric tradition of their predatory ancestry. During the twenty years of the peace period, the people of this green and pleasant land reached almost the level of imbecility in their striving after good relations with the Germans. ... Since the outbreak of war, every reflection on my experience makes me admit shame-facedly that I was a fool. That I was in the category of self-deception does not soften the bitterness of recollection."

It was obvious now that the key to the future of international reconstruction in Europe must be found in our relationship with Soviet Russia. And what a difficult key it has been to turn all these years!

In order to counteract the flood of Socialist propaganda (which had received great impetus from the valiant exploits of the Russian army) and the consequent lively interest in Russia, Geoffrey Lloyd proposed to produce a Conservative propaganda magazine to be known as the 'Birmingham Magazine'. Those of us in the Conservative Party who were Members of Parliament for Birmingham constituencies were asked to contribute, and for the first issue I wrote a few paragraphs upon the Birmingham Group in the House of Commons. I told how the Group had held regular Wednesday meetings ever since its foundation in 1935.

I spoke of our indefatigable secretary, Sir John Smedley Crooke, and how much we were indebted to him. I defined the functions of the Group, on the one hand careful examination of general legislative measures in their effect upon the economic and social life of Birmingham, on the other hand, suggestions and criticism applied to matters particularly effecting the city, such as complaints or appeals from individuals or bodies, decisions taken by the Municipal authorities, or problems such as the lack of housing. I do not believe that any other city in Great Britain had its affairs kept under closer observation than had Birmingham.

Now the end of the war was in sight, and although there

lay ahead of us all the overwhelming difficulties of reconstruction attendant upon the vast disturbances left in the wake of such a World War, we entered upon 1945 with prayers of thankfulness in our hearts. So, to end this chapter on a note of brightness I will quote a passage from the 'Recorder': -

"Lloyd George is the father of the House of Commons, but Paddy Hannon is the uncle, the benevolent uncle. Dickens would have delighted in him. As an innkeeper welcoming his guests when the coach arrived, Paddy would have 'turned the rain into sunshine'. But he would have lost money, for he would have insisted upon giving his guests the best wine and charging them nothing for it. His position in the House is unique. The other day he advised one of the Ministers on the Front Bench to speak up, to 'put some life into it', and to turn round and speak to the Members behind him occasionally. Only a fond uncle could have got away with it."

And in contrast to this jovial commendation, I will quote from a German book 'Hundert Familien Bescheren das Empire'. My son Desmond, who was working at S.H.A.E.F., came across the book and sent me an illustration from it of Sir Patrick Hannon playing golf, with the text: -

"Hannon is considered one of the most influential men in England. Many of the scandalous conditions in the 'black' areas can be traced back to his constant protests in debates on social questions in Parliament against an effective Social policy."

CHAPTER 16

"... those days when she and you and I lived in the land of dreams. In some respects I think we are all dreamers still, but the outlook of this topsy-turvy world is very far removed from the dreams we entertained at the beginning of the century. ... India is a shocking mess, Palestine is seething with the outlook of Civil War, and most of the rest of the world baffling and unsettling."

This extract from a letter I wrote to my good friend Colonel Shaen Magan in Ireland is so different from the letters one might have anticipated writing during the first months of peace, having won a victory over tremendous odds after six gruelling years of war. Sir Richard Cooper wrote to me in August: -

"My dear Paddy,

... You are right When you talk of the 'hell of a mess the democracy of England has made of itself', and I share your feeling for Winston, even though he has brought some of the trouble on himself. After all, the very clothes that the Socialists stand up in, as well as their own lives, they entirely owe to him. You may think it a boastful remark, but I knew last May that the Labour Party would get in power, and I won one or two little bets among my friends here on this calculation, although I did not expect that they would get a majority of more than fifty. There are many causes for this landslide, not the least of which is the complete ineptitude of the Central Office. The time has come when the Central Office must be democratised, and it must belong to the British people and not to a few unknown people whose only thought is their own vested interests. At the end of May last, they had not a sheet of paper by way of literature of the slightest help to an innocent candidate fighting an election, but they did suddenly get out some good stuff, too late and too crowded in its printing to be as useful as it might be ... What is more, it is a great victory at this particular moment for you to have held your seat at Birmingham when so many of our best friends went down, and it does seem to me to be a fact that those who were successful, won largely on their personality and life's record; otherwise, the widespread faith of the public in their political service to the country. This certainly applies to you, and long may you live to keep the flag flying and to help rebuild the Conservative Party; previous to which, it would be better if it could more or less die before its rebirth ...

My warmest regards, dear friend,
I am, yours sincerely,
Dick Cooper."

Certainly, the result of the immediate post-war election was a devastating blow to the prestige of our Party, and we all felt grieved and distressed at the ingratitude of the public to their mighty leader, Churchill. Perhaps as a Party we were too complacent in anticipating a Conservative victory. Perhaps we did not adequately weigh up our opponent's measure. But whatever the reason, the landslide bore away with it many able Members with whom I had conferred and arranged, planned and put into practice matters of some political and social importance. On July 29th, I sent a message to Churchill on behalf of the 'Birmingham Group': -

"Members of the Birmingham Group in the late Parliament, desire to express to you our profound regret and deep sorrow that you have been deprived of the leadership of the nation at this momentous stage in the advancement of international world peace, and tender you our affectionate gratitude for the delivery of civilisation from universal ruin and anarchy."

Sir Robert Cahill wrote to me on July 28th, complaining of terrible conditions in France, and asking about the election. His house in Bordeaux had been used as quarters for the German soldiery, and on his return to France he found it had been looted. "The price of food," he wrote, "was appallingly high." He knew of people queuing in the Gare de Lyon at 4 p.m. (in order to obtain travel vouchers at 7 a.m. to enable than to travel three days later. When I had commiserated with him, I said: - "We have had in the Tory Party a pretty cruel time under the recent tornado. The 'Yellow Jackets' of Gollancz, and the underground activities of Morrison, extending over several years, have had their unsavoury result. Anyhow, we are taking things like sportsmen, and must face up to the situation as it develops from day to day. For the moment, I think, our policy must be to support the Government on that part of our programme which, in fact, was the settled policy of the Coalition War. Cabinet. At the same time, we must, by every means possible, put the brake on their nationalisation schemes."

A few weeks before the Election, I had been presented with an illuminated address by the Moseley Division Unionist Association, in appreciation of my twenty years service to them, and now I was elected to continue to represent them in Parliament. The ceremony of Presentation made me both happy and proud. Happy in the evidence of the many friendships I had made in Birmingham and proud to have been of service to her people.

From Yugoslavia came sad letters from my old friends the Prpics. Josip Prpic wrote saying: - *"We are still in storm and distresses. After two months of deliberation nothing specially bad occurred to us, but my wife, daughter and I leave my house and all ... So here we are in Trieste."* And Mrs. Prpic wrote: - *"Oh, poor Yugoslavia, you will wonder about when you see it again. The great world war in the same time the guerrilla war with the worst concentration camps, and now, now after all, now in peace time, the whole land is a dark prison with new concentration camps and old fascistic methods. ... Only the time can do something, but in the meantime a lot of people lose their lives every day and our whole property will be gone."* Yes, it was hard to know where in the world to look for a cheerful, prosperous, peaceful country.

By 1946 we were growing accustomed to life in peacetime again and, alas, also accustomed to the fumbling and folly of the Labour Government, who in their sloppy and ignorant way were fast ruining the export trade and our commercial vitality. The introduction of Bill after Bill in the House was interrupting the work of the country. State control was now enveloping the life of the individual and, if carried on to a more serious extent, would (as I said in a speech): - *"... produce a nation consisting of a dictatorial bureaucracy, with the vast body of people more or less in the capacity of a colossal Civil Service."*

The housing situation in Birmingham and elsewhere was deplorable. I suspected that there was some confusion between the various departments, and I had no hesitation in attacking the Minister and demanding that adequate homes should be prepared as quickly as possible to house the many newly married couples and husbands and wives reunited after the separation of the war years. One year after the war had ended, a first delivery of steel houses was made in Birmingham, and aluminium houses were said to be on the agenda.

There were naturally many trials and inconveniences consequent upon the 'outbreak of peace' which could not be avoided; and the swing of the pendulum had created a dangerous trend of relaxation from the burden of economic effort. But Government blunders and muddles, and general

309

ineptitude, had increased the troubles and miseries of the people. We old campaigners were trying to stimulate fresh interest in the Conservative Party, and working together with new zest and enthusiasm for the time when we would once more be in power. Sir Herbert Wragg wrote asking for my practical help at his meeting in Swadlincote, and I replied: -

"Nothing could give me greater pleasure than to be associated with you again in some modest approach to the extermination of the Socialist Party, as the most dangerous evil in the public life of our time. I am booking in November 8th for your proposed meeting at Swandlincote, and will do my best to give effect to all the kindly sentiments you entertain for the destruction of the present administration." In the golden days before the war I was seldom seen at any function without a carnation in my buttonhole, but the Socialist regime had destroyed even this little patch of felicity in my declining years.

Having read with great interest a pamphlet on Joseph Chamberlain produced by David Eccles, I wrote to him on October 9th: -

"In every feature of his public life which you have analysed so thoughtfully, 'Joe' could never have been regarded as a Socialist in the limited, self-seeking and totalitarian qualities which adorn the rag-tag and bobtail Party now in power in this country, and whose national administration and Empire outlook should make his bones turn over in his modest tomb in Hockley Cemetery."

Captain Sir Donald Simson, with whom I had been associated in the 'Comrades', had been for several years the Honorary Director of the Empire Services League. He now had a splendid plan for creating and extending interest in our Colonies and Dominions by a system of Empire education. I wrote to him: -

"... You will recall, perhaps, that for many years I have, from time to time, in the House of Commons pressed upon the old Board of Education, and later on the present Ministry, the importance of Empire education. For a long time now, I think, text books have been available in primary and secondary schools on Empire subjects, but the weak feature in our educational programmes is the frequent indifference of the schoolmaster to Empire questions. Your plan should work usefully in factories and workshops where recreation and instruction would be carefully fused together. You know, of course, that the Federation of British Industries has a Committee on

Industrial Education, and you might send a copy of your plan to the President, Sir Clive Baillieu. I will gladly help in the N.U.M., but I think what would be more helpful than anything else would be if you had an interview with Creech Jones, the Under Secretary of State for the Colonies, and get the support of the Secretary of State and himself for the scheme. If you will send me a few copies of your plan I will gladly place them in the hands of both Ministers." Which I did! Creech Jones, in his reply to me, said that: -

"... if the scheme was in the charge of someone with first class organising capacity, and if it received the necessary financial support, it should do a great deal of good."

Addison, the Secretary of State, wrote: -

"As you may have seen from a speech which I made in the House of Lords on the 27th February, I am very much impressed with the desirability of stimulating in the people of Britain, an interest in other parts of the British Commonwealth, and I am glad to hear of the initiative which you and your friends are taking in putting forward a scheme with this object in view. If any of my officers can advise on points of detail when matters are further advanced, I should be glad to arrange for this to be done. I assume that you will be discussing the project with Sir Stafford Cripps as to its practical applicability. It is rather for him, than for me, to give any advice that you may be seeking in this field."

I was delighted that year to be sent a copy by Winston Churchill of his 'Secret Sessions' speeches. It had been my privilege to attend every Secret Session during the War, and the record of those days was most interesting to possess. What would we not have given for Churchill's presence at the International Conferences that were now taking place? Instead of fine, telling phrases, and decisive statements, we raised but feeble voices, and met a series of pin-pricking tactics to which we succumbed. Indeed, dissensions at these Conferences were hardly worthy of the squabbles of a local council.

During October the savage trial was held of Archbishop Stepinac of Zagreb, which resulted in his being condemned to death. The whole of Christianity was appalled at this barbarism, and I made an earnest appeal in Parliament for his release. I urged Bevin to make the decision of His Majesty's Government quite clear to the Tito Administration, that the Archbishop should be freed immediately. But the great persecution of Catholic priests continued and spread to other countries. Some years later, when Cardinal Mindszenty was imprisoned, there was a large Catholic rally of protest in the Albert Hall at which I submitted our resolution. In so doing, I declared that the refusal of the Hungarian Government to allow observers on the part of Great Britain and the United States to attend the trial was a direct insult to both nations. It was a tragic reflection upon the times in which we lived that a murderous clique in Budapest could treat with contempt representatives of two of the greatest civilised nations in the world. When during July, some nine months later, Archbishop Stepinac (though alive) was still in prison and, no doubt, in mental and physical suffering, a meeting was held in London at which Cardinal Griffen presided. He declared that the persecution of Catholics and Orthodox in Yugoslavia equalled in severity the Nazi tyranny.

Back in England, the inconveniences of post-war life were vociferously resented by many who were wholly forgetful of the unspeakable misery from which, under God's mercy, their rescue had been achieved. The latest irritation was the temporary stoppage of electricity for short lengths of time. In the Midlands this curtailment was seriously affecting industry. But what else could be done since the coal situation was to be regarded with something approaching despair. As I wrote in a letter to the 'Financial Times': -

"Every ton of coal at the service of industry means employment; every ton of coal of which industry is deprived by voluntary absenteeism or slackness means less earning capacity for a fellow worker, and increased misery for the housewife."

I pressed for an immediate debate in Parliament to prevent, if it were possible, matters becoming even more serious. But, far from there being an improvement in the situation, as 1947 dawned and died, electricity cuts became so general and so frequent that they were gradually accepted as part of the British way of life. Industry was also being hampered, indeed hamstrung, by taxation. We were, I believe, the most heavily taxed country in the world, and a factor that the Labour Government refused to realise was that one cannot cripple the purchasing expenditure of the individual without crippling the nation.

I headed a deputation from the N.U.M. to the President

of the Board (Sir Stafford Cripps) to plead the cause of the smaller firms, many of which were suffering from the high taxation and irritating controls. We stressed the fact that, in those present circumstances, they could play only an unimportant role in industry, and we presented our plans for enabling them to take a more effective part in the export drive. We were kindly received, and Sir Stafford Cripps promised to do what he could to help. Four days later he announced a very big programme for industry which, he declared, must be achieved, although the targets seemed apparently very high. Exports, he declared, must be raised to one third above the 1938 level, and he pressed for the greater development of Empire resources. In all it was an excellent speech.

I had previously complained of the lack of a positive policy of action by the Labour Government to counter our national economic crisis. There seemed to be a complete lack of dominance in leadership. It would have been a blessing if the best of the leaders of all Parties could have formed a Coalition Government to win the peace as they had won the war. The one criticism I had for Cripps' programme was that it came far too late. Leo Amery wrote to me next day: -

"You said yesterday the one thing that needed saying, namely, that all that Cripps said should have been said at least twelve months ago. What is more, if the policy of Empire and bi-lateral trade agreements is vital to our recovery, what could have been more crazy than accepting loan conditions which definitely vetoed any such policy, conditions which we are now compelled to repudiate in fact, if not in so many words."

During June, I wrote a letter to the 'Times' about the sad case of a former Member of Parliament, Mr. J.R. Clynes, who had been three times a Cabinet Minister. He was now in his late seventies and living in reduced circumstances because he drew a small superannuation allowance from the Trade Unions and, therefore, was ineligible for the House of Commons Members' Fund pension: -

"It is somewhat in the nature of a human political tragedy," I wrote, *"that a career so conspicuous in the public service of the nation for a generation, should suffer such bitter frustration in the conflict of life at the age of seventy-seven years."* In response to this letter I received many cheques and messages of sympathy which I gave to Mr. Clynes. And some weeks

later Attlee wrote to me, saying that he was personally interesting himself in the problem of pensions for ex-Ministers. I was somewhat surprised, however, when on the death of Mr. Clynes a few years later, I learned of the amount of money that he left.

In December, I announced that I myself would soon become an ex-Member of Parliament, or rather that I would not seek re-election at the next General Election, but would retire to make way for younger men. I was beginning to feel the combined burden of politics and industry weighing heavily on my shoulders, and also the revision of the areas of many Midland Parliamentary Divisions had disheartened me. For they proposed to remove my beloved Sparkhill from me, which would have caused me some unhappiness. In my letter to Horace Goodby, of King's Heath, I said: -

"This decision has been taken in the presence of circumstances which make it abundantly manifest that the burden of the future in the maintenance of the purpose and policy of the Conservative Party must be borne by younger men. Nothing is more stimulating in our recent political structure than the enthusiasm of the newer generation to undertake responsibility in public affairs.

The generous consideration extended to me during this long period by all sections of the people of the Constituency is warmly appreciated, and will be an abiding happy recollection during the remainder of my life. There is no phase in the life of the Constituency in which I have not taken some modest part. To you, and the Executive Committee, I am grateful beyond expression. Moseley has been a sublime example of friendship, goodwill and tolerance, and this applies to political opponents as well as political friends. While the present Parliament survives, I shall contrive to discharge my duties as heretofore."

The 'Sunday Express', commenting upon my proposed retirement said: -

"His excuse, and an utterly inadequate one, is that he is seventy-three and wants to make room for a younger man. There are no younger men than Paddy Hannon, unless it is Mr. Churchill who is his junior by a few months."

The 'Birmingham Mail' was kind enough to say of me: -

"Those who witnessed his introduction to the House of Commons in March 1921, will never forget the heartening impact of his coming. It was not a good Parliament. Lloyd George and his managers in the 1918 General Election had packed the House with

314

uninspiring newcomers. An older Member, destined later to become Prime Minister, described them as 'a hard-faced set of men who look as if they had done well out of the War.' Into this assembly came the genial and expansive presence of the new Member for Moseley, quite obviously a personality to be reckoned with. For more than a generation he has fulfilled the promise of that first impression. A loyal party man, if ever there was one, his peculiar province was to soften the acerbities of debate, to find the unity underlying diversity and (to quote Lord Baldwin again), 'to appreciate the many sidedness of truth'. He made politics more agreeable and entertaining, and sweetened controversy with a smile and a quip."

In response to my announcement, I was inundated with letters, telegrams and messages of goodwill. People were extraordinarily kind. Among the letters in my file is one from Leslie Hore-Belisha, who wrote: -

"Although it has not happened yet, I do not like to think of it, even in anticipation. Your statement is a generous one; but that is your characteristic. It is hard to visualise Parliament without you. May you and your wife have great happiness always. I know you will always find much of it in bringing the younger ones on.

Always,
Leslie."

And my old friend Sir Percy Hurd said in his letter: -

"Before you drop the M.P. from your title, I would send you a message of goodwill and good wishes. I recall that it was at your instance, and with your aid, that I fought the election in Frome in 1918, and then followed twenty-six years of crowded, and I hope useful, Parliamentary life, generally in your company. The causes in which we stood together include some which have helped to give Britain her place of leadership among the nations. I hope good health and good fortune may attend you in your more leisured hours."

One thing at any rate of which I am proud, and I am not ashamed to say so, is that I cannot recall any instance in which my public duty has been found wanting, nor my interest in the welfare of my constituents the subject of adverse comment. Of my feelings in the matter, they are best expressed in a letter I wrote to Brigadier Smith, of Canada: -

"It is, of course, a pretty testing ordeal to sever my connection with a constituency which I have represented for twenty-seven years. Politics in this country ... have become a whole-time job. I could not, with full personal regard for my responsibility to my various business interests, continue as a Member of the House of

Commons and do justice to my abilities outside. I am being followed in the Division by an ex-Cabinet Minister, and a very likeable personality, the Rt. Hon. Geoffrey Lloyd."

Lovely Magna Carta Island offered a very pleasant home to retire to, but it was not without its problems. For early that year, the Thames rose so much that the island was badly flooded. Water penetrated the lower rooms to a depth of six inches, and the servants were marooned there. The river besieged the house for a week before it decided upon invasion, bringing with it into our little home the usual friendly association of flotsam and jetsam.

Of happier events that year I recall a delightful wedding I attended between Alastair Nicholson and Barbara Creighton, which took place at the historic chapel of St George's, Windsor Castle, and a particularly interesting dinner at the Savoy given under the auspices of the Knights of the Round Table. The principal guests were the Archbishop of Canterbury, the Cardinal Archbishop of Westminster, the Moderators of the Free Churches and the Church of Scotland, and the Archbishop of Utrecht. I invited Hore-Belisha as my guest, saying: - *"I hope you won't be shocked with this array of sanctity."*

Hore-Belisha replied: -

"Do we have the pleasure of hearing all these great Ecclesiastics speak? In any event, it will be a delight to be with you and in the odour of sanctity."

It is true to say now, as it was equally true then, that only the Church stands as a real barrier to Communism. How can one contemplate Europe without fear for Christian people? In 1947, France was being menaced internally on the greatest scale since the Revolution. Italy was in the throes of a great Communist challenge. Trieste had become a festering sore of unrest. Poland was gradually being swamped by Communism. These events, if not perhaps so obvious now, have done their evil work, and the results are damming the soul of Europe. Communism, in the opinion of most sensible men, means the elimination of God from human thought, the destruction of personal liberty, and the extinguishing of the freedom of the Press.

At this time, and for some years to follow, the Government had its hands full with the problem or the civil war in Palestine. Most Christians must have been very distressed by this fighting in the Holy Land, and I asked in the Commons during February 1948 if steps could not be taken to prevent riots and bloodshed in Jerusalem. The answer I received, however, was that this was U.N.O.'s responsibility. Later on, I went so far as to declare that people all over the world would feel that the Government had muddled and messed the grave question of Palestine in a way which, in the verdict of future generations, would be one of the ugliest and darkest chapters in the history of the present administration. Sir Ralph Glyn also refused to let the matter rest. Whenever he raised the matter in the House, I supported him and, after a most unsatisfactory debate on March 10th, he wrote to me saying how concerned he was with the whole problem: -

"I notice in the paper today, that the United Nations, running away as usual from a difficult problem, have refused to deal with the matter before April 21st. This is far too late."

He suggested that I should write a letter to 'The Times', adding his signature. I quote an extract from the letter that we sent: -

"Civilisation has never been confronted by a more tragic example of the absence of vision and judgement in relation to a problem, the solution of which is of profound moment to the future peace of mankind. ... Mr. Bevin enjoys the respect and esteem of all Parties in the House of Commons, and he must have felt deeply the failure of his repeated efforts to conciliate conflicting elements within and without Palestine."

It was unfortunate that the Foreign Press, and especially that in America, should not only have wildly exaggerated every defect in the Government's policy in regard to Great Britain's relation to Palestine, but should have quite misunderstood our position. When the Moral Re-Armament Movement met at Caux in 1948, I had the privilege of making a speech of welcome to no less than forty-one senators and Members of the House of Representatives, who were on their way there from the States. I wrote to Miss Annie Yasserman, adding: -

"There was an immense demonstration at Los Angeles some months ago, to which I received an urgent invitation, including, if you please, a private luxury plane, and heaven knows what volume of special attention on my arrival! My years of discretion, combined with the inherited modesty of my race, prevented my acceptance ...

317

We are, of course, profoundly impressed in this country by the abounding interest shown by the U.S. A. in the rehabilitation of Europe, but especially the contribution which is being made to enable this old country, Great Britain, to survive its economic, tantalising worries and troubles. The extent to which we are indebted to the Marshall Aid Plan may be conveyed to you by saying that, unless Marshall Aid became effective during the current financial year in Great Britain, we probably would have had two million work-people unemployed during the coming Winter ... The greatest fact in the record of Human History would be the intimate association of America and ourselves in these grim and dread days."

The individual generosity of Americans to Europe showed itself in many ways, including the relief organisation C.A.R.E., which was too little known in this country. Numbers of food packages and other goods were contributed to ease the plight of less fortunate people.

When Mrs. Roosevelt came over to Great Britain in April, she was, among other activities, entertained to dinner at the Mansion House. My wife and I had the pleasure of attending the function. It was a joy to be among the guests invited to meet this great and remarkable lady. Ideally, we should have worked with the United States to save Western civilisation, but instead of a joint, all-out effort, our energies were forcibly spent on frustrating schemes of nationalisation of industry. As I said in one of my speeches during the spring: - *"Nationalisation was the outcome of ideological concepts by amateur persons engaged in politics having no proper notion of what industrial organisation meant."* I also deplored the swollen proportion of the public administration, both national and local, which had produced the fantastic position that, out of every nine employed persons, one was engaged in checking the activities of the other eight.

I remember being particularly annoyed when Mr. Herbert Morrison (who had come to Birmingham as guest at the Jewellers' annual banquet) criticised the management of industry there, and I did not hesitate to declare that I disliked Ministers coming down to Birmingham and coolly telling us that we were inefficient. Mindful of the Government's own inefficiency, Herbert Morrison had to defend himself by attacking us. A striking example of efficiency in organisation was shown in the 1948 British Industries Fair held in Birmingham. This was quite a phenomenal success, and possibly housed the most comprehensive display of heavy industries ever previously presented in Europe. On looking back to the great St. Louis Fair of1904, and other exhibitions in American cities and in Europe which I attended, I compared Birmingham's Fair as being superior in plan, organisation, display and business arrangements. The only blot on the landscape was the grievous shortage of hotel accommodation. The trade agreement signed in Havana in March caused us much concern, and we raised a fighting fund to oppose its ratification. Its restrictions and, as Amery put it in a stirring appeal, its' 'entangling, international control', might, we believed, be the cause of the death of Empire trade. In September, a big Empire rally was held in Westminster at which Mr. Menzies spoke, and in November the British Empire League (of which I was a Vice President) gave the former Australian Prime Minister a reception in the House of Commons.

In December, the country or my birth, Eire, broke the final bands of her somewhat anomalous position in the British Commonwealth of Nations and declared herself a true Republic. In a letter to my old friend Shaen Magan, dated December 1381, I wrote: -

"For over a quarter of a century there was little to distinguish between Eire as a member of the Commonwealth, and an independent nation. Indeed, she enjoyed privileges which no other independent community under the sun could remotely claim. It has been quite clear to many of us that the bitterness of seven hundred years could not be removed by anything less than complete severance of the Imperial Gordian Knot."

Yet it came as a shock to many Irish people, who had regarded Mr. Costello (to whose actions this severance was due) as a politician who looked with approval on this small link that held the two islands together. During the debate of the Ireland Bill, which took place later the following spring, there was a certain amount of restiveness concerning the Government's guarantee to Northern Ireland. Amendments were suggested, but were overruled. I declared at that time that I looked upon the detachment of Eire from the Commonwealth of Nations as a tragedy of the gravest kind in our time. But I was proud of the way in which the Bill had been presented by the Prime Minister. I was proud, too, when his late Majesty, King George VI, sent a telegram of good wishes to the President.

"Not since the days of the Roman Empire", I said, *"has a reigning monarch deliberately sent a message of goodwill and sympathy to the head of a new state over which his family had reigned for hundreds of years."*

That brilliant and unusual Irishman, Professor Walter Starkie, sent me an interesting letter that summer from the British Council in Spain, of which he was Representative: -

"At last," he wrote, *"there has been some recognition in England of all that has been achieved by the British Council's work in Spain. It has indeed been a long and bitter struggle, and more than once I have felt discouraged. I never forgot your kindness in giving that dinner in the House of Commons for me, a week after Dunkirk, when Lord Lloyd gave me my instructions for Spain. In those days I never imagined that it would have been possible to build up anything, as people even laughed at me in Madrid at the idea. I still find the going hard, and have to fight my way and be very watchful ... I have just been accompanying Sir Alexander Fleming, and arranging matters for him with the Spaniards. He has been a gigantic success. In fact, I never remember witnessing such scenes of enthusiasm, not only among the authorities, the doctors and the upper classes, but among the humble. In the streets there were spontaneous demonstrations with poor people coming up to kiss his hand; porters of institutions coming up and saying their lives had been saved by penicillin. There has never been, in my experience, any demonstration or sympathy towards a Briton to compare with what I have myself witnessed in the past few days with Sir Alexander Fleming ... A pro British Irishman is able to do a great deal, even these days, in the Spanish world."* In August of the following year a group was formed called, 'The Friends of Spain', of which I became a member. The President was Sir Alexander Roger. The group aimed at working for the re-establishment of full diplomatic relations with Spain, and for better cultural, social and economic understanding.

CHAPTER 17

An important decision for our export trade occurred in June 1949, with the formation of the Dollar Exports Board. Sir Graham Cunningham was elected Chairman, (a position which he held for a short time, resigning in favour of Sir Cecil Weir, former economic adviser to the Control Commission in Germany) and I agreed to sit on the Board as representative of the N.U.M., although I was finding difficulty in getting through all my various commitments. Industrial life had undergone some profound changes during the previous decade. On the credit side was the more intimate relationship between the man who worked with his hands, and the managerial staff. On the debit side stood our glaringly unfavourable trade balance. The problem of the dollar gap presented a grim outlook. There was also, consequent upon the trend to State monopoly, the danger of new discoveries not finding their way to the best place. Some decisive steps had to be taken, and so the Dollar Board was formed.

It was, also, most urgent that the Government should cease to put obstacles in our way, and co-operate more closely with industry. During the previous month the N.U.M. had raised a campaign to stimulate resistance against State interference in industry, and a booklet, 'An outline of policy for industry' was published. Our statement stressed that there seemed to be a complete disregard of facts by the Government, and an absence of reasoning in their frequent exhortation to greater productivity, while at the same time crushing industry with taxation which even hindered the buying of new equipment. The work of the new Board was to be financed by industry, but the Government might be called upon to supply certain services. In this way we hoped to gain a big impetus in exports to the Western Hemisphere.

Sir Graham, in referring to the Board by its initials D.E.B., jested that it was a debutante which would dig for dollars, not for gold. After a luncheon given by the Board to Mr. Hoffmann and his American colleagues in September, I had the following letter from Sir Stafford Cripps: -

"My dear Paddy,
... I entirely share your view that Mr. Hoffmann and his administration are sincerely anxious to help our exporters in every

possible way. I had an opportunity of seeing this for myself during the Washington discussions. Mr. Hoffmann's attitude could not have been more helpful."

Meanwhile Birmingham was endeavouring to increase her export trade by every possible means. A toy fair was staged, designed to catch the American eye. It ran for five days, and I opened it on February 21st amid considerable interest. I can guarantee that the following Christmas there was many a British toy delighting the American children. Leslie Hore-Belisha paid a visit to Birmingham in April as my guest, and I showed him our B.S.A. works, which were valiantly grinding out exports for the dollar market. He wrote to me afterwards in his ebullient manner: -

"My dear Paddy,

... We had such a whirlwind of a time in Birmingham and thereabouts, that I have not yet been able to sort out all my impressions. That Art Gallery, under Professor Bodkin, is one of the best I have ever seen, and I am so grateful to you for having had the original inspiration to think of taking a fellow politician there. I was also so pleased to meet him at dinner. All the B.S.A. factories I saw interested me, and I was delighted to meet the various people responsible. The fact that you came on the journey made it all the more delightful. The next day Mr. Leek gave are lunch at the Daimler works in Coventry, and I was glad to see the two works you have in that city.

The meeting in your constituency was really excellent and a tribute to your well-deserved popularity. You certainly amply rewarded any effort I made on your behalf by the comprehensiveness, variety and hospitality of the arrangements that you were good enough to make. Long may you with your courtesy and charm flourish!

... Leslie."

Sir Winston Churchill has been portrayed on canvas many times since he achieved world fame, and his portraits have roused much comment. One for which I have a particular regard is that painted by Frank Salisbury, depicting him delivering his famous 'Blood, toil, tears and sweat' speech, and it hangs in the Constitutional Club. In my capacity as President of the Constitutional, I had some hand in instigating this, arranging for the portrait to be painted, and arranging the presentation dinner in celebration. I wrote to him on September 9th 1949, concerning the final arrangements, and received the following reply: -

"My dear Paddy.

... I do not think I should unveil a picture of myself, but I would certainly be honoured to be present at the ceremony. If you would care to suggest to me dates, I will see if I can fit one in. A Wednesday when Parliament is sitting is most suitable for me.

Yours sincerely,
Winston S. Churchill."

A date in November was arranged, and I had the honour of unveiling the portrait. "This is, in cold hard fact, in the light of the history of this Club, our greatest hour," I declared. That evening was indeed a memorable one, so pleasant to recall. Churchill was in excellent spirits, a fact that guarantees the enjoyment of all about him, and his fighting ardour inspired us all when he spoke of the imminence of the General Election and our need to assert our strength and vitality. One of his statements that evening was this: - "I can assure you I have no personal ambitions. All mine have long ago been satisfied and far surpassed by the good fortune that has fallen upon me to be the bearer of the Standard of Britain in her most glorious hour." I had a letter of thanks, the following day from Viscount Simon: -

"My dear Pat.

... I must send to you, and through you to the Committee of the Constitutional Club, my warmest thanks for letting me share in the wonderful evening last night. Winston was brilliant and the enthusiasm was infectious. As he said, 'We can do it if we try'. And we will.

Yours ever,
John Simon."

I have known Sir Winston for well over fifty years now, first meeting him when I was appointed Director of Agricultural Organisation to Cape Colony. In his capacity as Under-Secretary for the Colonies he received me for an interview. After that our paths occasionally crossed in the course of our individual pursuits, until the day that I entered Parliament. So many Members have vanished from the scene since that far off day, but if they could, they would all agree that throughout the years that followed, Sir Winston was always a potent personage. Whether in debate or in a condition of potential eruption he made his presence felt. I often think that his greatest single contribution to Britain's name was his mobilisation of the Fleet on the outbreak of the First World War.

Devaluation of the pound sterling came in September 1949. It was not inevitable and could have been avoided, and I termed it (in all its drastic finality) 'the murder of the pound note'. Any firm which had subsidiary interests in the United States, (such as H.P. Sauce, with which I was associated for thirty years, thirteen of them as Chairman) was able to bear the increased costs following devaluation, but many industries were not in so fortunate a position.

The late Queen Mary, that great lady whose warm-hearted interest in the lives and welfare of the poor endeared her to all her subjects, was most anxious to do what she could to help the economic problem of the nation. The following letter, which I received from Lady Cynthia Colville, dated January 27th 1950, explains itself: -

"Dear Sir Patrick Hannon,

... I am commanded by Queen Mary to thank you warmly for the trouble and interest you have taken over the proposed export of Her Majesty's needlework carpet. The Queen is most grateful for your help,and has heard of the charming speech which you made at the Press Conference yesterday in appreciation of Her Majesty's gift. This dollar earning scheme, which the Queen has much at heart, will owe much to your kindly advice and experience, and to the time and thought which you have so generously bestowed upon the project.

Yours sincerely,

Cynthia Colville."

The Conference, over which Lady Reading presided, had been held at Burlington House, where the carpet was exhibited. Her Majesty's gracious gift to the nation helped not only to bring dollars to the National Exchequer, but also to direct attention upon our economic crisis and to stimulate the interest of the British people. Perhaps I had been spending too much time and thought on too many different projects, for my health began to feel the strain. On the day before the dissolution of Parliament, I held a farewell party for members of the staff of the House of Commons. Messengers, waiters, cleaners, porters, about forty people all told, were entertained to luncheon in an atmosphere of the greatest friendliness and good humour. "It was one of the warmest and most touching parties seen in the House for a long time" according to the 'Birmingham Post', and "the first of its kind in the history of Parliament."

All these people had been so helpful and cheerful and good tempered when times were difficult and I wanted to show that I appreciated them. Most of them were eager to say a few words when the time came for speech making, and kindly feelings prompted them to say that they would miss 'Old Paddy' in the days to come. Although I was not going to seek re-election, I took prominent part in an intensive campaign for the Conservative Party, during most of the first three weeks of February and before. On February 10th, the Speaker, Clifton-Brown, sent me this letter which I greatly treasure: -

"I feel that I cannot let you leave the House of Commons without saying how sorry I am and how much I shall miss you. We have been in the house together for so many years that I hate to think that you will no longer be there. I almost feel that I should visit the Carlton Club regularly on the chance of seeing you there. This is not, however, to say goodbye because I hope that we shall still meet occasionally, but I could not let you leave without saying how sorry I am."

This was the forerunner of quite a flood of letters I was shortly to receive because, on February 19th, I had to retire to a nursing home for observation and I quickly learned that my friends had not forgotten me. This was a sad way to end my political career, but I was fortunate in having been able to keep going during those last days while I was still a Member of Parliament. My good friend Lord Beaverbrook wrote immediately saying: -

"My dear Paddy,

... I am so very sorry to hear that you are ill and I would like to have news of your progress. If there is anything I can do for you, I am at your disposal.

With affectionate good wishes.

I am, yours ever,

Max."

His was one of the many letters I received during that tedious period. For a week later I was operated upon, and then came the dreary time of convalescence, which precluded me from taking part in the life of the world outside my nursing home until the second week of April.

While waiting for the surgeon's decision to operate, my thoughts dwelt upon the result of the General Election, and I visualised the new Parliament with its absence of some of the old, familiar faces and the presence of new, and as yet, untried men and women. On February 25th, two days after polling day, the 'Birmingham Gazette' published an article from my pen headed, 'Welcome to New Boys at Westminster', from which I have taken the following extract: -

"There are three stages in the period of exhilaration which a new candidate will experience in his process from the declaration of the poll till he is sworn in at the table. The announcement that he has become an M.P. gives a new sense of dignity and self-importance to even the humbled candidate, and I have never known, in my long experience in the House, a newly elected Member to arrive who didn't believe that his object in life was the accomplishment of great things. The second stage is his arrival at the House of Commons, making the acquaintance of the genial and kindly policemen, and being taken by some elder Member on a geographical survey of the Palace of Westminster.

It has been my pleasant duty for many years to take fresh Members of Parliament by the hand, and give them a gentle and kindly lesson on their attitude towards the servants of the House, their duty on passing through the Lobby to make a respectful bow to the tellers. I always bow to the teller of my own Party, but this is a practice which is not particularly followed by other M.P.'s.

The third stage is when he lines up to be received at the Table, to take the Bible in his hand and solemnly swear his duty to His Majesty the King, and his heirs and successors, and having signed the huge book on the Table, the Members Register, walks forward diffidently, and perhaps a little haltingly, and shakes hands with Mr. Speaker. The swearing process is arranged after a General Election on a series of days, and Mr. Speaker calls tier after tier alternately from the Government and Opposition benches to proceed to the Table.

The smoking room of the House of Commons is one of the most fascinating institutions in the public life of any nation. In a friendship-making atmosphere, Members become rapidly acquainted, and, with all that enthusiasm which attaches to the 'new boy', exchange views on the thrilling experience of the contest through which they have passed. I have a profound respect for the smoking room of the House of Commons, and although Members speak to one another of matters which are perhaps confidential, I have never known an instance in which intimate confidence has been revealed outside the smoking room.

Somehow or other, in the last Parliament, the sense of friendship and freedom in mutual confidence was on a lower level than in the previous Parliaments in which I have served. The new House of Commons will provide much greater facilities for the convenience of Members than was the character of the old Chamber destroyed on the 10th May 1941.

It is of course a matter of deep regret to me that I shall not be able to sit in the new Chamber of the House. I sat on the rehabilitation committee, and moved the appointment of Sir Gilbert Scott as architect."

The new Parliament quickly settled down, and I read the Government and Opposition speeches, the apt question, the measured reply, the witty twist given to some point, the biting retort, and felt a little out of things. It was good to read a letter one morning in the 'Birmingham Post' from Raymond Blackburn M.P., who said that he had been asked by many Members on all sides of the House to say how much they missed me.

After recuperating on the south coast, I returned to the hurly-burly of London life once more, to settle into a new routine. The Birmingham Unionist Association, the Constitutional Club and some other organisations were individually arranging presentations to be made to me. On June 29th, a luncheon was held in the Constitutional Club, at which I was presented with a cigar case and wallet. The toast was proposed by Lord Woolton, and Sir Anthony Eden sat on my right. Churchill, who could not be present, sent this message: -

"You are met today to honour, in Paddy Hannon, a man who has been a doughty fighter for the Conservative and Unionist Party for more than forty years. Closest to his heart have always been four causes: to develop the Empire and its trade with the Mother country; to protect and foster our home industries; to maintain the strength of the Royal Navy, and to improve the living conditions of the British people. I wish him well."

Yes, Churchill had very fairly summed up the objects of my life, and I was very gratified to be sent such a charming tribute. Eden, who said some delightful phrases in my honour, had a few weeks previously sent me the following note, which is so characteristic of his friendship: -

"My dear Paddy,

... It was good of you to send me such a charming telegram for

my birthday. I deeply appreciated it, and thank you so much. We miss you sadly in the House.

Yours ever,

Anthony Eden."

Later on in the year, I received three beautiful silver salvers at a joint presentation made to me in Moseley, and handed to me by Councillor Cross. It is a very pleasant custom that one should be the recipient of gifts and tributes upon retirement, and I have taken part in so many like presentations to my colleagues. They are ceremonies, however, which always hold a touch of sadness mingled with the good cheer, combining to create a slight emotional tension in which one responds with instant and exaggerated feeling to the spoken word.

During the summer of 1951, the arm of H.P. Sauce and its subsidiary companies commissioned Sir Gerald Kelly to paint my portrait, and Professor Bodkin gave me a letter of introduction to him. On June 23rd I received the following letter: -

"Dear Sir Patrick,

... Of course, I suggest that you should come and see me. In all these things I try to be as business like as possible. I don't know how big you want the picture to be, and how much you want to pay. You must tell me and then I will tell you what I am accustomed to receive for the size picture you want me to paint, and, here and now, I will warn you of one thing: I have always wanted a lot of sittings, and now as I grow older I do not paint my pictures any faster. I used to say a minimum of ten sittings. I should say, nowadays, that it is more like a minimum of fifteen. You must also tell me when you want to sit and by when you want the picture finished."

After a few sittings we became great friends, and his letter to me on August 11th begins: -

"My dear Paddy,

… We are off early tomorrow but I must just write and thank you for your good wishes. We are both very overdue for a holiday, and I expect, it will do us a lot of good. Your picture is going to be GREAT. It is going to please many, (your friends, I hope) and annoy no-one but Gerald Kelly, who'll be regretting it isn't much better."

As a matter of fact, the portrait was so splendidly painted that it was held back, postponing the presentation, to be exhibited at the Royal Academy the following summer, where it hung for about three months.

Apart from my resignation, illness, and the wonderful expressions of friendship combined with the presentation ceremonies, that year of grace, 1950, will always be memorable to me for the delightful visit my daughter, Dorothy, and I paid to Rome. The highlight of this trip, of course, was a special audience with the Holy Father at Castle Gandolfo, which it was my particular good fortune to be accorded. This notable event was arranged by the kindness and generosity of the Archbishop of Birmingham, and of Monsignor Tickle (Vice-Rector of the English College in Rome). His Holiness spoke perfect English, and for nearly a quarter of an hour he talked to us of his friendship for the people of England, recalling his visit to London when he represented the Vatican at the Coronation of the late King George and the Queen Mother; of his confidence in the success of the Hierarchy Centenary celebrations which were then taking place, and of his admiration for Winston Churchill, whom he regards as one of the saviours of Christian civilisation. Among other things he emphasised his deep regard for the spirit of tolerance among British people all over the world.

The personality of the Pope is unforgettable; so penetrating, such vigour mingled with benevolence. I left his presence with the feeling that he was the most powerful factor in our time for the preservation of world peace. On Wednesday afternoons during the celebration, hundreds of thousands of people of every race gathered in the great Piazza in front of St Peter's to receive the blessing of the Pope, and their demonstrations of affection and loyalty were unparalleled.

Indeed, I have been most fortunate in witnessing those scenes of intense Christian loyalty and, above all, to have had audiences, not only with the present Pope, but also with Popes Leo XIII, Pius X, Pius XI and Benedict XV. Among other churches Which my daughter and I visited on that occasion was that of St Gregorius, the Parish church in Rome of our late Cardinal, where we were pleased to see Cardinal Griffen's portrait occupying a conspicuous position, and also that fascinating little church built on the spot where St Peter is said to have been reproved by our Lord and, as result, to have turned back to Rome to meet his terrible martyrdom.

At one period in pre-war years the chapel had been sadly neglected, bits of torn paper lay scattered about, and the dust had accumulated sadly. I had mentioned this to the late Signor Marconi, who spoke to Mussolini about it. When I next saw that famous church it had undergone the process of thorough cleaning and tidying. Our holiday included trips to neighbouring towns to inspect factories, and a visit to Salerno where some of the basic materials for the manufacture of HP. sauce is obtained.

Soon after my return, Dulanty (on his retirement) was given a farewell dinner by the Prime Minister at 10, Downing Street, a most unusual gesture, signifying the exceptional esteem in which the Irish Ambassador was held. In writing to thank Mr. Attlee for the luncheon, I added: - *"I shall always recall with pleasure the appropriate and kindly tribute you paid to Dulanty. ... but much more still, your abounding friendship for the Irish people."* I have always found Mr. Attlee, in his official capacity, ever open to considering suggestions and comments, and in his courtesy and help and brilliance, I consider him to be one of the great gentlemen of our time. When I heard in September 1951, that the Chancellor of the Western Zone of Germany (Herr Adenauer) was to come to Britain at the invitation of H.M. Government, I wrote the following letter to Attlee: -

"The announcement of the contemplated visit of Herr Adenauer as the guest of the Government suggests to me the propriety of an invitation to him to meet some of the leaders of the Catholic body in this country. I met Herr Adenauer after the First World War, saw a good deal of him for some days, visited his home, and accompanied him to the Convent in Gotesburg which was endowed by the late Sir Ernest Cassel. Notwithstanding this remote acquaintance, I think I could take the liberty, if you and the Foreign Office approved, of inviting him to a luncheon at which the Cardinal Archbishop of Westminster would, I hope, be able to attend, the Apostolic delegate, and leading members of the Catholic Union, of whose Council I am a member. It would, I feel, be a friendly gesture to the Catholics of Western Germany, if the Chancellor were entertained by members of the Hierarchy and laity of the Catholic Church in this country. It may be that the Foreign Office will propose some function with the same objective as the submission I now make to you, but I am confident that a Catholic manifestation of friendship to the West German Chancellor will serve the cause of Anglo-German friendship and understanding."

In his reply he said: -

"Thank you very much for your letter of 7th September. I am

330

grateful to you for your suggestion of organising a luncheon party to be given to Dr Adenauer by the leaders of the Catholic body in this country. We are indeed most anxious that Dr Adenauer should meet as many people as possible from all sections; I am afraid, however, that the programme which has been drawn up is already rather full and, as it now stands, there are no free dates for luncheons."

He added, however, that the programme was not completely decided upon, and he suggested that I should discuss the matter with the Foreign Office and obtain details of the programme.

In October 1952, I was re-elected President of the National Union of Manufacturers for the eighteenth time, but I felt that I should not continue to hold the position for very much longer. Accordingly, with reluctance and some sadness, I handed in my resignation the following year. The annual dinner, at which I was generously presented with an inscribed silver salver, was made memorable by the presence of his Royal Highness, the Duke of Edinburgh, who was guest of honour. In welcoming him to our assembly, I said: -

"Speaking on behalf of five thousand, five hundred of the smaller manufacturers, I would like to say that never has the relationship between the Crown and the people been so deep and warm. ... You, Sir, are doing a profound service to the industrial life of the nation, in your exalted capacity, by taking a live interest in the productivity of the people."

The Duke, in one of his forceful speeches, delivered with his usual charm and wit, said that he: - *"… would like to congratulate you all on your really tremendous efforts to get things going after the war. ... It has been rather like pulling oneself up by ones bootlaces. But you have done it. … You must literally live by your wits. Judging on the past achievements of this country, I do not think our worst enemies would say that we are a nation of nitwits. In my opinion the working formula is Happiness plus Efficiency equals Hjgh Productivity."* A sentiment with which we were all in entire agreement. As a public speaker His Royal Highness is a model whom most of us would do well to emulate. Not for him the dreary platitudes woven into long, intricate sentences, the would-be humorous anecdotes which have no possible connection with the subject but are tediously intruded in order to rouse the listeners' interest. No, the Duke is always clear, concise and convincing, presenting his facts in a crisp form without making a demand on the intelligence of his audience.

Apart from Sir Winston Churchill, the outstanding speaker of my time was the late Lord Birkenhead. He possessed a mental flexibility rarely surpassed and, no matter what his subject, one listened to his words with unflagging and increasing interest. With regard to my own humble efforts, I was amused to learn from the lips of the late Ernest Bevin that we encountered one another verbally as far back as 1910. For, while I was endeavouring to give one of my earlier political speeches when standing for Bristol East, he was practising the art of heckling at my expense! On his entry into Parliament, so much later in life, his forcefulness and 'bulldoggedness' were immediately recognised, and given their place of fulfilment. His is one of those mighty names that will ever live in the history of British war statesmanship.

As I have mentioned elsewhere, Association Football has always given me the keenest pleasure (as an onlooker) and it has been a continual source of joy to me to have been a President of the Aston Villa Football Club over a great number of years. The late Fred Normansell (who was for twenty years the Chairman) was a man for whom I entertained a deep affection. His social and charitable work in the city of Birmingham, and his interests in so many different movements there, gained him the admiration of all, and every phase of life in the city was represented at his funeral, along with a large contingent of Aston Villa Footballers.

In the long course of my full life I have met a bewildering variety of personalities, many of whom achieved fame, some of whom moved in the quiet waters of semi obscurity. It would be impossible to mention even half of those who, at one time or another, were my friends, acquaintances and colleagues. But I cannot close this humble account of a life of over four-score years without speaking of the memory I treasure of two delightful ladies, Julia Neilson-Terry, and Lady de Frece. The vitality and liveliness of the former could hardly be shown to better advantage than in a letter written to me after celebrating her eighty-third birthday. Perhaps it may give my younger readers some idea of the personality of that great lady: -

"Darling Sir Patrick,

... I think you're an angel to drop me a line about my birthday, and I

333

greatly appreciated your bothering to do such a thing. I ought to be ashamed of myself not answering your dear note until now, but I have not been too well, acute arthritis, and I am afraid it has made me a little lazy, shall I say, and if you could see my correspondence now you would forgive me being so dilatory in writing to thank you for my eighty-third birthday wishes. Bless you. I hope one day we shall meet again at lunch here."

Lady de Frece (the lovable, fascinating Vesta Tilly) resembled her strongly in one respect, her joy of living. She was my guest in Birmingham many years ago, when a giant demonstration was organised in support of the National Savings movement, and she received an uproarious welcome from the citizens. Our route from the Queen's Hotel (where I had entertained her and a large, but select, party to luncheon) to Bingley Hall was thronged with cheering multitudes, through which mounted policemen had difficulty in clearing a way for us, and the hall itself was, of course, crowded to suffocation. I have seldom seen Birmingham so roused.

The highly individualistic personalities of the past are unlikely to appear in other forms in the future, for our race has become stereotyped, educational advantages are widely spread, and too many people excel in the same line. Nevertheless, the rock-and-rolling youngsters of today have a great future before them, more particularly if they can direct some of their liveliness into spiritual channels, and not allow themselves to be swept headlong in the mad race of science for further fantastic achievements. Youth has come too much into the limelight during the last two decades. A Parliamentary candidate, for instance, should not, as a general rule, be less than twenty-five years old. Mature judgement in politics, as in other walks of life, is in danger of being cast aside in favour of the voice of eagerness and inexperience.

History has shown us that the follies of one generation can never, with all the good will in the world, be completely eradicated in the lifetime of the succeeding generation. Therefore, let our young men and women of today consider well the outcome of their schemes before they put them into action. That is the advice that I would wish to offer, for I should like them to one-day feel, as I do, that in some small and modest measure we have contributed to the happiness and welfare of our island community.

POSTSCRIPT
By Fiona Hannon

Sir 'Paddy', my great-grandfather, had celebrated what he (and the family) believed to be his 92nd birthday in March 1962, although records give his birth as 1874, making him 88. Family meant more to him than anything in his crowded life. His 92nd birthday was celebrated with a family party — his three sons and their wives, his three grandchildren and two of his six great-grandchildren.

He died the following year, on January 10th 1963, at his home in Queen's Gate Gardens, Kensington. Of the many tributes paid to him, I would like to quote from a few. Mr. Geoffrey Lloyd, President of Birmingham Conservative Association and M.P. for Sutton Coldfield, said: -

"'Paddy' Hannon, as he was known to all at Westminster, had a wonderful life. Irish charm, ceaseless application, shrewdness, genuine good nature — these were the secrets of his great success. By them he rose through hard early struggles and adventures to his eminent position in public life."

Mr C.S. Buckley, Chairman of Aston Villa football club said: -

"He was a great personality and will be badly missed by the club. He kept in touch with the club and knew everything that was going on. He was always a tower of strength to the Board and took an interest in everything — the financial position, transfers and the welfare of the players."

The political correspondent of the Birmingham Post wrote: -

"Raising frequently from the Back Benches a voice with an unmistakeable Irish brogue and himself exhibiting more than a trace of Irish temperament, Sir Patrick Hannon was, during his 29 years in the Commons, an indefatigable debater.

He had a warmth of heart which caused his rather indignant style of speech often to melt into a rosy smile, while he brushed back a wealth of white locks and asked the House to forgive his depth of feeling.

He launched, founded or was a member of more organisations than probably any other Member in living history.

He is remembered for giving a party when he left the Commons in 1950 for all the House servants who had served under him in his 29 years' membership. They said of him then, 'Who but he would have thought of it.'"

Also mentioning personal features, in addition to listing his many interests and achievements, the obituary in the Times (and also in the Irish Times) included the following:

"Sir Patrick was an impenitent and incurable individualist, excepting in his readiness to collaborate with others in pursuing his favourite causes. ... In the Commons he was, it could be fairly said, both an institution and a phenomenon, with his fresh pink complexion and his white hair — white for so many years before he grew old — and his twinkling dancing eyes which suggested, quite rightly, that he was always ready for a quip or a joke."

The Birmingham Mail made mention of his sense of style in one of its features, Day by Day, printed the day after his death: -

"But to look at the man more intimately is to see him as the Last of the Beaux. He had been, in his day, something of a dandy. At the height of his fashion consciousness — he created fashion rather than followed it — he sported shepherd's plaid trousers, braided tailcoats, elaborate cravats and distinctive hats that sometimes turned one's thought to O'Connell Street."

As his great-granddaughter, I am particularly heartened by the tributes referring to his kindness.

Cyril Aynsley wrote in the Daily Express: -

"They still remember Sir Patrick Hannon in the House of Commons as a member who in nearly 30 years never made an enemy. ... For he was a kind man."

At his funeral, a friend and former colleague in the House of Commons, Sir Harry Brittain, also made reference to my great-grandfather's popularity when he gave a tribute saying: -

"He did not have a single enemy. I do not think any man in the House was more beloved by M.P.s of all parties."

His funeral was held on January 14th at the Roman Catholic Church of the Holy Name in Denham, Buckinghamshire, followed by interment at St. Joseph's Roman Catholic Carmelite Church, Gerrards Cross. Requiem Masses took place at the Roman Catholic Church of the English Martyrs, Sparkhill, Birmingham the following day and at Westminster Roman Catholic Cathedral on January 16th. As a small child of 6 years I was the only Great-Grandchild present and clearly remember being overawed at seeing, and being introduced to, so many people who filled the Cathedral to pay their respects to Great-Grandpa.

Who's Who of 1963 catalogues the enormous range of Sir Patrick's services to the business community and to public life, but I would like to close these Memoirs with a quote from an unnamed friend of his in the Tablet newspaper: -

"A man of incorruptible character, unspoiled by life, Sir Patrick gave and won much affection, and enlivened all those who were privileged to enjoy his friendship."